Adapted Reading and Study Wo...

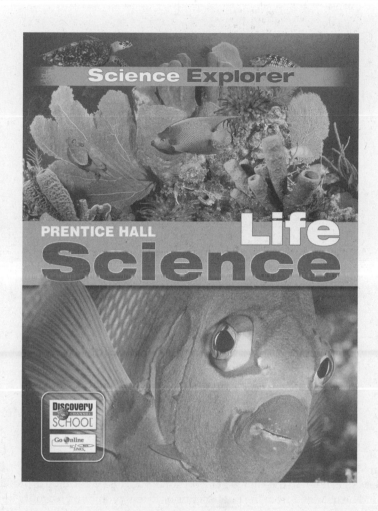

Science Explorer

PRENTICE HALL

Life Science

PEARSON

Prentice
Hall

Boston, Massachusetts
Upper Saddle River, New Jersey

ISBN 0-13-166594-4
5 6 7 8 9 10   09 08 07

Life Science

Introduction to Life Science

What Is Science? (pages 6–13)

Observing (page 7)

Key Concept: **Scientists use the skill called observing to learn more about the world.**

- **Science** is a way of learning about the natural world.

- **Observing** means using your senses to gather information. Your senses include sight, hearing, touch, taste, and smell.

- You can make either quantitative observations or qualitative observations.

- **Quantitative observations** deal with numbers—the amount of something. When you observe how many gears you have on your bike, you are making a quantitative observation.

- **Qualitative observations** deal with descriptions that do not include numbers. When you observe the color of your bike, you are making a qualitative observation.

Answer the following questions. Use your textbook and the ideas above.

1. Draw a line from each term to its meaning.

Term	Meaning
observing	**a.** observations that deal with numbers
quantitative observations	**b.** using your senses to gather information
qualitative observations	**c.** observations that deal with descriptions that do not include numbers

Introduction to Life Science

2. The picture below shows a spider called a tarantula. Circle the letter of a quantitative observation about this animal.

   a. A tarantula is scary.

   b. A tarantula has eight legs.

   c. A tarantula eats insects.

Inferring (page 8)

Key Concept: **Scientists use the skill called inferring to learn more about the world.**

- **Inferring** is explaining or interpreting the things you observe. When you infer, you make an inference.

- Making an inference does not mean guessing wildly. When you infer, you use reasoning. You make an inference from what you already know about something.

- You make inferences all the time. For example, if you see a friend smile after taking a test, you infer that your friend did well on the test.

Answer the following questions. Use your textbook and the ideas above.

3. Explaining or interpreting the things you observe

   is called _____.

Introduction to Life Science

4. Circle the letter of each sentence that is true about inferring.

    a. When you infer, you use reasoning.

    b. Making an inference is like guessing wildly.

    c. Making an inference does not mean guessing wildly.

Predicting (page 9)

***Key Concept:* Scientists use the skill called predicting to learn more about the world.**

- **Predicting** means making a forecast of what will happen in the future. You make a prediction based either on what you have experienced in the past or on current evidence.

- You make predictions all the time. Based on past experience, you may predict that you will eat dinner at a certain time tonight.

- Predictions and inferences are closely related. Inferences attempt to explain what *has* happened. Predictions attempt to explain what *will* happen.

Answer the following questions. Use your textbook and the ideas above.

5. Making a forecast of what will happen in the future is

    called _____.

6. Circle the letter of each sentence that is true about predicting.

    a. You make predictions all the time.

    b. Predictions and inferences are closely related.

    c. Predictions may be based on past experience.

Introduction to Life Science

Classifying (page 10)

Key Concept: **Scientists use the skill called classifying to learn more about the world.**

- **Classifying** is grouping together things that are alike in some way.

- You classify information and objects all the time. When you put papers in a notebook, you might classify them by subject or by date. You might classify information you hear on the radio as information about sports or information about music.

Answer the following questions. Use your textbook and the ideas above.

7. The process of grouping together items that are alike in some way is called _____.

8. Is the following sentence true or false? You are classifying when you put socks in one drawer and shirts in another drawer. _____

Making Models (page 11)

Key Concept: **Scientists use the skill called making models to learn more about the world.**

- **Making models** is creating something that represents a complicated object or process.

- Models help people understand things that are complex or that cannot be observed directly.

- Sometimes models are physical objects. For example, a globe is a model.

- Sometimes models are not physical objects. For example, a model on a computer might be used to design a new building.

Introduction to Life Science

Answer the following questions. Use your textbook and the ideas on page 8.

9. When you create a representation of an object, you are making a(an) _____.

10. Is the following sentence true or false? Models can be made on computers. _____

Working in Life Science (pages 12–13)

Key Concept: **Many different jobs involve knowing about life science.**

- **Life science** is the study of living things. Life science is also called biology.

- Scientists who study living things are called biologists.

- You do not need to be a biologist to use life science in your job. Many jobs use life science. People working in such places as forests, laboratories, farms, and hospitals all use life science.

Answer the following questions. Use your textbook and the ideas above.

11. Circle the letter of each term that describes the study of living things.
   a. biology
   b. life science
   c. physical science

12. Is the following sentence true or false? You must be a biologist to use life science in your job. _____

Introduction to Life Science

Scientific Inquiry (pages 14–18)

The Scientific Process (pages 14–17)

Key Concept: **Scientific inquiry refers to the diverse ways in which scientists study the natural world and propose explanations based on the evidence they gather. Scientists propose hypotheses that can be proved or disproved with an investigation.**

- **Scientific inquiry** is a process used by scientists to study the natural world. Thinking and questioning is the start of the scientific inquiry process.

- To answer a scientific question, a scientist develops a hypothesis. A **hypothesis** (plural: *hypotheses*) is a possible explanation or answer to a scientific question.

- After stating a hypothesis, you are ready to design an experiment to test it.

- When you think about the data collected in an experiment, you draw a conclusion about whether the data support or disprove your hypothesis.

- Scientific inquiry does not usually end with an experiment. The results of an experiment often lead to new questions.

- Scientists must share the results of their studies. **Communicating** is the sharing of ideas and results of experiments.

Answer the following questions. Use your textbook and the ideas above.

1. The process used by scientists to study the natural world is called _____.

2. Circle the letter of a possible explanation or answer to a scientific question.

    a. inference

    b. observation

    c. hypothesis

3. Circle the letter of each sentence that is true about scientific inquiry.

    a. Thinking and questioning is the start of the inquiry process.

    b. You design the experiment before stating a hypothesis.

    c. After collecting data, you draw a conclusion about your hypothesis.

4. The diagram below is a model of the scientific inquiry process. Circle the step in the process where scientific inquiry usually begins.

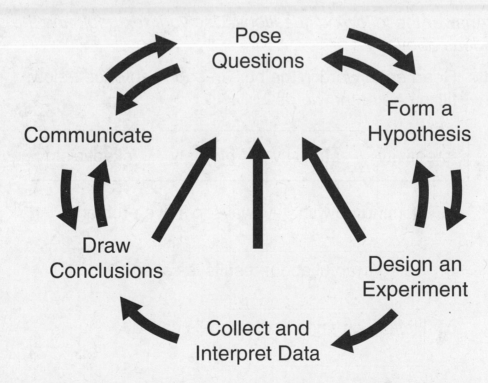

Pose Questions

Communicate

Form a Hypothesis

Draw Conclusions

Design an Experiment

Collect and Interpret Data

5. The sharing of ideas and the results of experiments is called _____.

Introduction to Life Science

Scientific Attitudes (page 18)

Key Concept: **Successful scientists possess certain important attitudes, or habits of mind, including curiosity, honesty, open-mindedness, skepticism, and creativity.**

- Good scientists have certain attitudes when doing their work.

- Good scientists are very curious and eager to learn more.

- Honesty is very important when results go against earlier ideas or predictions.

- Having an attitude of doubt is called skepticism. A scientist combines being open-minded with being skeptical. That is being open to new ideas but with some doubt about whether a new idea will work.

- Creativity is important to find an answer. Creativity means coming up with new ways to solve problems.

Answer the following questions. Use your textbook and the ideas above.

6. Read each word in the box. In each sentence below, fill in one of the words.

creativity	curiosity	honesty	skepticism

   a. Coming up with new ways to solve problems

   is_____.

   b. Being truthful about results is called

   _____.

   c. Having an attitude of doubt is called

   _____.

7. Is the following sentence true or false? Good scientists are eager to learn. _____

Introduction to Life Science

Understanding Technology
(pages 19–22)

What Is Technology? (page 20)

Key Concept: **The goal of technology is to improve the way people live.**

- **Technology** is how people change the world around them. People create technology to meet their needs and to solve problems.

- Technology includes more than modern inventions. New knowledge about how things work is technology. So is the ability to make things and move them from place to place.

- Other examples of technology are football helmets, refrigerators, and contact lenses.

Answer the following questions. Use your textbook and the ideas above.

1. People create _____ to meet their needs and to solve problems.

2. Is the following sentence true or false? Knowing about how things work is not considered an example of technology. _____

3. Circle the letter of each sentence that is true about technology.
   a. The goal of technology is to improve the way people live.
   b. Making things is one example of technology.
   c. A refrigerator is an example of technology.

Introduction to Life Science

Comparing Technology and Science (page 21)

Key Concept: Science is the study of the natural world to understand how it functions. Technology, on the other hand, changes, or modifies, the natural world to meet human needs or solve problems.

- The purposes of science and technology are very different. Science is the study of the natural world. In contrast, technology changes the natural world in order to solve problems.

- For example, a scientist studies insects to learn about how they live. An **engineer**, a person who develops technology, studies insects to keep them from destroying food plants.

- Advances in science often depend on advances in technology. And, advances in technology often depend on advances in science.

Answer the following questions. Use your textbook and the ideas above.

4. Circle the letter of each sentence that is true about the relationship of science and technology.

   a. Technology changes the natural world in order to solve problems.

   b. Advances in technology often depend on advances in science.

   c. The purposes of science and technology are very similar.

5. A person who develops technology is a(an)

   _____.

Introduction to Life Science

Impact on Society (page 22)

Key Concept: **Technology can have both positive and negative consequences for individual people and for society as a whole.**

- A society is a group of people who live together in an area and have things in common. For example, Americans form a society.

- Technology can have both good and bad effects on society.

- For example, chemicals that kill insects allow farmers to grow more food. However, these chemicals can harm plants and animals, and people, if they are not used properly.

- Before using technology, people must decide if it will cause more harm than good.

Answer the following questions. Use your textbook and the ideas above.

6. A group of people who live together in an area and have things in common is a(an)

   _____.

7. Circle the letter of each risk of using chemicals that kill insects.

   a. Farmers grow more food.
   b. Animals eat food that has chemicals in it.
   c. Rain washes chemicals into lakes and rivers.

8. Is the following sentence true or false? All technology causes harm. _____

Introduction to Life Science

Safety in the Science Laboratory (pages 23–26)

Safety During Investigations (pages 23–25)

Key Concept: **Good preparation helps you stay safe when doing science activities.**

- You should begin preparing the day before the lab. Make sure you understand all the directions. Read the safety guidelines for any equipment you will be using.

- When performing a lab, the most important safety rule is: Always follow your teacher's instructions and the textbook directions exactly.

- Make sure you are familiar with all the safety symbols.

- Never do a field investigation alone.

- You may have safety problems in the field. For example, you might have bad weather or touch poison ivy.

Answer the following questions. Use your textbook and the ideas above.

1. Circle the letter of when you should start preparing for a lab.
   a. the day before the lab
   b. an hour before the lab
   c. when the lab begins

2. Each of the pictures below is a laboratory safety symbol. Circle the letter of the safety symbol that warns you not to touch broken glassware.

a.   b.   c.

Introduction to Life Science

3. Circle the letter of each sentence that is true about safety during investigations.

   a. Follow your teacher's instructions.

   b. There will not be safety problems in the lab or in the field.

   c. You should never do a field investigation alone.

In Case of an Accident (page 26)

Key Concept: When any accident occurs, no matter how minor, notify your teacher immediately. Then, listen to your teacher's directions and carry them out quickly.

- Tell your teacher right away if there is an accident.

- Make sure you know where emergency equipment is in your lab room. Learn how to use the emergency equipment.

- Know what to do in if you cut yourself, burn yourself, spill something on your skin, or put something in your eye. For example, if you spill something on your skin, you and your teacher should pour large amounts of water on your skin.

Answer the following questions. Use your textbook and the ideas above.

4. Circle the letter of what you should do immediately if an accident occurs in the laboratory.

   a. Find emergency equipment.

   b. Ask another student what to do.

   c. Tell your teacher.

5. Is the following sentence true or false? Only the teacher needs to know where emergency equipment is in the laboratory. _____

What Is Life? (pages 34–40)

The Characteristics of Living Things
(pages 34–35)

Key Concept: **All living things have a cellular organization, contain similar chemicals, use energy, respond to their surroundings, grow and develop, and reproduce.**

- An **organism** is a living thing. You are an organism. So are trees and ants.

- A **cell** is the building block of structures in an organism. **Unicellular** organisms are made of only one cell. **Multicellular** organisms are made of many cells.

- Living things react to what happens around them. A **stimulus** is a change in an organism's surroundings. Light is a stimulus. A **response** is an action or behavior an organism takes when it reacts to a stimulus. A plant bending toward light is a response.

- Living things grow and develop. When a living thing grows, it gets larger. **Development** produces a more complex organism. When organisms grow and develop, their cells use energy to make new cells.

- Living things produce offspring like the parents.

Answer the following questions. Use your textbook and the ideas above.

1. Circle the letter of the building block of structures in all living things.

   a. stimulus

   b. organism

   c. cell

2. The picture shows a plant growing toward light. What is the stimulus? _____

3. Is the following sentence true or false? When a living thing develops, it becomes more complex.

_____

Life Comes From Life (pages 36–37)

Key Concept: **Living things arise from living things through reproduction.**

- Four hundred years ago, people thought living things could come from nonliving things. For example, people thought flies could come from rotting meat.

- Francesco Redi set up an experiment to show that rotting meat does not produce flies.

- Louis Pasteur carried out an experiment that showed bacteria could be produced only from bacteria.

- These experiments helped people understand that living things could not come from nonliving things. Living things come only from other living things through reproduction.

Living Things

Answer the following question. Use your textbook and the ideas on page 19.

4. Circle the letter of each sentence that is true about where living things come from.

    a. Living things can come from nonliving things.

    b. Redi showed that flies do not come from rotting meat.

    c. Pasteur showed that bacteria come from nonliving materials.

The Needs of Living Things (pages 38–40)

Key Concept: **All living things must satisfy their basic needs for water, food, living space, and stable internal conditions.**

- Living things must have water to live. Water dissolves body chemicals and carries the chemicals through the body.

- Living things need food to get the energy to live.

- Some living things use the energy from sunlight to make food. Living things that make their own food are **autotrophs** (AW toh trohfs). Plants are autotrophs.

- Living things that cannot make their own food are **heterotrophs** (HET uh roh trohfs). Heterotrophs get energy by feeding on other living things. Animals are heterotrophs.

- All living things need a place to live. Living things must get food, water, and shelter from where they live.

- A living thing must be able to keep the conditions inside its body stable, even when conditions around it change. For example, your body temperature stays the same even when the air temperature changes.

Answer the following questions. Use your textbook and the ideas on page 20.

5. Read each word in the box. In each sentence below, fill in tho corroct word.

autotrophs	heterotrophs	organisms

a. Living things that get energy by feeding on other living things are _____.

b. Living things that use the energy from sunlight to make food are _____.

6. Read each word in the box. Use the words to complete the concept map about the needs of living things.

Food	Living space	Sunlight	Water

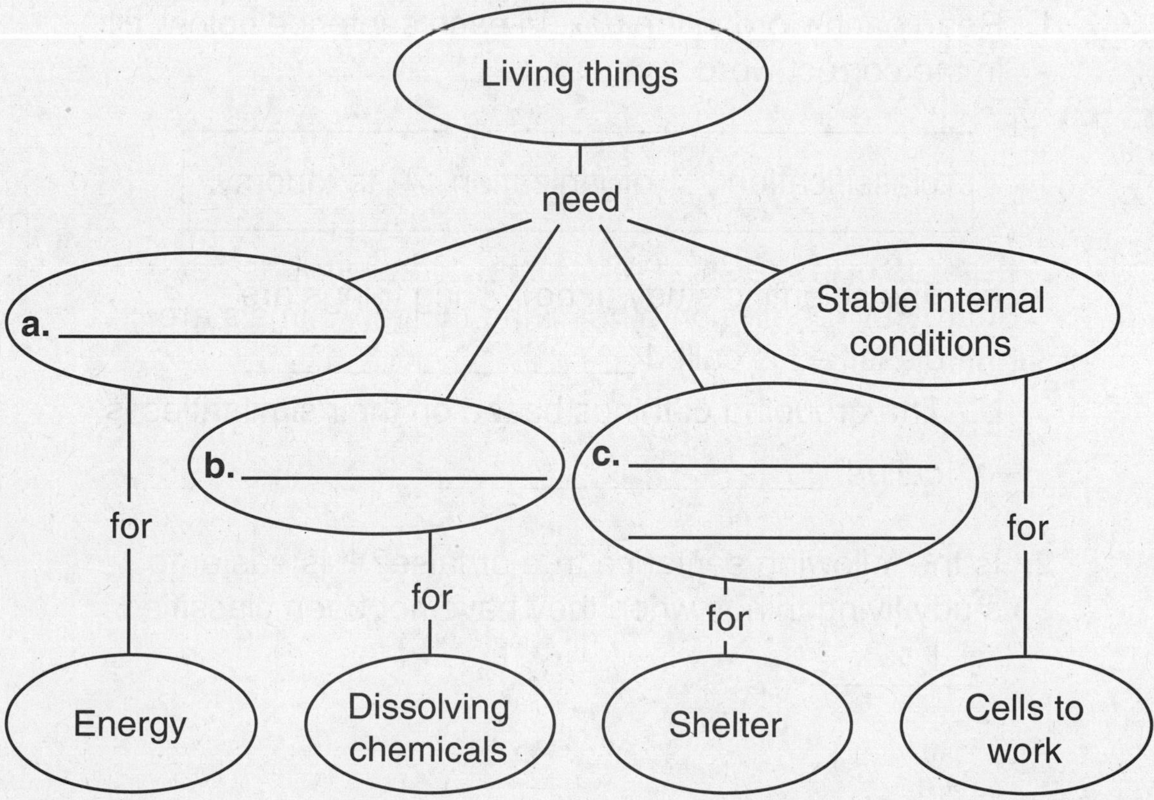

Living things

need

a. _____

b. _____

c. _____ _____

Stable internal conditions

for

for

for

for

Energy

Dissolving chemicals

Shelter

Cells to work

Living Things

Classifying Organisms (pages 42–49)

Why Do Scientists Classify? (page 43)

Key Concept: Biologists use classification to organize living things into groups so that the organisms are easier to study.

- Biologists put living things into groups based on how the living things are alike. **Classification** is grouping things based on their similarities.

- The scientific study of how living things are classified is called **taxonomy** (tak SAHN uh mee). Taxonomy is useful because once a living thing is classified, a biologist knows a lot about it. For example, if a crow is classified as a bird, you already know that a crow has feathers and lays eggs.

Answer the following questions. Use your textbook and the ideas above.

1. Read each word in the box. In each sentence below, fill in the correct word.

classification	organization	taxonomy

    a. The scientific study of how living things are

    classified is called _____.

    b. The grouping of things based on their similarities is

    called _____.

2. Is the following sentence true or false? It is easier to study living things when they have not been classified.

    _____

Living Things

The Naming System of Linnaeus (pages 44–45)

Key Concept: **Carolus Linnaeus devised a system of naming organisms in which each organism has a unique, two-part scientific name.**

- Linnaeus gave each living thing a scientific name with two parts. The first part of the name is the genus. A **genus** (JEE nus) is a group of similar organisms. For example, all cats belong to the genus *Felis.*

- The second part of a scientific name often describes a distinctive feature of the organism. Together, the two words in a scientific name make up the species. A **species** (SPEE sheez) is a group of similar organisms that can mate and produce offspring that can also mate and reproduce. House cats and lions are in the same genus, but are different species.

- Scientific names make it easier for scientists to talk about organisms. For example, woodchucks are also called groundhogs and whistlepigs. But this animal has only one scientific name—*Marmota monax.*

Answer the following questions. Use your textbook and the ideas above.

3. The scientific name for pumas is *Felis concolor.* Circle the letter of the genus to which pumas belong.

    a. *Felis*

    b. *concolor*

    c. puma

4. Circle the letter of each sentence that is true about scientific names.

    a. Scientific names have two parts.

    b. Organisms in the same species cannot mate and produce offspring.

    c. Scientific names make it easier for scientists to talk about an organism.

Living Things

Levels of Classification (pages 45–46)

Key Concept: **The more classification levels that two organisms share, the more characteristics they have in common.**

- The classification system that scientists use has more groups than just genus and species. Scientists use a series of eight levels to classify organisms. The eight levels are: domain, kingdom, phylum, class, order, family, genus, and species.

- Organisms are grouped by characteristics that they have alike. Organisms with the same classification at lower levels share more characteristics.

- The highest level in the classification system is the domain. The living things In a domain are very wide-ranging. A domain has the largest number of organisms.

- The lowest level in the classification system is the species. The characteristics of a species are very specific. Only one kind of organism is in the species level.

Answer the following questions. Use your textbook and the ideas above.

5. Is the following sentence true or false? Organisms with the same classification at lower levels share more

   characteristics. _____

6. Circle the letter of the classification level where you would find the most different kinds of organisms.
   a. species
   b. family
   c. domain

Living Things

Domains and Kingdoms (page 47)

Key Concept: **Organisms are placed into domains and kingdoms based on their cell type, their ability to make food, and the number of cells in their bodies.**

- The three domains are Bacteria, Archaea, and Eukarya.

- Members of the domain Bacteria are single-celled living things.

- Bacteria are prokaryotes. **Prokaryotes** (proh KA ree ohtz) are living things whose cells do not have a nucleus. A **nucleus** (NOO klee us) is a dense area in a cell that holds genetic material.

- Some bacteria make their own food. These bacteria are autotrophic. Other bacteria cannot make their own food. They are heterotrophic.

- Members of the domain Archaea (ahr KEE uh) live in harsh environments like hot springs.

- Archaea are single-celled organisms that do not have a nucleus. Some archaea make their own food. Others cannot make their own food.

- Archaea have a different chemical makeup than bacteria have.

Answer the following questions. Use your textbook and the ideas above.

7. Circle the letter of the best description of members of the domain Bacteria.

    a. are single-celled

    b. are many-celled

    c. have a nucleus

Living Things

8. Circle the letter of each sentence that is true about prokaryotes.

   a. Prokaryotes hold genetic material in a nucleus.

   b. Prokaryotes do not have a nucleus.

   c. Prokaryotes do have genetic material.

9. Draw lines to show how archaea compare to bacteria.

Archaea	**Characteristic**
like bacteria	a. single-celled
	b. do not have nucleus
different from bacteria	c. chemical makeup

10. Is the following sentence true or false? All archaea are autotrophs, which make their own food. _____

Domain Eukarya (pages 48–49)

Key Concept: **Scientists classify organisms in the domain Eukarya into one of four kingdoms: protists, fungi, plants, or animals.**

- All members of the domain Eukarya have cells that contain a nucleus. **Eukaryotes** (yoo KA ree ohtz) are living things with cells that have a nucleus.

- Members of the domain Eukarya are classified into one of four kingdoms. These kingdoms are protists, fungi, plants, and animals.

- A protist (PROH tist) is any eukaryote that cannot be classified as a fungi, plant, or animal. Most protists are single-celled.

Living Things

- Fungi (FUN jy) are eukaryotes that cannot make their own food. Most fungi are many-celled.

- Plants are many-celled eukaryotes that can make their own food.

- Animals are many-celled eukaryotes that cannot make their own food.

Answer the following questions. Use your textbook and the ideas on page 26 and above.

11. Circle the letter of the *best* description of all members of the domain Eukarya.

    a. can make their own food

    b. have bodies made of many cells

    c. have cells with a nucleus

12. Fill in the table below about members of the domain Eukarya.

Domain Eukarya		
Kingdom	**Cell Number**	**Able to Make Food?**
Protists	single-celled and many-celled	yes and no
a. _____	single-celled and many-celled	no
Plants	many-celled	**b.** _____
Animals	**c.** _____	no

Living Things

Discovering Cells (pages 50–57)

An Overview of Cells (page 51)

Key Concept: **Cells are the basic units of structure and function in living things.**

- **Cells** make up the structures in all living things. Cells also carry out all of the functions, or jobs, of living things.

- Living things look like they do because of the different ways cells are put together.

- The different things that living things do are all done by cells. For example, digesting food, moving, and growing are all done by cells.

- Cells are so small that they cannot be seen with your eyes alone.

Answer the following questions. Use your textbook and the ideas above.

1. Read each word in the box. In each sentence below, fill in the correct word.

functions	structures	units

   a. Cells make up the _____ in all living things.

   b. Cells carry out all the _____ of living things.

2. Is the following sentence true or false? You can see cells with just your eyes alone. _____

Living Things

First Observations of Cells (pages 51–53)

Key Concept: **The invention of the microscope made it possible for people to discover and learn about cells.**

- A **microscope** is a tool that makes small objects look larger.

- Many microscopes work by using curved pieces of glass or plastic to focus light.

- Robert Hooke was an English scientist who was one of the first people to see a cell with a microscope.

Answer the following question. Use your textbook and the ideas above.

3. Circle the letter of what a microscope does.
   a. makes large objects look smaller
   b. makes small objects look larger
   c. makes faraway objects look closer

Development of the Cell Theory
(pages 54–55)

Key Concept: **The cell theory states the following: All living things are composed of cells. Cells are the basic units of structure and function in living things. All cells are produced from other cells.**

- As more and more scientists used microscopes to observe cells, they learned that cells are the building blocks of living things.

- Many different scientists worked together to develop the cell theory. The **cell theory** explains the relationship between cells and living thing.

- The cell theory is true for all living things. Scientists can study cells to learn how living things function and grow.

Answer the following question. Use your textbook and the ideas on page 29.

4. Circle the letter of each sentence that is true about cells.

    a. Not all living things are made of cells.

    b. The cell theory explains how cells are made.

    c. Scientists learn how living things function by studying cells.

Light and Electron Microscopes

(pages 55–57)

Key Concept: **The lenses in light microscopes magnify an object by bending the light that passes through them. Electron microscopes use a beam of electrons instead of light to produce a magnified image.**

- Microscopes magnify objects. To magnify means to make things look larger than they are.

- Light microscopes have lenses. A lens is a piece of curved glass or plastic. The lens bends light that passes through it. When the light hits your eyes, your eyes see the object larger than it really is.

- Electron microscopes use electrons to make an image. Electrons are very tiny particles. You can see things with an electron microscope that are too small to see with a light microscope.

Answer the following question. Use your textbook and the ideas above.

5. Circle the letter of each type of microscope.

    a. electron microscope

    b. light microscope

    c. telescope

Living Things

Looking Inside Cells (pages 60–67)

Enter the Cell (page 61)

Key Concept: **A plant's cell wall helps to protect and support the cell. The cell membrane controls what substances come into and out of a cell.**

- An **organelle** is a structure in the cell that has a specific function.

- The **cell wall** is a stiff layer that protects and supports the cell. Animal cells do not have cell walls.

- The **cell membrane** forms the boundary between the cell and its environment. The cell membrane controls what goes in and out of a cell.

Answer the following questions. Use your textbook and the ideas above.

1. A structure inside a cell that has a specific function

   is a(an) _____.

2. Read each word in the box. In each sentence below, fill in the correct word or words.

cell membrane	cell wall	organelle

   a. A stiff layer that protects and supports the cell is

      the _____.

   b. The cell boundary that controls what goes in and

      out of a cell is the _____.

3. Is the following sentence true or false? Animal cells do

   not have a cell wall. _____

Sail on to the Nucleus (page 62)

Key Concept: **Think of the nucleus as the cell's control center, directing all of the cell's activities.**

- The cell nucleus is the control center of the cell.

- The nucleus is protected by a membrane called the nuclear envelope.

- The nucleus holds the genetic information. The genetic information controls what the cell does.

Answer the following question. Use your textbook and the ideas above.

4. Circle the letter of each sentence that is true about the nucleus.

    a. The nucleus is the control center of the cell.

    b. The cell membrane protects the nucleus.

    c. The nucleus holds the genetic information.

Organelles in the Cytoplasm (pages 63–66)

Key Concept: **The cytoplasm has many organelles that carry out the life functions of a cell.**

- The **cytoplasm** (cy tuh PLAZ um) is the thick, gel-like fluid found between the cell membrane and the nucleus. The cytoplasm has many organelles.

- **Mitochondria** (my tuh KAHN dree uh) are rod-shaped organelles known as the "powerhouses" of the cell. Mitochondria change food to energy.

- **Ribosomes** (RY buh sohm) are very small grainlike structures that make proteins.

- Plant cells have chloroplasts. **Chloroplasts** (KLOR uh plasts) are green organelles that capture the energy from sunlight and use it to make food.

Living Things

Answer the following questions. Use your textbook and the ideas on page 32.

5. Circle the letter of the gel-like fluid found between the cell membrane and the nucleus.

   a. organelle

   b. cytoplasm

   c. nuclear envelope

6. Draw a line from each organelle to its function.

Organelle	Function
mitochondria	**a.** make proteins
ribosomes	**b.** capture the energy from sunlight
chloroplasts	**c.** change food to energy the cell can use

7. The picture shows two different cells. One cell is an animal cell. The other cell is a plant cell. Read the labels for the cell parts. Circle the letter of the plant cell.

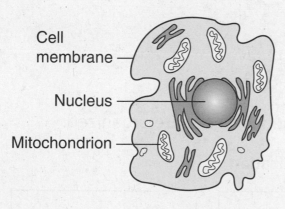

a.

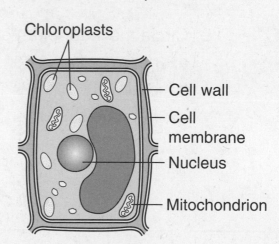

b.

Living Things

Specialized Cells (page 67)

Key Concept: **In many-celled organisms, cells are often organized into tissues, organs, and organ systems.**

- In a many-celled organism, cells are often very different from each other. These cells have different shapes and different jobs.

- A tissue is a group of cells that work together to do a specific job. For example, nervous tissue is made up of nerve cells.

- A group of different tissues is an organ. Your brain is an organ.

- An organ system is a group of organs working together. Your brain is part of the nervous system.

Answer the following questions. Use your textbook and the ideas above.

8. Is the following sentence true or false? In a many-celled organism, all the cells look the same.

   _____

9. Circle the letter of an organ.
   a. nerve cells
   b. brain
   c. nervous system

10. Complete the flowchart about how cells are organized.

Cell Organization

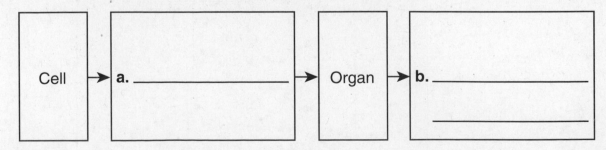

Cell Processes and Energy

Chemical Compounds
in Cells (pages 74–78)

Elements and Compounds (pages 74–75)

Key Concept: **An element is any substance that cannot be broken down into simpler substances. When two or more elements combine chemically, they form a compound.**

- Elements are the basic substances that everything is made of. An **element** cannot be broken down into simpler substances. Oxygen and hydrogen are two elements.

- A **compound** is made of two or more elements that are joined together in a chemical reaction. Water is a compound made of the elements hydrogen and oxygen.

- Most chemical reactions in cells take place in water. Some chemical reactions use water in the reaction itself.

- Many of the compounds that make up living things contain the element carbon. Compounds that contain carbon are called organic compounds.

Answer the following questions. Use your textbook and the ideas above.

1. Any substance that cannot be broken down into simpler substances is a(an) _____.

2. Two or more elements that are joined together chemically are called a(an) _____.

3. Is the following sentence true or false? Many of the chemical reactions in cells take place in carbon. _____

Cell Processes and Energy

Carbohydrates (page 76)

Key Concept: **One important group of organic compounds found in living things is carbohydrates.**

- A **carbohydrate** (kahr boh HY drayt) is a compound made of the elements carbon, hydrogen, and oxygen. Carbohydrates give energy.

- Sugars and starches are carbohydrates. When plants make food, they make sugar. Plants store extra sugar as starch.

- All cells use carbohydrates for energy. Carbohydrates also make up the cell wall and the cell membrane.

Answer the following questions. Use your textbook and the ideas above.

4. Circle the letter of each sentence that is true about carbohydrates.
   a. Carbohydrates have the element nitrogen.
   b. Cells use carbohydrates for energy.
   c. Carbohydrates make up some cell parts.

5. Two carbohydrates are sugar and

   _____.

Lipids (page 76)

Key Concept: **Lipids are one important group of organic compounds found in living things.**

- **Lipids** are energy-rich compounds made of carbon, hydrogen, and oxygen. Fats, oils, and waxes are examples of lipids.

- Lipids have more energy than carbohydrates.

- Cells store energy as lipids for later use.

- Cell membranes are made mostly of lipids.

Cell Processes and Energy

Answer the following questions. Use your textbook and the ideas on page 36.

6. Is the following sentence true or false? Carbohydrates have more energy than lipids. _____

7. Cell membranes are made mostly of

_____.

Proteins (page 77)

Key Concept: **Proteins are one important group of organic compounds found in living things.**

- **Proteins** are large organic compounds. Meat, eggs, fish, and nuts are foods that are high in protein.

- Proteins are made up of many smaller compounds called **amino acids**. There are 20 different amino acids. Cells combine the amino acids in different ways to form thousands of different proteins.

- Most cell structures are made of proteins.

- Proteins called **enzymes** speed up the chemical reactions that take place in cells. Without enzymes, many chemical reactions would not happen.

Answer the following question. Use your textbook and the ideas above.

8. Draw a line from each term to its meaning.

Term	Meaning
amino acid	**a.** speeds up chemical reactions
enzyme	**b.** found in foods such as meat, eggs, and fish
protein	**c.** makes up proteins

Cell Processes and Energy

Nucleic Acids (page 78)

***Key Concept:* Nucleic acids are one important group of organic compounds found in living things.**

- **Nucleic acids** are long organic compounds that instruct cells in carrying out all their functions.

- One kind of nucleic acid is deoxyribonucleic (dee ahk see ry boh noo KLEE ik) acid, or DNA. **DNA** is the genetic material that carries information about an organism. DNA is passed from parents to offspring. DNA is in the nucleus of the cell.

- The information in DNA directs the cell's activities.

- Ribonucleic (ry boh noo KLEE ik) acid, or **RNA**, helps make the proteins that a cell needs. RNA is in the cytoplasm and in the nucleus.

Answer the following questions. Use your textbook and the ideas above.

9. Circle the letter of a function of nucleic acids.

   a. carry information about the cell

   b. provide energy

   c. make up cell structures

10. Fill in the table about nucleic acids.

Nucleic Acids		
Type	**Role in the Cell**	**Location in the Cell**
DNA	carries information about living things	a. _____
RNA	b. _____ _____	cytoplasm and nucleus

The Cell in Its Environment

(pages 80–85)

Diffusion (pages 81–82)

Key Concept: **Diffusion is the main method by which small molecules move across the cell membrane.**

- The cell membrane lets only some substances pass through it. Oxygen, food, waste products, and water are substances that can pass through the cell membrane.

- **Diffusion** (dih FYOO zhun) is when substances move from an area of high concentration to an area of low concentration. It is like when people spread out from a crowded space to a less crowded space.

Answer the following questions. Use your textbook and the ideas above.

1. Is the following sentence true or false? In diffusion, substances move from areas of high concentration to areas of low concentration. _____

2. The pictures show particles of a substance spread inside and outside a cell. Circle the letter of the picture that shows how the particles look before diffusion has taken place.

a.

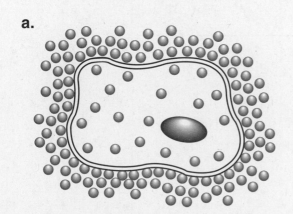

b.

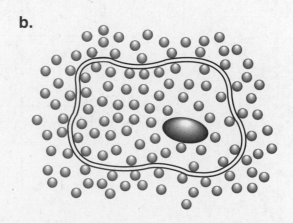

Cell Processes and Energy

Osmosis (pages 82–83)

Key Concept: **Because cells cannot function properly without adequate water, many cellular processes depend on osmosis.**

- **Osmosis** (ahz MOE sis) is the diffusion of water across a cell membrane.

- In osmosis, water moves by diffusion through the cell membrane to an area of low water concentration.

- Water moves out of the cell if there is more water inside the cell than outside the cell. Cells shrink when water moves out.

- Water moves into the cell if there is more water outside the cell. Cells swell, or get larger, when water moves in.

Answer the following questions. Use your textbook and the ideas above.

3. Circle the letter of how water moves in osmosis.
    a. across a cell membrane
    b. to areas where there is more water
    c. downhill

4. Read each word in the box. In each sentence below, fill in the correct word or words.

shrinks	stays the same	swells

   a. When water moves into a cell, the cell

   _____.

   b. When water moves out of a cell, the cell

   _____.

Cell Processes and Energy

Active Transport (pages 84–85)

Key Concept: **Active transport requires the cell to use its own energy, while passive transport does not.**

- In **passive transport**, substances move back and forth through the cell membrane without the use of energy. Diffusion and osmosis are examples of passive transport.

- In **active transport**, cells use energy to move substances through the cell membrane. Cells use active transport to take in substances that are already in higher concentrations inside the cell than outside.

- Calcium, potassium, and sodium are some substances that move in and out of cells by active transport.

Answer the following questions. Use your textbook and the ideas above.

5. Fill in the table below to compare active transport and passive transport in cells.

Cell Transport		
Type	**Needs Energy?**	**Direction Materials Move**
Passive	**a.** _____	to lower concentration
Active	yes	to **b.** _____ concentration

6. Cells use energy to move substances through the cell membrane in _____ transport.

Cell Processes and Energy

Photosynthesis (pages 86–90)

Sources of Energy (page 87)

Key Concept: **Nearly all living things obtain energy either directly or indirectly from the energy of sunlight captured during photosynthesis.**

- **Photosynthesis** (foh toh SIN thuh sis) is what happens when cells take in the energy in sunlight and use it to make food.

- Plants make their own food by photosynthesis. Plants get energy directly from sunlight.

- Animals cannot make their own food. Animals get food by eating plants or by eating other animals that eat plants. So, animals get the sun's energy indirectly.

Answer the following questions. Use your textbook and the ideas above.

1. Circle the letter of what happens in photosynthesis.
   a. Animals get food.
   b. Plants make food using the sun's energy.
   c. The sun shines on plants.

2. Look at the picture of the zebra eating grass. Which gets energy indirectly from the sun, the grass or the zebra? _____

Cell Processes and Energy

The Two Stages of Photosynthesis

(pages 88–90)

Key Concept: During photosynthesis, plants and some other organisms use energy from the sun to convert carbon dioxide and water into oxygen and sugars.

- In the first stage, or part, of photosynthesis, plants take in the energy in sunlight. Remember, plant cells have special organelles called chloroplasts. Chloroplasts absorb the energy in sunlight.

- In the second stage of photosynthesis, plant cells use the captured energy to make food. To do this, plant cells need water and carbon dioxide.

- Plants get water by absorbing it from the soil with their roots. Carbon dioxide gas enters the leaves through small openings on the leaves.

- Inside the chloroplasts, water and carbon dioxide go through a series of chemical reactions. The energy captured from the sun powers these reactions.

- One product of these chemical reactions is sugar. Plant cells use the energy from some of this sugar to carry out cell activities. Some of this sugar is changed to carbohydrates that make up plant structures. Any unused sugar is stored in the plant for later use.

- The other product of photosynthesis is oxygen. Oxygen goes out of the leaf through the same small openings that carbon dioxide entered the leaf.

Answer the following questions. Use your textbook and the ideas above.

3. Is the following sentence true or false? In the first stage of photosynthesis, plant cells make sugar. _____

Cell Processes and Energy

4. Draw a line from each event in photosynthesis to the stage of photosynthesis in which it occurs. Stages of photosynthesis may be used more than once.

Stage of Photosynthesis

first stage

second stage

Event in Photosynthesis

a. series of chemical reactions

b. oxygen released

c. energy captured

5. Fill in the concept map below about photosynthesis.

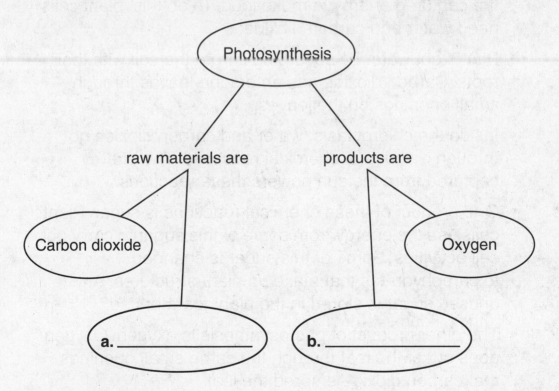

Cell Processes and Energy

Respiration (pages 91–94)

What Is Respiration? (pages 91–93)

Key Concept: During respiration, cells break down simple food molecules such as sugar and release the energy they contain.

- **Respiration** is how cells get energy from sugar.

- Respiration takes place in both plant cells and animal cells. Respiration happens all the time because cells always need energy. Respiration has two stages.

- The first stage of respiration takes place in the cytoplasm of the cell. There, sugar from food is broken down into smaller particles. Just a little energy is released.

- The second stage of respiration takes place in the mitochondria. There, the small sugar particles from the cytoplasm are broken down into even smaller particles. These chemical reactions must have oxygen to take place. Oxygen comes from the air you breath.

- A lot of energy is released during the second stage of respiration. Carbon dioxide and water are also made. They are given off as wastes.

- Photosynthesis and respiration are the opposite of each other. Photosynthesis uses carbon dioxide, water, and energy and makes oxygen and sugar. Respiration uses sugar and oxygen and gives off carbon dioxide, water, and energy.

- Together, photosynthesis and respiration form a cycle that keeps the levels of oxygen and carbon dioxide about the same in Earth's atmosphere.

Cell Processes and Energy

Answer the following questions. Use your textbook and the ideas on page 45.

1. Is the following sentence true or false? Respiration takes place only in animal cells. _____

2. Draw a line from each event in respiration to the stage of respiration in which it takes place. Stages and events of respiration may be used more than once.

Stage of Respiration

first stage

second stage

Event in Respiration

a. takes place in the mitochondria

b. takes place in the cytoplasm

c. gives off energy

d. must have oxygen

3. Fill in the cycle diagram about photosynthesis and respiration.

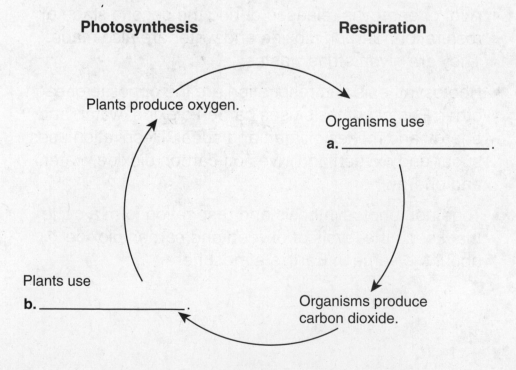

Photosynthesis   **Respiration**

Plants produce oxygen.

Organisms use
a. _____.

Plants use
b. _____.

Organisms produce carbon dioxide.

Cell Processes and Energy

Fermentation (pages 93–94)

Key Concept: Fermentation provides energy for cells without using oxygen.

- **Fermentation** is when the energy from sugar is released without using oxygen.

- Fermentation produces less energy from sugar than respiration does.

- Fermentation takes place in yeast and some other single-celled living things. The products of fermentation are carbon dioxide gas, alcohol, and a little bit of energy.

- Bakers use fermentation to make bread. Yeast breaks down sugar, forming carbon dioxide. Carbon dioxide causes the bread dough to rise. When the dough is baked, the carbon dioxide leaves tiny holes in the bread.

Answer the following questions. Use your textbook and the ideas above.

4. Circle the letter of the best description of fermentation.

   a. releases energy from sugar without oxygen

   b. releases more energy than respiration

   c. produces sugar and oxygen

5. Read each word in the box. In each sentence below, fill in the correct word or words.

carbon dioxide	energy	yeast

   a. Fermentation takes place in some single-celled

   living things such as _____.

   b. Bread dough rises because of the

   _____ given off during

   fermentation.

Cell Processes and Energy

Cell Division (pages 95–102)

Stage 1: Interphase (page 96)

Key Concept: **During interphase, the cell grows, makes a copy of its DNA, and prepares to divide into two cells.**

- For living things to grow, their cells must grow and divide over and over. The regular series of growth and division that cells undergo is called the **cell cycle**.

- The cell cycle is divided into three main stages: interphase, mitosis, and cytokinesis.

- **Interphase** is the first stage of the cell cycle. Interphase takes place before the cell divides.

- In the first part of interphase, the cell grows to its full size. The cell also makes all the cell structures and organelles that it needs.

- In the second part of interphase, the cell makes an exact copy of its DNA molecule in a process called **replication**. At the end of DNA replication, the cell has two identical sets of DNA, or genetic material.

- At the end of interphase, the cell makes the structures it will need to divide.

Answer the following questions. Use your textbook and the ideas above.

1. Circle the letter of each sentence that is true about cell growth.
   a. For living things to grow, their cells must grow and divide.
   b. After interphase is over, cells grow to their full size.
   c. Cells divide during interphase.

Cell Processes and Energy

2. Read each word in the box. In each sentence below, fill in the correct word or words.

| cell cycle | division | interphase | replication |

   a. The regular series of growth and division in a cell is called the _____.

   b. The first stage of the cell cycle is called _____.

   c. When a cell makes an exact copy of its DNA, it is called _____.

3. Is the following sentence true or false? During the first part of interphase, the cell grows to its full size.

   _____

Stage 2: Mitosis (pages 97–99)

Key Concept: **During mitosis, one copy of the DNA is distributed into each of the two daughter cells.**

• The second stage of the cell cycle is mitosis. **Mitosis** (my TOH sis) is the stage when the cell's nucleus divides into two new nuclei.

• In mitosis, the threadlike DNA shortens and thickens to form **chromosomes**. Each chromosome is made up of two rods held together. The two rods are made of DNA that are an exact copy of each other.

• During mitosis, the two chromosome rods separate from each other and move to opposite sides of the cell.

• At the end of mitosis, a new nucleus forms around each group of chromosomes, creating two new nuclei. Each new nucleus has one copy of DNA.

Cell Processes and Energy

Answer the following questions. Use your textbook and the ideas on page 49.

4. Look at the two cells below. Circle the letter of the cell that has just finished mitosis.

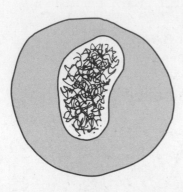 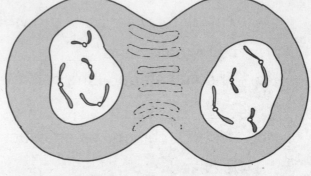

     a.   **b.**

5. Circle the letter of each sentence that is true about mitosis.

    a. The nucleus of the cell divides into two nuclei.

    b. One copy of DNA is given to each new nuclei.

    c. The chromosomes do not divide.

Stage 3: Cytokinesis (page 100)

Key Concept: **During cytokinesis, the cytoplasm divides. The organelles are distributed into each of the two new cells.**

- **Cytokinesis** (sy toh kih NEE sis) is the final stage in the cell cycle. In cytokinesis, the cytoplasm divides. The organelles are divided up between the two new cells.

- When cytokinesis is over, two new cells, called daughter cells, have formed. Each daughter cell has the same number of chromosomes as the original parent cell.

- At the end of cytokinesis, each new cell enters interphase. The cell cycle begins again.

Cell Processes and Energy

Answer the following questions. Use your textbook and the ideas on page 50.

6. During cytokinesis, the _____ divides.

7. After cytokinesis, each _____ has the same number of chromosomes as the parent cell.

Structure and Replication of DNA

(pages 101–102)

Key Concept: **Because of the way in which the nitrogen bases pair with one another, the order of the bases in each new DNA molecule exactly matches the order in the original DNA molecule.**

- Remember that DNA replication takes place in interphase. Because the DNA molecule replicates, each new daughter cell has genetic information to direct the cell's activities.

- DNA looks like a twisted ladder. The sides of the ladder are the DNA backbone.

- The rungs of the ladder are made of four nitrogen bases. The bases on one side of the ladder pair up with bases on the other side of the ladder.

- Only certain bases pair with other bases. Adenine (A) pairs only with thymine (T). Guanine (G) pairs only with cytosine (C).

- DNA replication begins when DNA unwinds and separates. DNA separates between the paired bases.

- Nitrogen bases floating in the nucleus pair up with the unpaired bases on each half of the separated DNA. When the new bases attach, two new DNAs are formed. The new DNA is an exact copy of the original DNA.

Name _____ Date _____ Class _____

Cell Processes and Energy

Answer the following questions. Use your textbook and the ideas on page 51.

8. The picture shows the structure of DNA. Circle the nitrogen bases.

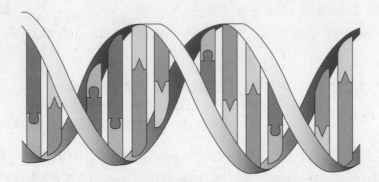

9. Which nitrogen base pairs up with adenine? Circle the letter of the correct answer.

    a. guanine

    b. cytosine

    c. thymine

10. Fill in the flowchart to show what happens during DNA replication.

DNA Replication

The DNA unwinds and **a.** _____.

⬇

Nitrogen bases floating in the nucleus pair up with the unpaired

b. _____ on each half of the separated DNA.

⬇

When the new bases attach, two new

c. _____ are formed.

Genetics: The Science of Heredity

Mendel's Work (pages 110–115)

Mendel's Experiments (pages 111–112)

Key Concept: In all of Mendel's crosses, only one form of the trait appeared in the F_1 generation. However, in the F_2 generation, the "lost" form of the trait reappeared in about one fourth of the plants.

- In the mid 1800s, Gregor Mendel used garden peas to study how traits were passed from parents to offspring. A **trait** is a characteristic, such as seed color.

- The passing of traits from parents to offspring is called **heredity**. The study of heredity is called **genetics**.

- Mendel started his experiments with purebred pea plants. A **purebred** always produces offspring that have the same trait.

- In one experiment, Mendel crossed purebred tall plants with purebred short plants. When Mendel crossed the plants, he took pollen from a flower on the tall plant and used it to pollinate a flower on a short plant. He collected the seeds that formed and grew them. All the offspring plants were tall. The trait for shortness seemed to disappear.

- Mendel allowed the offspring plants to pollinate themselves. When he planted the seeds, he saw some short plants. About one fourth of the plants were short.

Answer the following questions. Use your textbook and the ideas above.

1. The passing of traits from parents to offspring is called

   _____.

2. The study of heredity is called

   _____.

Genetics: The Science of Heredity

3. Circle the letter that explains why Mendel used purebred plants.

   a. Purebred plants produce many offspring.

   b. Purebred plants produce offspring with different traits.

   c. Purebred plants produce offspring with the same trait.

4. Fill in the flowchart about Mendel's first experiment with pea plants.

Mendel's Experiment

> Mendel crossed purebred tall plants with purebred
>
> a. _____ plants.

↓

> The offspring were all b. _____.

↓

> Mendel allowed the offspring to pollinate themselves.

↓

> This second group of offspring were both
>
> c. _____.

Genetics: The Science of Heredity

Dominant and Recessive Alleles (pages 113–115)

Key Concept: An organism's traits are controlled by the alleles it inherits from its parents. Some alleles are dominant, while other alleles are recessive.

- Mendel concluded that separate factors control how traits are inherited. These factors are in pairs, with one factor from the mother and one from the father.

- Today, scientists call the factors that control traits **genes**. The different forms of a gene are called **alleles** (uh LEELZ). For example, the gene for stem height in pea plants has two alleles—one for tall stems and one for short stems.

- A **dominant** allele always shows up in an organism, even when the other allele is present. A **recessive** allele is hidden whenever the dominant allele is present.

- In Mendel's crosses, the purebred parent plants had two alleles for tall stems. The purebred short plants had two alleles for short stems. The offspring plants had one allele for tall stems from the tall parent and one allele for short stems from the short parent.

- The offspring plants from Mendel's crosses are called hybrids. A **hybrid** (HY brid) has two different alleles for a trait. All the offspring plants were tall because the dominant allele for tall stems covers up the recessive allele for short stems.

- Geneticists use letters to represent alleles. A dominant allele has a capital letter. The allele for tall plants is *T*. A recessive allele has the lowercase letter. The allele for short plants is *t*. A purebred tall plant is *TT*. A purebred short plant is *tt*. A hybrid tall plant is *Tt*.

Genetics: The Science of Heredity

Answer the following questions. Use your textbook and the ideas on page 55.

5. Is the following sentence true or false? Factors that control traits are called genes. _____

6. Fill in the table about alleles of genes.

Alleles of Genes		
Type of Allele	**Description**	**Represented by**
Dominant	always shows up when present	a. _____ _____
Recessive	b. _____ _____	lowercase letter, *t*

7. Look at the two pea plants in the picture. Circle the letter of the plant that could be a hybrid.

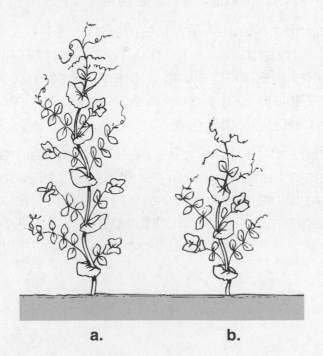

a.   b.

Genetics: The Science of Heredity

Probability and Heredity (pages 118–123)

Principles of Probability (pages 118–119)

***Key Concept:* Probability is a number that describes how likely it is that an event will occur.**

- **Probability** is a number that tells how likely it is that something will happen.

- In a coin toss, the coin will land either tails up or heads up. Each event is equally likely to occur.

- The probability that the coin will land heads up is one event in two possible events, or 1 in 2.

- A 1 in 2 probability can be described as a fraction, 1/2. It can also be described as a percent—50 percent.

- Probability predicts what is likely to occur, not what will actually occur. If you tossed a coin 20 times, you might expect the coin to land heads up 10 times and tails up 10 times. Your actual tosses will likely be different.

- The more coin tosses you make, the closer your actual results will be to the results predicted by probability.

- Each coin toss is an independent event. That is, one coin toss does not affect the results of the next coin toss.

Answer the following questions. Use your textbook and the ideas above.

1. Circle the letter of each sentence that is true about probability.
   a. In a coin toss, the coin will land heads up most of the time.
   b. Probability predicts what events will actually occur.
   c. One coin toss does not affect the results of the next coin toss.

Genetics: The Science of Heredity

2. What is the probability that a tossed coin will land tails up? Circle the letter of the correct answer.
   a. 1 in 2
   b. 2 in 1
   c. 1 in 4

Probability and Genetics (pages 120–121)

Key Concept: **In a genetic cross, the allele that each parent will pass on to its offspring is based on probability.**

- A **Punnett square** is a chart that shows all the possible combinations of alleles that can occur in a genetic cross. Geneticists use Punnett squares to predict the results of a cross.

- The boxes in a Punnett square represent the possible combinations of alleles that offspring can inherit from their parents.

- You can use a Punnett square to find the probability that offspring will have a certain combination of alleles.

- In a cross between two hybrid pea plants with round seeds (*Rr*), the Punnett square gives four possible combinations of alleles in the offspring. These combinations are *RR,* two *Rr,* and *rr.*

Answer the following questions. Use your textbook and the ideas above.

3. Fill in the Punnett square to show the possible allele combinations from a cross between two hybrid pea plants with round seeds (*Rr*).

	R	r
R	RR	a. _____
r	Rr	b. _____

4. In the cross between two hybrid pea plants with round seeds (*Rr*), what is the probability that a pea plant will have seeds that are wrinkled (*rr*)? Circle the letter of the correct answer.

   a. 3 in 4, or 75 percent

   b. 2 in 4, or 50 percent

   c. 1 in 4, or 25 percent

Phenotypes and Genotypes (page 122)

Key Concept: **An organism's phenotype is its physical appearance, or visible traits. An organism's genotype is its genetic makeup, or allele combinations.**

- **Phenotype** (FEE noh typ) is the way an organism looks. You can see that pea pods are smooth. Smooth pea pods is a phenotype.

- **Genotype** (JEN uh typ) is the genetic makeup, or combination of alleles in an organism. The genotype for smooth pea pods can be either *SS* or *Ss*.

- An organism that has two of the same alleles for a trait is **homozygous** (hoh moh ZY gus). A pea plant with smooth pods is homozygous when its genotype is *SS*. A pea plant with pinched pods is always homozygous, *ss*.

- An organism with two different alleles for a trait is **heterozygous** (het ur oh ZY gus). A hybrid plant is heterozygous. A pea plant with smooth pods is heterozygous when it has the alleles *Ss*.

Answer the following questions. Use your textbook and the ideas above.

5. Circle the letter of the homozygous genotype.

   a. Ss

   b. SS

   c. smooth pea pods

Genetics: The Science of Heredity

6. Draw a line from each term to its meaning.

Term	Meaning
phenotype	**a.** an organism with two different alleles for a trait
genotype	**b.** the way an organism looks
heterozygous	**c.** an organism with two of the same alleles for a trait
homozygous	**d.** an organism's genetic makeup

Codominance (page 123)

Key Concept: **In codominance, the alleles are neither dominant nor recessive. As a result, both alleles are expressed in the offspring.**

- Not all alleles for a trait are simply dominant or recessive.

- In **codominance**, the alleles are neither dominant nor recessive. Neither allele is hidden by the other allele. The phenotypes of both alleles can be seen in the offspring with both alleles, which are the heterozygous offspring.

Answer the following question. Use your textbook and the ideas above.

7. Circle the letter of each sentence that is true about codominance.
   a. All traits have either dominant or recessive alleles.
   b. Heterozygous offspring show the phenotype for both alleles.
   c. One allele is hidden by the other allele.

Genetics: The Science of Heredity

The Cell and Inheritance (pages 126–130)

Chromosomes and Inheritance (page 127)

Key Concept: **According to the chromosome theory of inheritance, genes are carried from parents to their offspring on chromosomes.**

- Egg cells and sperm cells have half the number of chromosomes as body cells. For example, grasshopper body cells have 24 chromosomes. Grasshopper sex cells (egg and sperm) have 12 chromosomes.

- When an egg and a sperm join during fertilization, the fertilized egg has exactly the same number of chromosomes as each of the parents.

- The chromosomes in body cells are in pairs. One chromosome in each pair came from the father. The other chromosome in the pair came from the mother.

- The chromosomes carry genes from parents to offspring. This is related to the pairs of alleles for each trait. One set of alleles comes from the mother. The other set of alleles comes from the father.

Answer the following question. Use your textbook and the ideas above.

1. Circle the letter of each sentence that is true about chromosomes.

   a. Sex cells have the same number of chromosomes as body cells have.

   b. The chromosomes in body cells are in pairs.

   c. The chromosomes carry genes from parents to offspring.

Genetics: The Science of Heredity

Meiosis (pages 128–129)

Key Concept: During meiosis, the chromosome pairs separate and are distributed to two different cells. The resulting sex cells have only half as many chromosomes as the other cells in the organism.

- A cell produces sex cells with half the number of chromosomes during **meiosis**. Sex cells are sperm cells and egg cells.

- In meiosis, chromosome pairs separate and move into new sex cells. The sex cells end up with half the number of chromosomes found in the parent cells. Each sex cell has one chromosome from the original pair of chromosomes.

- When sex cells join, the offspring have the normal number of chromosomes.

- A Punnett square shows how the alleles separate during meiosis. When the chromosome pairs separate and go into different sex cells, so do the alleles carried on each chromosome. One allele from each chromosome pair goes to each sex cell.

Answer the following questions. Use your textbook and the ideas above.

2. The picture shows two cells from the same living thing. One cell is a parent cell. One cell is a sex cell. Circle the letter of the sex cell.

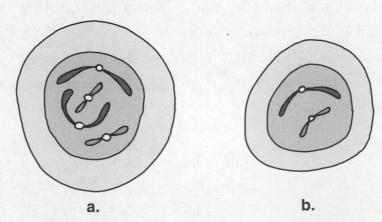

a.   b.

Genetics: The Science of Heredity

3. Fill in the cycle diagram about meiosis.

Meiosis

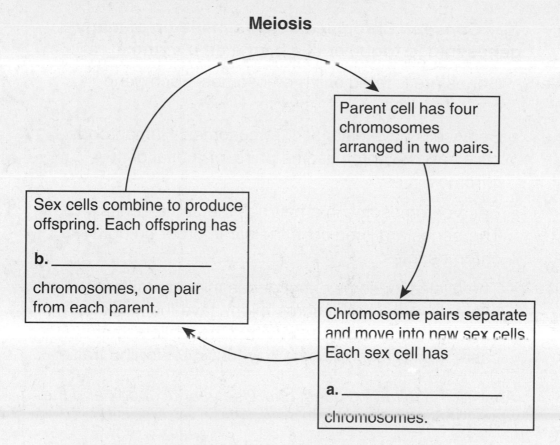

Parent cell has four chromosomes arranged in two pairs.

Chromosome pairs separate and move into new sex cells. Each sex cell has

a. _____

chromosomes.

Sex cells combine to produce offspring. Each offspring has

b. _____

chromosomes, one pair from each parent.

4. A male parent (father) is heterozygous for a trait, *Tt*. What alleles for the trait could the sperm cells have? Circle the letter of the correct answer.

   a. All sperm cells would have *T*.

   b. All sperm cells would have *t*.

   c. The sperm cells could have *T* or *t*.

Genetics: The Science of Heredity

A Lineup of Genes (page 130)

Key Concept: **Chromosomes are made up of many genes joined together like beads on a string.**

- Genes are located on chromosomes. Each gene controls a trait.

- Body cells have pairs of chromosomes. Human body cells have 23 chromosome pairs, or a total of 46 chromosomes.

- Each chromosome in a pair has the same genes. The genes are lined up in the same order on both chromosomes.

- The alleles for some of the genes might be different. For example, one chromosome might have the *A* allele, while the other chromosome has the *a* allele. In this case, the organism is heterozygous (*Aa*) for the trait.

Answer the following questions. Use your textbook and the ideas above.

5. Read each word in the box. In each sentence below, fill in the correct word.

| alleles | chromosomes | genes |

   a. Genes are located on _____.
   b. Each chromosome in a pair has the same

   _____.

6. Is the following sentence true or false? In a chromosome pair, the alleles for some genes might be different. _____

Genetics: The Science of Heredity

The DNA Connection (pages 131–137)

The Genetic Code (page 132)

Key Concept: The order of the nitrogen bases along a gene forms a genetic code that specifies what type of protein will be produced.

- Chromosomes are made mostly of DNA. DNA has four different nitrogen bases—adenine, guanine, thymine, and cytosine.

- Each gene is located at a specific place on a chromosome.

- A gene is a section of DNA with a specific order of nitrogen bases.

- A group of three DNA bases codes for a specific amino acid. The order of the three-base groups is a genetic code. This genetic code determines the order in which amino acids are joined to make a protein.

- Proteins help to determine the traits of living things.

Answer the following questions. Use your textbook and the ideas above.

1. Circle the letter of each sentence that is true about the DNA code.
   a. Chromosomes are made mostly of DNA.
   b. A gene has a specific order of amino acids.
   c. Proteins help determine the traits of a living thing.

2. What does a group of three DNA bases code for? Circle the letter of the correct answer.
   a. gene
   b. amino acid
   c. chromosome

Genetics: The Science of Heredity

How Cells Make Proteins (pages 133–135)

Key Concept: **During protein synthesis, the cell uses information from a gene on a chromosome to produce a specific protein.**

- The cell makes proteins in a process called protein synthesis. Protein synthesis takes place in the ribosomes. Remember, the ribosomes are organelles in the cytoplasm.

- The DNA stays in the nucleus. RNA carries the DNA code into the cytoplasm.

- RNA is like DNA, except RNA has only one strand. Like DNA, RNA has the nitrogen bases adenine, guanine, and cytosine. However, RNA has uracil (YOOR uh sil) instead of thymine.

- Protein synthesis begins when messenger RNA is made from the DNA inside the nucleus. **Messenger RNA** carries the code to the cytoplasm. In the cytoplasm, messenger RNA attaches to a ribosome.

- As the ribosome moves along the strand of messenger RNA, the ribosome holds the three-letter codes so that the transfer RNA can match up with them. The **transfer RNA** carries specific amino acids to the ribosome and adds them to the growing protein.

- The amino acid chain grows until the ribosome comes to a three-letter code that acts as a stop sign. The ribosome releases the completed protein.

Answer the following questions. Use your textbook and the ideas above.

3. Is the following sentence true or false? Proteins are made in the nucleus in structures called ribosomes.

_____

Genetics: The Science of Heredity

4. Fill in the table to show how DNA and RNA are alike and different.

Comparing Nucleic Acids			
Nucleic Acid	**Location**	**Number of Strands**	**Nitrogen Bases**
DNA	a. _____	two	adenine, guanine, cytosine, thymine
RNA	moves from nucleus to cytoplasm	b. _____	adenine, guanine, oytosine, c. _____

5. The picture shows transfer RNA matching up to the three-letter code in messenger RNA. Circle the transfer RNA.

Genetics: The Science of Heredity

Mutations (pages 136–137)

Key Concept: **Mutations can cause a cell to produce an incorrect protein during protein synthesis. As a result, the organism's trait, or phenotype, may be different from what it normally would have been.**

- A **mutation** is any change in a gene or chromosome.

- Sometimes mutations happen when DNA is copied or when RNA is made. The wrong base might be added, an extra base might be added, or one base might be removed. These mutations can cause the cell to make the wrong protein. The wrong protein can change the organism's phenotype, or traits.

- Sometimes mutations happen when chromosomes do not separate correctly during meiosis. When this happens, a cell might have too many or too few chromosomes.

- Mutations are harmful if they reduce the organism's chance to survive and reproduce.

- Mutations are helpful if they help an organism survive and reproduce better.

Answer the following questions. Use your textbook and the ideas above.

6. Circle the letter of what may happen when chromosomes do not separate correctly during meiosis.

   a. An extra base is added to DNA.

   b. The wrong base is added to DNA.

   c. A cell might have too many chromosomes.

7. Is the following sentence true or false? All mutations are harmful. _____

Modern Genetics

Human Inheritance (pages 144–150)

Patterns of Human Inheritance (pages 145–146)

Key Concept: **Some human traits are controlled by single genes with two alleles, and others by single genes with multiple alleles. Still other traits are controlled by many genes that act together.**

- Many human traits are controlled by one gene with one dominant allele and one recessive allele. These traits have two specific phenotypes. For example, the allele for a widow's peak in the hairline is dominant over the allele for a straight hairline.

- Some human traits are controlled by one gene that has more than two alleles. Genes with more than two alleles have **multiple alleles**. Even though a gene has multiple alleles, a person can have only two of the alleles. This is because a person has chromosomes in pairs. Each chromosome in the pair carries only one allele for a gene. Human blood type is controlled by a gene with multiple alleles.

- Some human traits are controlled by many genes. These traits have a wide range of phenotypes because the genes act as a group to produce a single trait. Height and skin color are controlled by many genes.

Answer the following questions. Use your textbook and the ideas above.

1. Circle the letter of each sentence that is true about human traits.

   a. All human traits are controlled by one gene.

   b. Even though a gene has multiple alleles, a person can have only two alleles for the trait.

   c. Traits controlled by many genes have a wide range of phenotypes.

Modern Genetics

2. Draw a line from each example to the pattern of inheritance.

Example	Pattern of Inheritance
human blood type	a. single gene with two alleles
height	b. single gene with multiple alleles
widow's peak	c. many genes

The Sex Chromosomes (pages 147–149)

Key Concept: **The sex chromosomes carry genes that determine whether a person is male or female. They also carry genes that determine other traits.**

- The **sex chromosomes** are one pair of the 23 pairs of human chromosomes.

- Sex chromosomes are the only chromosomes that do not always exactly match. Females (women) have two X chromosomes. Males (men) have one X chromosome and one Y chromosome. The Y chromosome is much smaller than the X chromosome.

- When sex cells form, the sex chromosomes separate just like the other chromosomes. All egg cells have an X chromosome. Half of the sperm cells have an X chromosome and half have a Y chromosome.

- When a sperm cell with an X chromosome fertilizes an egg cell, the fertilized egg develops into a girl. When a sperm cell with a Y chromosome fertilizes an egg cell, the fertilized egg develops into a boy.

- Genes for some human traits are also carried on the sex chromosomes. These genes are called **sex-linked genes** because their alleles are passed from parents to child on a sex chromosome. One sex-linked trait is red-green colorblindness.

Modern Genetics

Answer the following questions. Use your textbook and the ideas on page 70.

3. When a sperm cell with an Y chromosome fertilizes an egg cell, the fertilized egg develops into a(an)

   _____.

4. Women have two _____ chromosomes.

5. The Punnett square below shows the possible phenotypes of the children whose mother has one allele for colorblindness. Normal vision (X^C) is dominant over colorblindness (X^c). The Y chromosome does not carry a gene for color vision. Circle the genotypes of the children that will be colorblind.

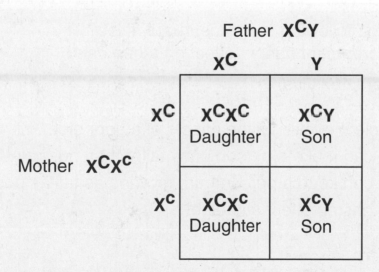

6. Look again at the Punnett square above. What is the probability that this couple will have a daughter who is colorblind? Circle the letter of the correct answer.
   a. No daughters will be colorblind.
   b. The daughters have a 50 percent chance of being colorblind.
   c. All the daughters will be colorblind.

Modern Genetics

The Effect of Environment (page 150)

Key Concept: **Many of a person's characteristics are determined by an interaction between genes and the environment.**

- The phenotypes of all living things are not the result of their genes alone. A living thing's environment, or surroundings, also affects the living thing's characteristics.

- Height is determined by several genes that work together. However, people's diets also influence height. A poor diet or poor health can keep a person from growing as tall as might be possible.

Answer the following questions. Use your textbook and the ideas above.

7. Is the following sentence true or false? The environment has an effect on a person's

   characteristics. _____

8. Circle the letter of the effects of a poor diet.
   a. can make a person grow taller than possible
   b. can keep a person from growing as tall as possible
   c. has no affect on height

Modern Genetics

Human Genetic Disorders (pages 151–155)

Causes of Genetic Disorders (page 152)

Key Concept: **Some genetic disorders are caused by mutations in the DNA of genes. Other disorders are caused by changes in the overall structure or number of chromosomes.**

- A **genetic disorder** is an abnormal condition that a person inherits through genes or chromosomes.

- Some genetic disorders are caused by a change in DNA. Cystic fibrosis is caused by a mutation in a gene. People with cystic fibrosis have abnormally thick mucus in their lungs. The allele for cystic fibrosis is recessive to the normal allele.

- Other genetic disorders are caused by changes in chromosome number or structure. In Down syndrome, a person has one extra copy of chromosome 21. People with Down syndrome may have some mental retardation as well as heart problems.

Answer the following questions. Use your textbook and the ideas above.

1. Circle the letter of each cause of a genetic disorder.
   a. changes in the environment
   b. changes in DNA
   c. changes in chromosome number or structure

2. Circle the letter of each genetic disorder.
   a. Down syndrome
   b. chicken pox
   c. cystic fibrosis

Modern Genetics

Pedigrees (page 153)

Key Concept: **One important tool that geneticists use to trace the inheritance of traits in humans is a pedigree.**

- A **pedigree** is a chart or "family tree" that tracks the members of a family that have a certain trait.

- Geneticists use pedigrees to follow a human trait through several generations of a family. This helps geneticists learn how the trait is inherited.

- In a pedigree, a circle stands for a female (woman). A square stands for a male (man). A line connecting a square and circle shows that the man and woman are married. Children are connected to their parents by a line and a bracket.

- A shaded square or circle stands for a person who has the trait. A half-shaded square or circle stands for a person who carries just one allele for the trait, but does not show the trait. A person who carries one allele for a trait, but does not have the trait is called a carrier. A circle or square that is not shaded stands for a person who does not have the trait.

Answer the following questions. Use your textbook and the ideas above.

3. What is a chart that follows a trait through several generations of a family? Circle the letter of the correct answer.
   a. Punnett square
   b. allele combinations
   c. pedigree

Modern Genetics

4. Look at the symbol below.

   a. Does this symbol stand for a male or a female?

      _____

   b. Does this symbol stand for a person who has the
      trait or one who is a carrier for the trait?

      _____

5. The chart below follows hemophilia in a family.
   Hemophilia is a genetic disorder in which the blood
   does not clot normally. How many males (men) have
   hemophilia? Circle the letter of the correct answer.

   a. 1
   b. 2
   c. 3

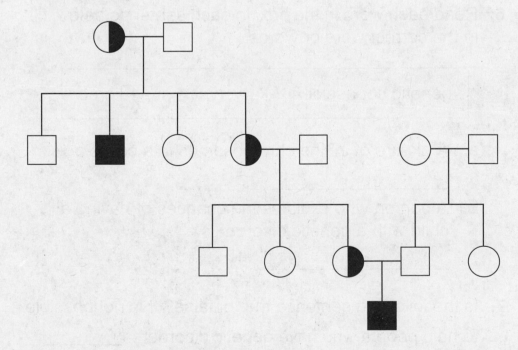

Managing Genetic Disorders
(pages 154–155)

Key Concept: Doctors use tools such as karyotypes to help diagnose genetic disorders. People with genetic disorders are helped through medical care, education, job training, and other methods.

- A **karyotype** is a picture of all the chromosomes in a cell. A karyotype shows whether or not a person has the correct number of chromosomes.

- Genetic counselors help couples understand their chances of having a child with a genetic disorder. Genetic counselors use karyotypes, pedigree charts, and Punnett squares in their work.

- People with genetic disorders live active, productive lives. Some people might need medical care. Others might need education and job training.

Answer the following questions. Use your textbook and the ideas above.

6. Read each word in the box. In each sentence below, fill in the correct word or words.

genetic counselor	karyotype	pedigree

   a. A picture of all the chromosomes in a cell is a

   _____.

   b. A person who explains the chances of having a child with a genetic disorder is a

   _____.

7. Is the following sentence true or false? It is not possible to help people who have genetic disorders. _____

Advances in Genetics (pages 157–162)

Selective Breeding (page 158)

Key Concept: **Selective breeding is one method for developing organisms with desirable traits.**

- **Selective breeding** is when organisms with desired traits are chosen to be the parents of the next generation. At least some of the offspring may have the desired traits.

- Corn plants that produced the most and the best food were developed by selective breeding.

Answer the following question. Use your textbook and the ideas above.

1. When organisms with desired traits are chosen to be the parents of the next generation, it is called

   _____.

Cloning (page 159)

Key Concept: **Cloning is one method for developing organisms with desirable traits.**

- A **clone** is an organism that has exactly the same genes as the organism from which it was produced.

- Some plants are very easy to clone. Just cut a stem from the plant and put the stem in soil. The stem will grow into a new plant. The new plant is genetically identical to the plant the stem was cut from.

- Scientists have cloned some animals. Cloning animals is more difficult than cloning plants. The nucleus of an animal's body cell is used to produce an animal clone.

Answer the following questions. Use your textbook and the ideas on page 77.

2. Which is an example of a clone? Circle the letter of the correct answer.

   a. Corn developed by selective breeding.

   b. A plant grown from the stem cut from a plant.

   c. Kittens that look different from their mother.

3. Is the following sentence true or false? Animals are easier to clone than plants. _____

Genetic Engineering (pages 160–161)

Key Concept: **Genetic engineering is a method for developing organisms with desirable traits.**

- In **genetic engineering**, genes from one organism are put into the DNA of another organism.

- Scientists use genetic engineering to create bacteria that can make useful human proteins such as insulin. The human insulin gene is put into a bacterial cell. The bacterial cell makes the insulin. Then scientists collect the insulin, which is used to treat a disease.

- In **gene therapy**, scientists put copies of a needed gene directly into a person's cells. For example, scientists could replace the allele of the gene that causes cystic fibrosis with a copy of the normal allele.

Answer the following questions. Use your textbook and the ideas above.

4. Circle the letter of each sentence that is true about genetic engineering.

   a. Scientists put bacteria into human cells.

   b. Scientists put human proteins into bacterial cells.

   c. The bacterial cells make the human protein.

Modern Genetics

5. Scientists put genes directly into a person's cells in a process called _____.

6. Scientists transfer genes from one organism into the DNA of another organism in _____.

Learning About Human Genetics (page 162)

Key Concept: The main goal of the Human Genome Project has been to identify the DNA sequence of every gene in the human genome.

- A **genome** is all the DNA in one cell of an organism.

- In the Human Genome Project, scientists are working to identify the sequence, or order, of nitrogen bases for all the genes on the human chromosomes.

- Every person has a different sequence of nitrogen bases in their DNA, except for identical twins.

Answer the following question. Use your textbook and the ideas above.

7. Draw a line from each term to its description.

Term	Description
genome	**a.** have the same DNA sequence
Human Genome Project	**b.** all the DNA in one cell of an organism
identical twins	**c.** identify the base sequence for all human genes

Darwin's Theory (pages 172–179)

Darwin's Observations (page 173)

Key Concept: **Charles Darwin's important observations included the diversity of living things and the remains of ancient organisms.**

- In 1831, Charles Darwin left from England on a ship that made many stops along the coast of South America. Darwin's job was to learn about the living things he saw.

- Darwin saw many plants and animals that he had never seen before. The living things he saw in South America were all very different from those in England.

- A **species** is a group of similar living things that can mate with each other and produce offspring.

- Darwin saw fossils in South America. A **fossil** is the preserved remains of an organism that lived long ago.

Answer the following questions. Use your textbook and the ideas above.

1. Is the following sentence true or false? Darwin saw that living things in South America were just like those in England. _____

2. Read each word in the box. In each sentence below, fill in the correct word or words.

fossil	living thing	species

   a. The preserved remains of an organism that lived long ago is a _____.

   b. A group of similar living things that can mate and produce offspring is a _____.

Galápagos Organisms (pages 174–175)

Key Concept: **Darwin's important observations included the characteristics of organisms on the Galápagos Islands.**

- Darwin saw that the plants and animals on the Galápagos Islands were much like those on the mainland of South America.

- The Galápagos plants and animals did have some very important differences from those on the mainland. For example, Galápagos iguanas had larger claws than mainland iguanas.

- Darwin thought that some plants and animals came to the Galápagos Islands from the mainland. Eventually, the offspring of these plants and animals became different from their mainland relatives.

- Darwin also saw that tortoises and finches were different from one Galápagos island to the next. Finches, for example, had different beak shapes.

- Beak shape is an example of an adaptation. An **adaptation** is a trait that helps an organism survive and reproduce.

Answer the following questions. Use your textbook and the ideas above.

3. Is the following sentence true or false? Darwin thought that some plants and animals came to the Galápagos Islands from the mainland. _____

4. What is an adaptation? Circle the letter of the correct answer.
   a. a difference between two animals
   b. a trait that helps an organism survive and reproduce
   c. a way for plants and animals to get to an island

Changes Over Time

Evolution (page 176)

Key Concept: Darwin reasoned that plants or animals that arrived on the Galápagos Islands faced conditions that were different from those on the mainland. Perhaps, Darwin hypothesized, the species gradually changed over many generations and became better adapted to the new conditions.

- The gradual change in a species over time is called **evolution**.

- Darwin concluded that the living things that came to the Galápagos Islands from the mainland had changed over time. The living things changed so that they could live better in the island environment.

- Darwin's ideas are often called the theory of evolution. A **scientific theory** is a well-tested idea.

Answer the following questions. Use your textbook and the ideas above.

5. Is the following sentence true or false? The Galápagos plants and animals changed over time so that they could live better in the island environment. _____

6. Read each word in the box. In each sentence below, fill in the correct word or words.

adaptation	evolution	scientific theory

a. A well-tested idea is a(an) _____.

b. The gradual change in a species over time is called _____.

Changes Over Time

Natural Selection (pages 177–179)

Key Concept: **Darwin proposed that, over a long time, natural selection can lead to change. Helpful variations may gradually accumulate in a species, while unfavorable ones may disappear.**

- Darwin suggested that evolution happens because of natural selection. In **natural selection**, individuals that are better adapted to their environment are more likely to survive and reproduce.

- Factors that affect natural selection are overproduction, competition, and variation.

- Most species produce far more offspring than can possibly survive. Overproduction makes it more likely that some offspring will survive.

- Food and other resources are limited. Members of a species must compete with each other for these resources. Some members of a species may not find enough to eat, so they do not survive.

- Any difference between individuals of the same species is called a **variation**.

- Some variations make individuals better adapted to their environment. Individuals that are better adapted are more likely to live and produce more offspring. Their offspring may inherit these helpful variations. After many generations, more members of the species will have the helpful variations.

- Variations in characteristics are caused by mutations and the shuffling of alleles during meiosis.

Answer the following questions. Use your textbook and the ideas above.

7. Evolution happens because of

_____.

Changes Over Time

8. Look at the picture of the turtle eggs above. Circle the letter of the factor affecting natural selection that the picture shows.

   a. competition

   b. overproduction

   c. variation

9. Draw a line from each factor that affects natural selection to its meaning.

Factor	Meaning
competition	a. difference between individuals of the same species
overproduction	b. caused by limited food and other resources
variation	c. produce more offspring than can survive

Evidence of Evolution
(pages 182–187)

Interpreting the Evidence (pages 183–184)

Key Concept: Fossils, patterns of early development, and similar body structures all provide evidence that organisms have changed over time.

- Fossils show that living things from the past were very different from the living things of today.

- Scientists study what organisms look like when they are just beginning to develop. For example, the early stages of all animals with backbones all look similar. Patterns of early development can show that animals are related. These animals share a common ancestor that evolved over time into different species.

- How bones are arranged in the body also gives clues to evolution. Many animals with backbones have body structures that do different things, but the bones are arranged in the same way. This shows that the animals evolved from a common ancestor.

Answer the following questions. Use your textbook and the ideas above.

1. Circle the letter of each sentence that is true about evidence for evolution.

   a. Fossils show that living things are the same as they were in the past.

   b. Animals that develop with the same patterns share a common ancestor.

   c. Animals with body structures that look alike have different ancestors.

Changes Over Time

2. Fill in the graphic organizer about the evidence that supports the theory of evolution.

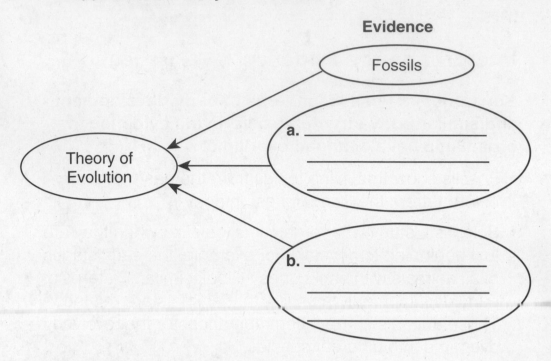

Inferring Species Relationships

(pages 185–186)

Key Concept: **Scientists have combined the evidence from DNA, protein structure, fossils, early development, and body structure to determine the evolutionary relationships among species.**

• Fossils, early development, and body structures give evidence that evolution has occurred and also give clues to how different species are related.

• DNA and proteins also give clues to how different species are related. The more alike DNA and protein structures are, the more closely related the species are.

• After studying DNA and protein structures, along with fossils, early development, and body structures, scientists have a good idea about how species are related. To show these relationships, scientists draw branching tree diagrams.

Name _____ Date _____ Class _____

Changes Over Time

Answer the following questions. Use your textbook and the ideas on page 86.

3. Read each word in the box. In each sentence below, fill in the correct word or words.

branching tree proteins species

    a. Scientists compare DNA and proteins to find

       out how _____ are related.

    b. Scientists show the relationships among species

       using a diagram called a _____.

4. The branching tree shows how scientists think raccoons, lesser pandas, giant pandas, and bears are related. Are bears more closely related to raccoons or giant pandas? _____

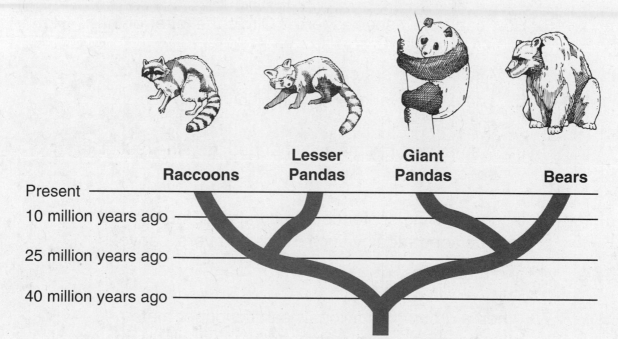

Changes Over Time

How Do New Species Form? (pages 186–187)

Key Concept: **A new species can form when a group of individuals remains isolated from the rest of its species long enough to evolve different traits.**

- Rivers, canyons, and mountains can separate a small group of individuals from the rest of it species.

- Over time the small group will evolve traits that are different from the rest of the species.

- If the small group stays separate from the rest of its species, the small group may become so different that it will become a separate species.

- The small group has become a separate species when the group can no longer mate and produce offspring with members of the original species.

Answer the following questions. Use your textbook and the ideas above.

5. How can a new species form? Circle the letter of the correct answer.
    a. A species overproduces.
    b. There is no variation among individuals in a species.
    c. A small group remains separated from the rest of its species.

6. Is the following sentence true or false? Small groups may be separated by such things as rivers, canyons, and mountains. _____

7. When a group of individuals can no longer mate and produce offspring with members of the original species, the group has become a separate

    _____.

Changes Over Time

The Fossil Record (pages 189–197)

How Do Fossils Form? (page 190)

Key Concept: **Most fossils form when organisms that die become buried in sediments.**

- Usually only the hard parts of an organism, such as the bones or shells of animals, can form fossils.

- Most fossils form when a dead organism is covered in layers of sediment—soil and small pieces of rock.

- Over millions of years, the sediments harden and become rock. The bones or shells of the dead organism become fossils.

- When the rock wears away, the fossil can be seen on the surface of the rock.

Answer the following question. Use your textbook and the ideas above.

1. Complete the flowchart about how a fossil forms.

Fossil Formation

A crocodile dies and sinks in the water.

↓

Layers of **a.** _____ cover the crocodile's body.

↓

The sediments harden and become rock. The remains of the crocodile become a **b.** _____.

Changes Over Time

Determining a Fossil's Age (pages 191–192)

Key Concept: **Scientists can determine a fossil's age in two ways: relative dating and radioactive dating.**

- When scientists learn the age of fossils, they can figure out when past events occurred. Scientists can also learn how organisms have changed over time.

- One way to learn the age of a fossil is based on where the fossil is found. A fossil found near the top of a canyon is younger than fossils found near the bottom of a canyon. The layers on the bottom of the canyon are older, because they were formed first. This method does not give the actual age of a fossil.

- Scientists learn the actual age of fossils by analyzing the different elements that make up the rocks around the fossils.

Answer the following questions. Use your textbook and the ideas above.

2. Is the following sentence true or false? Scientists use the age of fossils to learn how organisms changed

over time. _____

3. The picture shows layers of rock in a canyon wall. Some of the rock layers have fossils. Circle the youngest fossils.

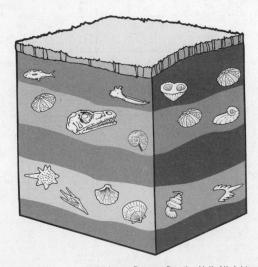

Changes Over Time

What Do Fossils Reveal? (pages 192–195)

Key Concept: The calendar of Earth's history is sometimes called the Geologic Time Scale.

- The millions of fossils that scientists have found are called the **fossil record**.

- Almost all of the species found as fossils are now extinct. A species is **extinct** if no members of that species are still alive.

- By studying the fossil record, scientists have created a "calendar" of Earth's history. Scientists have divided the history of Earth into units of time called eras and periods. The calendar of Earth's history is called the Geologic Time Scale.

Answer the following questions. Use your textbook and the ideas above.

4. Read each word in the box. In each sentence below, fill in the correct word or words.

extinct	fossil record	Geologic Time Scale

  a. If no members of a species are still alive, then

   the species is _____.

  b. The "calendar" of Earth's history is called the

   _____.

5. Circle the letter of each sentence that is true about Earth's history.

  a. The fossil record is made up of all the fossils that have been collected.

  b. Most species found as fossils are now extinct.

  c. Earth's history is divided into years and centuries.

Changes Over Time

Unanswered Questions (pages 196–197)

Key Concept: Two unanswered questions about evolution involve the causes of mass extinctions and the rate at which evolution occurs.

- Most living things died without leaving fossils behind. So the fossil record is not complete. An incomplete fossil record leaves many questions unanswered.

- During Earth's history, some mass extinctions have happened. A mass extinction is when many types of living things become extinct at the same time.

- Scientists are not sure what causes mass extinctions. Many scientists think major changes in Earth's climate caused these extinctions.

- Scientists are also not sure how quickly species change. Most scientists think that evolution can occur at different rates. Sometimes evolution is slow and steady. At other times, evolution happens very rapidly.

Answer the following questions. Use your textbook and the ideas above.

6. Is the following sentence true or false? All living things that became extinct left behind fossils. _____

7. Draw a line from each cause to its effect.

Cause	Effect
climate change	**a.** questions about Earth's history
missing fossils	**b.** mass extinction
sometimes slow, sometimes fast	**c.** speed of evolution

Viruses, Bacteria, Protists, and Fungi

Viruses (pages 210–215)

What Is a Virus? (pages 210–211)

Key Concept: **The only way in which viruses are like organisms is that they can multiply. All viruses have two basic parts: a protein coat that protects the virus and an inner core made of genetic material.**

- A tiny, nonliving thing that can enter a living cell and reproduce inside the cell is a **virus**.

- Viruses are not living things because viruses are not made of cells. Viruses also cannot make or use food.

- The only way that viruses are like living things is that viruses can make more viruses. But viruses make new viruses only when they are inside a living cell.

- Viruses act like parasites. A **parasite** (PA ruh syt) is an organism that lives on or in a host organism, causing it harm. A **host** is an organism that supplies energy to a virus or another organism. Almost all viruses kill the host cells in which they multiply.

- The genetic material in a virus has the instructions for making new viruses.

- The protein coat protects the genetic material. The proteins that make up the coat also help the virus attach to the cells that the virus will infect.

- A virus can infect only certain cells. The virus's protein coat will fit into only certain proteins on the surface of a cell. Not all cells have the proteins that will fit the virus's proteins.

Viruses, Bacteria, Protists, and Fungi

Answer the following questions. Use your textbook and the ideas on page 93.

1. Is the following sentence true or false? A virus is not a living organism because it is not made of cells.

_____

2. Draw a line from each term to its meaning.

Term	Meaning
virus	**a.** supplies energy to a virus or another organism
parasite	**b.** tiny, nonliving thing that enters a cell to reproduce
host	**c.** lives on or in another organism, causing it harm

3. The picture shows the two parts of a virus. Circle the letter of the part that has the instructions for making new viruses.

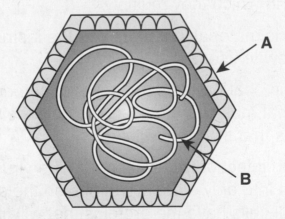

4. Circle the letter of what is NOT a function of the virus's protein coat.

a. protects genetic material

b. has instructions for making new viruses

c. helps a virus attach to the right cell

Viruses, Bacteria, Protists, and Fungi.

How Viruses Multiply (pages 212–213)

Key Concept: Once inside a cell, a virus's genetic material takes over many of the cell's functions. It instructs the cell to produce the virus's proteins and genetic material. These proteins and genetic material then assemble into new viruses.

- Some viruses are active as soon as they enter a cell. The genetic material of an active virus takes over the functions of the cell right away and starts making new viruses. The cell dies when the new viruses burst out.

- Other viruses are not active right away. A hidden virus may stay inactive for years. When conditions are right, the virus's genetic material suddenly becomes active. It takes over the cell's functions and begins making new viruses. When the cell is full of new viruses, the cell bursts open and dies.

Answer the following questions. Use your textbook and the ideas above.

5. Draw a line from each virus to its description. The descriptions may be used more than once.

Virus

active virus

hidden virus

Description

a. The virus's genetic material takes over the cell's functions.

b. The virus multiplies as soon as it enters the cell.

c. The virus may stay inactive for a long time.

6. Is the following sentence true or false? A cell does not die when the new viruses leave the cell. _____

Viruses, Bacteria, Protists, and Fungi

Viruses and Disease (pages 214–215)

Key Concept: **Resting, drinking plenty of fluids, and eating well-balanced meals may be all you can do while you recover from a viral disease.**

- Viruses cause diseases in people and other living things. For example, viruses cause colds and flu in people and rabies in dogs and cats.

- Some diseases caused by viruses can be spread through contact with an object handled by an infected person. Some viruses travel in tiny drops of moisture that an infected person sneezes or coughs into the air.

- One of the best ways to keep from getting a viral disease is by getting a vaccine. A **vaccine** causes the body to produce chemicals that destroy certain viruses.

- Keeping your body healthy prevents disease. Eat healthful foods. Get enough sleep. Drink lots of fluids. Wash your hands.

- When you are sick, get plenty of rest. Try not to spread your disease to other people.

Answer the following questions. Use your textbook and the ideas above.

7. Circle the letter of each sentence that is true about viruses.

    a. Viruses cause diseases only in people.

    b. Colds and flu are caused by viruses.

    c. Some viruses can be spread through objects handled by an infected person.

8. If you wanted your body to produce chemicals that destroy certain viruses, you would get a(an)

_____.

Viruses, Bacteria, Protists, and Fungi

Bacteria (pages 217–225)

The Bacterial Cell (pages 217–219)

Key Concept: **Bacteria are prokaryotes. The genetic material in their cells is not contained in a nucleus.**

- **Bacteria** are single-celled organisms that do not have a nucleus.

- The outside of a bacterial cell is usually protected by a stiff cell wall.

- Just inside the cell wall is the cell membrane. The cell membrane controls what can go in and out of the bacterial cell.

- The area inside the cell membrane is the cytoplasm. The cell's genetic material is in the cytoplasm. The genetic material looks like a tangled string.

- Some bacteria have a flagellum attached to the outside of the membrane. A **flagellum** (fluh JEL um) is a long, whiplike structure that helps a cell to move. Bacteria without a flagellum are carried by the wind or water.

Answer the following questions. Use your textbook and the ideas above.

1. The picture shows different parts of a bacterial cell.
   a. Circle the letter of the cytoplasm.
   b. Underline the letter of a flagellum.

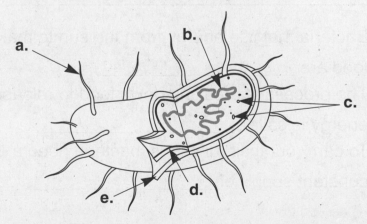

Viruses, Bacteria, Protists, and Fungi

2. Is the following sentence true or false? Bacteria are living things made up of many cells. _____

Obtaining Food and Energy (page 219)

Key Concept: **Bacteria must have a source of food and a way of breaking down the food to release its energy.**

- Bacteria need energy to live. This energy comes from food.

- Some bacteria can make their own food. Autotrophic bacteria either use energy from the sun or chemicals in the environment to make food.

- Other bacteria cannot make their own food. Heterotrophic bacteria get food by eating other organisms or the food made by other organisms.

- Breaking down food to release its energy is called respiration.

Answer the following question. Use your textbook and the ideas above.

3. Read each word in the box. In each sentence below, fill in the correct word.

autotrophic	energy	heterotrophic
respiration		

    a. Bacteria that use energy from the sun to make food are _____.

    b. The process of breaking down food to release its energy is called _____.

    c. To carry out their functions, bacteria need a constant supply of _____.

Viruses, Bacteria, Protists, and Fungi

Reproduction (pages 220–221)

Key Concept: **When bacteria have plenty of food, the right temperature, and other suitable conditions, they thrive and reproduce frequently.**

- Bacteria reproduce in the right conditions. The right conditions include plenty of food and water and the right temperature.

- Bacteria reproduce by binary fission. In **binary fission**, one cell divides to form two identical cells.

- Binary fission is a form of asexual reproduction. **Asexual reproduction** involves only one parent. The parent produces offspring that are identical to it.

- Sometimes bacteria undergo conjugation. In **conjugation** (kahn juh GAY shun), one bacterial cell transfers some genetic material into another bacterial cell.

- Conjugation is a form of sexual reproduction. **Sexual reproduction** involves two parents. The offspring of sexual reproduction are genetically different from either parent.

Answer the following questions. Use your textbook and the ideas above.

4. Circle the letter of when bacteria will reproduce.

   a. anytime

   b. only when water dries up

   c. when there is plenty of food and the temperature is right

Viruses, Bacteria, Protists, and Fungi

5. Read each word in the box. Use the words to complete the concept map about reproduction in bacteria.

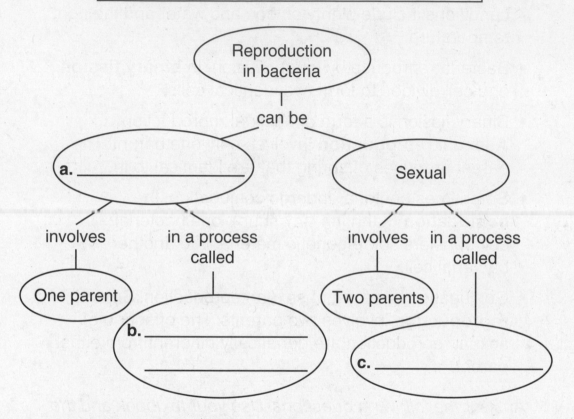

Asexual	Binary fission	Conjugation
Reproduction		

The Role of Bacteria in Nature (pages 222–225)

Key Concept: **Bacteria are involved in oxygen and food production, environmental recycling and cleanup, and in health maintenance and medicine production.**

- You might think that bacteria are only harmful because they cause disease. However, most bacteria are harmless. Some are even helpful to people.

- When bacteria make food with the sun's energy, they release oxygen into the air. These bacteria help keep the right amount of oxygen in the air.

Viruses, Bacteria, Protists, and Fungi

- Foods like vinegar, yogurt, and cheeses are made with the help of bacteria. Other kinds of bacteria cause food to spoil. Eating spoiled food can make you sick.

- Some bacteria break down the chemicals in dead organisms. Plants use these broken down chemicals to grow.

- Bacteria can help clean up oil spills. The bacteria make the poisonous chemicals in oil harmless.

- You have bacteria in your intestines. These bacteria help you to digest food.

Answer the following question. Use your textbook and the ideas on page 100 and above.

6. Fill in the table below. Write *helpful* if the role played by bacteria is helpful to people. Write *harmful* if the role is harmful to people.

The Roles of Bacteria	
Role	**Helpful or Harmful to People?**
Cause diseases	a. _____
Give off oxygen	b. _____
Used to make foods	c. _____
Spoil foods	d. _____
Break down dead organisms	e. _____
Clean up oil spills	f. _____

Viruses, Bacteria, Protists, and Fungi

Protists (pages 226–235)

What Is a Protist? (page 227)

Key Concept: **Protists are eukaryotes that cannot be classified as animals, plants, or fungi.**

- **Protists** are eukaryotes, or living things whose cells have a nucleus. Any eukaryote that is not classified as an animal, plant, or fungus is classified as a protist.

- All protists live in moist places.

- Most protists are unicellular—just one cell. Some protists are multicellular—made up of many cells.

- Some protists can move. Others cannot move.

- Scientists group protists based on the characteristics they share with animals, plants, or fungi.

Answer the following questions. Use your textbook and the ideas above.

1. Circle the letter of each sentence that is true about protists.

   a. Protists, like bacteria, do not have a nucleus in their cells.

   b. All protists live in moist places.

   c. All protists can move.

2. The picture below shows a protist. Is this protist unicellular or multicellular? _____

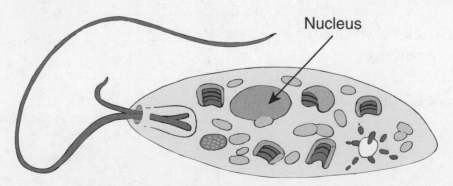

Nucleus

Viruses, Bacteria, Protists, and Fungi

Animal-Like Protists (pages 227–230)

Key Concept: **Like animals, animal-like protists are heterotrophs, and most are able to move from place to place to obtain food.**

- Animal-like protists are called protozoans. **Protozoans** (proh tuh ZOH unz) are single-celled eukaryotes that cannot make their own food. Most protozoans move to get food. Eukaryotes are living things with a nucleus in their cells.

- Some protozoans get food by forming pseudopods. **Pseudopods** (SOO duh pahdz) are temporary bulges of the cell. Pseudopods form when cytoplasm flows toward one direction and the rest of the organism follows.

- Other protozoans have cilia. **Cilia** (SIL ee uh) are hairlike structures that move with a wavelike motion. Cilia act like tiny oars to move an organism. Cilia also sweep food into the organism.

- Another group of protozoans use long, whiplike flagella to move.

Answer the following questions. Use your textbook and the ideas above.

3. Circle the letter of a single-celled eukaryote that cannot make its own food.

   a. bacteria   **b.** virus   **c.** protozoan

4. The pictures show two different protozoans. Circle the picture of the protozoan that has cilia.

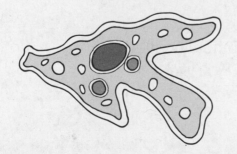
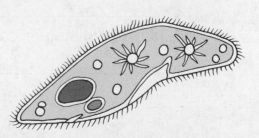

Viruses, Bacteria, Protists, and Fungi

Plantlike Protists (pages 231–233)

Key Concept: Like plants, algae are autotrophs.

- **Algae** (AL jee) are protists that use the sun's energy to make their own food. Autotrophs are living things that can make their own food.

- Some algae are unicellular. Other algae are multicellular.

- Algae can be green, yellow, red, brown, orange, or black. Algae have these different colors because algae contain pigments. Pigments are chemicals that produce color.

- Scientists have divided algae into different groups based on their color and structure.

Answer the following questions. Use your textbook and the ideas above.

5. Is the following sentence true or false? All plantlike protists are unicellular. _____

6. Read each word in the box. In each sentence below, fill in the correct word.

| algae   autotrophs   pigments   protozoans |

a. Because plantlike protists can make their own food, they are _____.

b. Chemicals that produce color are called _____.

c. Plantlike protists are commonly called _____.

Viruses, Bacteria, Protists, and Fungi

Funguslike Protists (pages 234–235)

Key Concept: Like fungi, funguslike protists are heterotrophs, have cells walls, and use spores to reproduce.

- Funguslike protists cannot make their food. Heterotrophs are living things that cannot make their own food.

- Funguslike protists have cell walls. Cell walls make cells very stiff. Plant cells also have cell walls.

- Funguslike protists use spores to reproduce. A **spore** is a tiny cell that grows into a new organism.

- All funguslike protists can move at some point in their lives.

Answer the following questions. Use your textbook and the ideas above.

7. Circle the letter of each characteristic of funguslike protists.
   a. cannot make their own food
   b. have cell walls
   c. cannot move at all

8. A tiny cell that grows into a new organism is a(an)

   _____.

Viruses, Bacteria, Protists, and Fungi

Fungi (pages 236–241)

What Are Fungi? (pages 236–237)

Key Concept: **Fungi are eukaryotes that have cell walls, are heterotrophs that feed by absorbing their food, and use spores to reproduce.**

- **Fungi** are living things that cannot make their own food. Fungi have cells with a nucleus and a cell wall.

- Fungi grow in warm, moist places.

- Fungi can be single-celled or many-celled. Many-celled fungi have cells arranged in structures called hyphae. **Hyphae** (HY fee) are branching, threadlike tubes that make up the body of fungi.

- Fungi do not take food inside their bodies. Hyphae ooze chemicals that break down their food. Then the hyphae absorb the smaller food particles.

Answer the following questions. Use your textbook and the ideas above.

1. Circle the letter of how fungi get food.

   a. Hyphae sweep bits of food into the cells.

   b. Hyphae make food using the sun's energy.

   c. Hyphae ooze chemicals that break down food.

2. The picture shows the structures of a mushroom. Draw arrows that point to hyphae.

Viruses, Bacteria, Protists, and Fungi

Reproduction in Fungi (page 238)

Key Concept: Fungi usually reproduce by making spores. The lightweight spores are surrounded by a protective covering and can be carried easily through air or water to new sites.

- Fungi reproduce asexually when there is enough food and water. In asexual reproduction, cells at the tips of the hyphae divide to form spores. The spores grow into fungi that are identical to the parent.

- Fungi produce millions of spores. Wind and water carry spores to new places. Only a few spores fall in places where they can grow.

- Fungi reproduce sexually when there is not much food and water. In sexual reproduction, hyphae from two fungi grow together. Then the fungi trade genetic material. A new structure grows from the joined hyphae and makes spores. The spores grow into fungi that are different from either parent.

Answer the following questions. Use your textbook and the ideas above.

3. Draw a line from each type of reproduction to its description. The descriptions can be used more than once.

Type of Reproduction	Description
asexual	a. produces spores
	b. offspring different from parents
sexual	c. offspring identical to parent

4. Is the following sentence true or false? All spores produced by a fungus grow into new fungi. _____

Viruses, Bacteria, Protists, and Fungi

The Role of Fungi in Nature (pages 239–241)

Key Concept: **Many fungi provide foods for people. Fungi play important roles as decomposers and recyclers on Earth. Some fungi cause disease while others fight disease. Still other fungi live in symbiosis with other organisms.**

- Yeast is a fungus used to make bread and wine. Molds are used to make cheeses. Mushrooms are eaten in salads and on pizza.

- Many fungi break down the chemicals in dead organisms. This process returns nutrients to the soil.

- Some molds produce chemicals that kill bacteria. Penicillin is an antibiotic that is made from a mold.

- Some fungi cause disease in plants and animals. Dutch elm disease is a fungus that has killed millions of elm trees.

- Some fungi grow around plant roots. Their hyphae absorb nutrients and water for the plant. The fungus feeds on extra food stored in the plant's roots.

- Fungi that grow together with certain algae or bacteria form an organism called a **lichen** (LY kun). Lichens are flat, crusty patches that grow on tree bark or rocks. The fungus gets food made by the algae or bacteria. The algae or bacteria get shelter, water, and minerals from the fungus.

Answer the following question. Use your textbook and the ideas above.

5. Circle the letter of each sentence that is true about the roles of fungi.

   a. A fungus is used to make bread and wine.

   b. Fungi do not cause any diseases in people.

   c. Fungi help some plants by growing on their roots.

The Plant Kingdom (pages 250–255)

What Is a Plant? (pages 250–251)

Key Concept: **Nearly all plants are autotrophs, organisms that produce their own food. All plants are eukaryotes that contain many cells. In addition, all plant cells are surrounded by cell walls.**

- Plants make their own food in a process called photosynthesis. In photosynthesis, a plant uses the energy in sunlight to make food.

- All plants are made up of many cells. The cells in a plant are organized into tissues. Tissues are groups of cells that have a specific job. For example, many plants have tissues that move water through their bodies.

- All plant cells have a nucleus and a stiff cell wall.

- All plant cells have chloroplasts. Chloroplasts (KLAWR uh plasts) are the structures in which food is made.

Answer the following questions. Use your textbook and the ideas above.

1. Draw a line from each term to its meaning.

Term	Meaning
photosynthesis	a. structure in a plant cell in which food is made
tissue	b. a group of cells that have a specific job
chloroplast	c. the process in which plants make food

2. The picture shows a plant cell. Circle the letter of the
cell structure that is the cell wall.

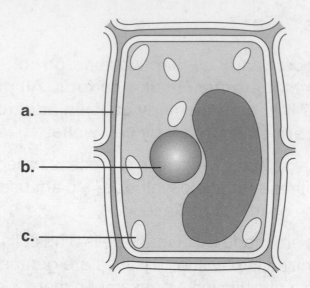

Adaptations for Living on Land
(pages 251–252)

Key Concept: **For plants to survive on land, they must
have ways to obtain water and other nutrients from
their surroundings, retain water, transport materials in
their bodies, support their bodies, and reproduce.**

- Plant leaves can easily lose water to the air. To keep
  from losing water, most plant leaves are covered with a
  cuticle. A **cuticle** is a waxy, waterproof layer of a leaf.

- Plants move water, nutrients, and wastes through their
  bodies. Large plants have tissues that move these
  materials. **Vascular tissue** is a system of tubes inside a
  plant that water and food move through.

- Large and tall plants need support to hold their leaves
  up to the sun. Stiff cell walls and vascular tissue
  strengthen and support the bodies of large plants.

- All plants reproduce by sexual reproduction. In the
  process of fertilization, a sperm cell from the male
  parent joins with an egg cell from the female parent. The
  fertilized egg cell is called a **zygote**.

Plants

Answer the following questions. Use your textbook and the ideas on page 110.

3. Circle the letter of each sentence that is true about plants.

    a. The cuticle helps support tall plants.

    b. Water and food move through vascular tissue.

    c. All plants reproduce by sexual reproduction.

4. Read each word in the box. In each sentence below, fill in the correct word.

fertilization	photosynthesis	zygote

    a. A fertilized egg cell is called a

    _____.

    b. A sperm cell joins with an egg cell in the

    process of _____.

Classifying Plants (pages 253–254)

Key Concept: **Scientists informally group plants into two major groups—nonvascular plants and vascular plants.**

- **Nonvascular plants** are plants that do not have a system of tubes for moving water and food.

- Nonvascular plants are low-growing plants. They also do not have true roots, stems, or leaves. These plants get water directly from their surroundings. Nonvascular plants grow in damp, shady places.

- **Vascular plants** have a system of tubes for moving water and food. Vascular plants can grow very tall because vascular tissue also gives the plant support.

Plants

Answer the following questions. Use your textbook and the ideas on page 111.

5. Plants that do not have a system of tubes for moving water and food are called _____ plants.

6. Fill in the table about the two major groups of plants.

Classification of Plants		
Group	**Vascular System**	**Size**
Nonvascular	**a.** _____	short
Vascular	yes	**b.** _____

Complex Life Cycles (pages 254–255)

Key Concept: **Plants have complex life cycles that include two different stages, the sporophyte stage and the gametophyte stage.**

- In the **sporophyte** (SPOH ruh fyt) stage, the plant produces spores. Spores are tiny cells that can grow into new organisms.

- A spore grows and develops to become the gametophyte. In the **gametophyte** (guh MEE tuh fyt) stage, the plant produces two kinds of sex cells: sperm cells and egg cells.

- When a sperm cell and egg cell join, they form a zygote. The zygote grows and develops into a sporophyte. The sporophyte produces spores, which grow into gametophytes. The gametophyte produces sperm cells and egg cells. And the cycle begins again.

Name _____ Date _____ Class _____

Plants

Answer the following question. Use your textbook and the ideas on page 112.

7. Read each word in the box. Use the words to complete the cycle diagram about the plant life cycle.

gametophyte	spores	sporophyte	zygote

Plant Life Cycle

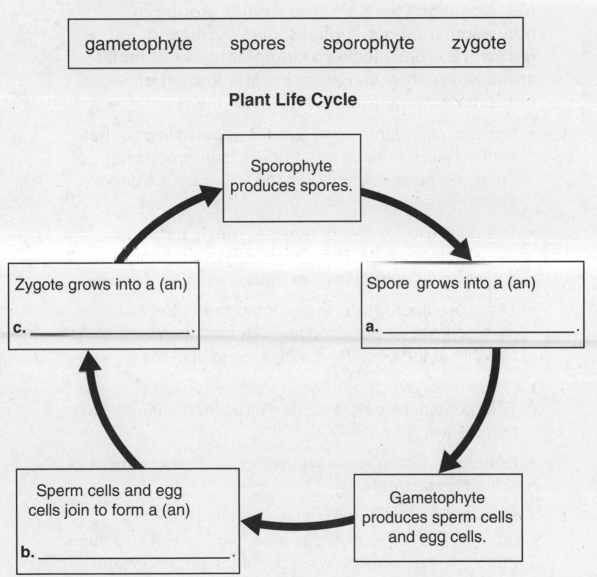

Sporophyte produces spores.

Spore grows into a (an)

a. _____.

Gametophyte produces sperm cells and egg cells.

Sperm cells and egg cells join to form a (an)

b. _____.

Zygote grows into a (an)

c. _____.

Plants Without Seeds (pages 256–260)

Nonvascular Plants (pages 256–257)

Key Concept: There are three major groups of nonvascular plants: mosses, liverworts, and hornworts. These low-growing plants live in moist areas where they can absorb water and other nutrients directly from their environment.

- Nonvascular plants need a moist place to live so that sperm cells can swim to egg cells for reproduction. These plants also absorb water and nutrients directly into their cells.

- The green, fuzzy part of a moss plant is the gametophyte stage. The gametophyte is low-growing. It has structures that look like roots, stems, and leaves.

- The moss sporophyte stage grows out of the gametophyte. The sporophyte is a long, thin stalk. A capsule at the end of the stalk makes spores.

- Liverworts have sporophytes that are too small to see. The gametophytes are leaflike structures shaped like a human liver.

- Liverworts often grow as a thick crust on moist rocks or soil along a stream.

- Hornworts have gametophytes that lie flat on the ground. The sporophytes are slender, curved structures that look like horns growing out of the gametophyte.

- Hornworts usually grow in moist soil, often mixed in with grass plants.

Answer the following questions. Use your textbook and the ideas above.

1. Is the following sentence true of false? Nonvascular plants can absorb water and nutrients directly into their cells. _____

2. Why do nonvascular plants need a moist home? Circle the letter of the correct answer.

    a. They can grow taller.

    b. Their spores can spread.

    c. They can reproduce.

3. The picture shows a moss plant. Identify the gametophyte stage and the sporophyte stage of the plant.

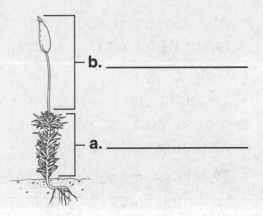

b. _____

a. _____

4. Draw a line from each nonvascular plant to its description. The plants may have more than one description.

Nonvascular Plant	Description
liverwort	**a.** Sporophytes look like horns.
hornwort	**b.** Gametophytes are shaped like a human liver.
	c. Grows on moist rocks or along streams.
	d. Grows in moist soil mixed with grass plants.

Seedless Vascular Plants (pages 258–260)

Key Concept: Ferns, club mosses, and horsetails have true vascular tissue, and they do not produce seeds. Instead of seeds, these plants reproduce by releasing spores.

- All seedless vascular plants have a system of tubes that move water and food through the plant. These plants all reproduce with spores. They do not make seeds.

- Vascular plants are tall because vascular tissue easily moves food and water through the plant. Vascular tissue also supports the plant.

- Seedless vascular plants must grow in moist places. Seedless vascular plants release spores. The spores grow into gametophytes. When the gametophytes produce sperm cells and egg cells, there must be enough water for the sperm to swim to the eggs.

- Ferns have true stems, roots, and leaves. Most ferns have underground stems. Roots anchor a fern to the ground and absorb water and nutrients from the soil.

- Fern leaves, or **fronds**, are divided into many smaller parts.

- A fern plant with fronds is the sporophyte stage of the plant. Spores develop on the undersides of fronds. Wind and water carry the spores away.

- If a spore lands in moist, shaded soil, the spore develops into a gametophyte. Fern gametophytes are tiny plants that grow low to the ground.

Answer the following questions. Use your textbook and the ideas above.

5. All seedless vascular plants have a system of

_____ that move water and food through the plant.

6. Circle the letter of each sentence that is true about vascular plants.

    a. Vascular plants are short so that food and water can move through them more easily.

    b. Vascular tissue gives plants support.

    c. Seedless vascular plants need water to reproduce.

7. Seedless vascular plants produce spores that grow

into _____.

8. Circle the letter of each characteristic of ferns.

    a. true stems, roots, and leaves

    b. underground stems

    c. seeds

9. The picture shows a fern plant. Circle a frond.

10. Is the following sentence true or false? A fern plant with fronds is the gametophyte stage of the plant.

_____

The Characteristics of Seed Plants (pages 262–271)

What Is a Seed Plant? (pages 262–263)

Key Concept: **Seed plants share two important characteristics. They have vascular tissue, and they use pollen and seeds to reproduce.**

- All seed plants have roots, stems, and leaves.

- In seed plants, the plant that you see is the sporophyte stage of the plant. The gametophyte stage is very small.

- Seed plants have vascular tissue. There are two kinds of vascular tissue:
    1. **Phloem** (FLOH um) is the vascular tissue that food moves through. Food is the sugar made in the leaves during photosynthesis.
    2. **Xylem** (ZY lum) is the vascular tissue that water moves through. The roots take up water from the soil.

- Seed plants can live any place. Seed plants do not need water for sperm cells to swim to egg cells.

- Seed plants produce pollen. **Pollen** has the cells that become sperm cells. Pollen carries sperm cells directly to the egg cells.

- After sperm cells fertilize the eggs, seeds form. A **seed** is a young plant inside a covering. Seeds protect the young plant from drying out.

Answer the following questions. Use your textbook and the ideas above.

1. Is the following sentence true or false? In seed plants, the plant that you see is the gametophyte stage.

_____

2. Draw a line from each term to its meaning.

Term	Meaning
phloem	**a.** a young plant inside a protective covering
xylem	**b.** vascular tissue that water moves through
pollen	**c.** vascular tissue that food moves through
seed	**d.** structure that carries sperm cells to egg cells

How Seeds Become New Plants

(pages 264–266)

Key Concept: **Inside a seed is a partially developed plant. If a seed lands in an area where conditions are favorable, the plant sprouts out of the seed and begins to grow.**

- A seed holds a young plant that has tiny roots, stems, and leaves. The young plant also has seed leaves called **cotyledons** (kaht uh LEED unz). In some seeds, the cotyledons have stored food.

- The outer covering of a seed is called the seed coat. The seed coat keeps the young plant from drying out.

- After seeds form, they are scattered far from the plant. Seeds are scattered by animals, water, and wind.

- After a seed is scattered, the seed stays inactive until it absorbs water. **Germination** (jur muh NAY shun) occurs when the young plant begins to grow and pushes out of the seed. The young plant uses stored food to grow.

Answer the following questions. Use your textbook and the ideas on page 119.

3. Read each word in the box. In each sentence below, fill in the correct word or words.

> cotyledon   germination   seed coat

a. A seed leaf inside the seed is a
   _____.

b. When a plant begins to grow and pushes out of the seed, the process is called _____.

4. Fill in the concept map to show ways that seeds are scattered.

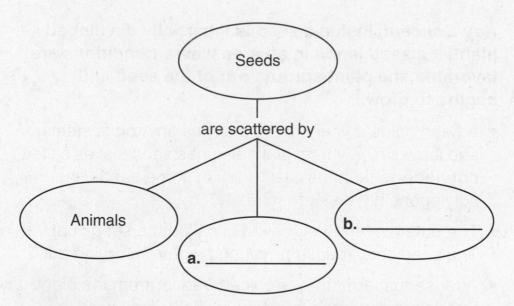

Seeds

are scattered by

Animals

a. _____

b. _____

5. Circle the letter of each sentence that is true about seeds becoming new plants.

a. The seed coat keeps the young plant from drying out.

b. After seeds are scattered, they germinate right away.

c. The young plant uses stored food to grow.

Plants

Roots (pages 266–267)

***Key Concept:* Roots anchor a plant in the ground, absorb water and minerals from the soil, and sometimes store food.**

- Plants have two kinds of root systems:
    1. A fibrous root system has many roots of the same size. Grass has fibrous roots.
    2. A taproot root system has one long main root. Smaller roots branch off the main root. Carrots have taproots.

- Root hairs grow out of a root's surface. Root hairs absorb water and minerals from the soil. Root hairs also help hold a plant in the soil.

- Xylem in the roots moves water and minerals from the soil up to the stems and leaves.

- Phloem moves food that was made in the leaves down to the roots. Roots use the energy from food to grow. Extra food is sometimes stored in roots.

Answer the following questions. Use your textbook and the ideas above.

6. The picture shows two plants with different kinds of root systems. Circle the letter of the plant with a taproot root system.

a.

b.

Plants

7. Draw a line from each term to its function in a root.

Term	Function
root hairs	a. moves water and minerals to the leaves
xylem	b. anchor the plant and absorb water and minerals
phloem	c. moves food into the roots

Stems (pages 268–269)

Key Concept: **The stem carries substances between the plant's roots and leaves. The stem also provides support for the plant and holds up the leaves so they are exposed to the sun.**

- A stem has two main jobs:
  1. The stem moves food and water between the roots and the leaves.
  2. The stem also supports the plant and holds up leaves to the light.

- Stems can be herbaceous (hur BAY shus) or woody. Herbaceous stems are soft and green. Tomato plants have herbaceous stems. Woody stems are hard and stiff. Trees have woody stems.

Answer the following questions. Use your textbook and the ideas above.

8. Circle the letter of each job of a stem.
    a. moving water between the roots and leaves
    b. supporting the plant
    c. absorbing water from the soil

9. Is the following sentence true or false? Woody stems are soft and green. _____

Leaves (pages 270–271)

Key Concept: **Leaves capture the sun's energy and carry out the food-making process of photosynthesis.**

- Every part of a leaf helps the leaf make food.

- Chloroplasts contain the green pigment chlorophyll. Chlorophyll traps the sun's energy to use in photosynthesis. Cells with the most chloroplasts are found near the upper surface of a leaf.

- Carbon dioxide enters a leaf through open stomata. Stomata are small openings in the surface layer of a leaf. Oxygen made during photosynthesis goes out of the leaf through the stomata.

- Water can be lost to the air through the leaves. When stomata close, they keep the plant from losing water.

Answer the following questions. Use your textbook and the ideas above.

10. Is the following sentence true or false? Leaves make food for the plant in the process of photosynthesis.

_____

11. Circle the letter of each function of stomata.

    a. absorbing energy from the sun

    b. letting carbon dioxide enter a leaf

    c. keeping water in a leaf

Gymnosperms and Angiosperms (pages 272–281)

Gymnosperms (pages 272–273)

Key Concept: **Every gymnosperm produces naked seeds. In addition, many gymnosperms have needle-like or scalelike leaves, and deep-growing root systems.**

- A **gymnosperm** (JIM nuh spurm) is a seed plant that produces naked seeds. The seeds are naked because they are not inside a fruit. Like all seed plants, gymnosperms have vascular tissue.

- Most gymnosperms have needle-like or scalelike leaves. Gymnosperms also have roots that grow far down.

- The most common group of gymnosperms are the conifers. Conifers are gymnosperms that have cones. Pine trees are conifers.

Answer the following questions. Use your textbook and the ideas above.

1. Which is a characteristic of all gymnosperms? Circle the letter of the correct answer.
   a. naked seeds
   b. fruit
   c. shallow root systems

2. Is the following sentence true or false? Gymnosperms do not have vascular tissue. _____

3. The most common group of gymnosperms are the

   _____.

Plants

Reproduction in Gymnosperms (pages 274–275)

Key Concept: **First, pollen falls from a male cone onto a female cone. In time, a sperm cell and an egg cell join together in an ovule on the female cone.**

- In most gymnosperms, seeds form in structures called **cones**. Cones are covered with scales. Male cones produce pollen. Female cones have an egg cell at the base of each scale.

- **Pollination** is when pollen moves from the male cone to the female cone. Wind often carries pollen from male cones to female cones. Female cones are sticky so the pollen easily sticks to them.

- Once pollination occurs, the sperm cell from the pollen fertilizes the egg cell. The fertilized egg develops into the young plant inside a seed.

- When the seeds have formed, the scales of the cone open. The wind shakes the seeds out of the cone and carries them away.

Answer the following questions. Use your textbook and the ideas above.

4. Draw a line from each term to its description.

Term	Description
scale	**a.** produces pollen
	b. covers a cone
male cone	
	c. produces egg cells
female cone	

5. Which carries pollen from male cones to female cones? Circle the letter of the correct answer.

   a. wind

   b. water

   c. animals

Plants

6. Complete the cycle diagram about the life cycle of gymnosperms.

Life Cycle of Gymnosperms

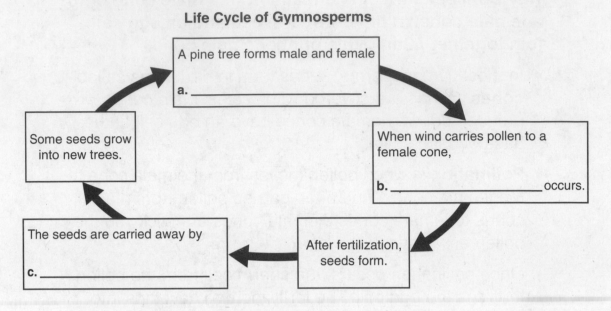

A pine tree forms male and female

a. _____ .

When wind carries pollen to a female cone,

b. _____ occurs.

After fertilization, seeds form.

The seeds are carried away by

c. _____ .

Some seeds grow into new trees.

Angiosperms (page 276)

Key Concept: **All angiosperms, or flowering plants, share two important traits. First, they produce flowers. Second, in contrast to gymnosperms, which produce uncovered seeds, angiosperms produce seeds that are enclosed in fruits.**

- An **angiosperm** (AN jee uh spurm) is a plant that forms seeds protected by a fruit.

- All angiosperms produce flowers.

- Angiosperms live almost everywhere on Earth.

Answer the following question. Use your textbook and the ideas above.

7. Circle the letter of each sentence that is true about angiosperms.

   a. Angiosperms produce naked seeds.

   b. Angiosperms have flowers.

   c. Angiosperms can grow only in hot, dry places.

Plants

The Structure of Flowers (pages 276–277)

Key Concept: **Flowers come in all sorts of shapes, sizes, and colors. But, despite their differences, all flowers have the same function—reproduction.**

- A **flower** is the structure in which seeds form. **Petals** are the colorful leaflike parts of a flower.

- Most flowers have both male and female parts.

- The **stamens** (STAY munz) are the male parts of a flower. The stamens make pollen. Pollen holds sperm cells.

- The female part of a flower is the **pistil** (PIS tul). Egg cells form in the pistil.

- The color, shape, and scent of flowers attract insects, birds, and bats. These animals pollinate flowers by moving pollen as they visit flowers to get food.

Answer the following questions. Use your textbook and the ideas above.

8. Read each word in the box. In each sentence below, fill in the correct word.

flower   petal   pistil

   a. The structure in which seeds form in an

     angiosperm is a _____.

   b. The leaflike part of a flower that is colorful is a

     _____.

9. The picture shows the parts of a flower. Label the pistil, which is the female part of the flower, and the stamens, which are the male parts of the flower.

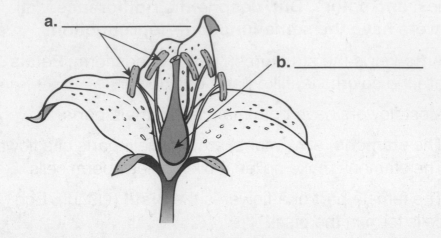

a. _____

b. _____

10. Insects, birds, and bats help to

_____ flowers.

Reproduction in Angiosperms (pages 278–279)

Key Concept: **Reproduction in angiosperms begins when pollen falls on a flower's stigma. In time, the sperm cell and egg cell join together in the flower's ovule. The zygote develops into the embryo part of the seed.**

- A flower is pollinated when a pollen grain falls onto the sticky top of a pistil.

- After pollination, a sperm cell from the pollen grain joins with an egg cell inside the pistil. The fertilized egg, or zygote, develops into the young plant that will be inside the seed.

- As the seed develops, part of the pistil becomes the fruit. A **fruit** contains one or more seeds.

- Fruits are a way angiosperm seeds are scattered. Animals that eat fruits spread the seeds. Other fruits are scattered by wind or water.

Answer the following question. Use your textbook and the ideas on page 128.

11. Circle the letter of each sentence that is true about reproduction in angiosperms.

    a. During pollination, pollen falls onto the stamen.

    b. Part of the pistil becomes a fruit.

    c. Only wind scatters angiosperm seeds.

Types of Angiosperms (page 280)

Key Concept: **Angiosperms are divided into two major groups: monocots and dicots.**

- "Cot" is short for *cotyledon.* Cotyledons, or seed leaves, store food used by young plants when seeds sprout.

- **Monocots** have seeds with only one seed leaf. Monocots include corn, lilies, and tulips. Monocots have flower petals in multiples of three. Their leaves are long and slender with parallel veins. Their vascular tissue is scattered throughout the stem.

- **Dicots** have seeds with two seed leaves. Some dicots are roses, oak trees, and beans. Dicot flowers have petals in multiples of four or five. Dicot leaves are wide with branching veins. Dicot stems have bundles of vascular tissue arranged in a ring.

Answer the following questions. Use your textbook and the ideas above.

12. Seeds with one seed leaf are

    _____.

13. Seeds with two seed leaves are

    _____.

Plants

14. Fill in the table below to compare monocots and dicots.

Comparing Monocots and Dicots		
Plant Part	**Monocots**	**Dicots**
Leaf	a. _____	branching veins
Stem	vascular tissue scattered	b. _____
Flower Parts	c. _____	in fours or fives

Seed Plants in Everyday Life (page 281)

Key Concept: **Seed plants are an important source of products and food.**

- Gymnosperms provide useful products such as paper and the lumber used to build homes.

- Both people and animals depend on flowering plants for food. Vegetables, fruits, grains, and grasses are all angiosperms.

- Clothing is made from parts of both gymnosperms and angiosperms. Both also provide wood used to make furniture.

Answer the following question. Use your textbook and the ideas above.

15. Circle the letter of each item that comes from seed plants.

   a. clothing

   b. steel

   c. furniture

Plants

Plant Responses and Growth
(pages 284–287)

Tropisms (pages 284–285)

Key Concept: **Touch, light, and gravity are three important stimuli to which plants show growth responses, or tropisms.**

- A **tropism** (TROH piz um) is a plant's growth response toward or away from a stimulus.

- Some plants respond to touch. For example, as vines grow, they coil around any object they touch.

- Plants respond to light. The leaves, stems, and flowers of plants grow toward light. This helps a plant get the energy needed for photosynthesis.

- Plants also respond to gravity. Roots grow down into the soil, toward the pull of gravity. Stems grow up toward the sun, away from the pull of gravity.

- Plants can respond to touch, light, and gravity because they make hormones. **Hormones** are chemicals that control how plants grow and develop.

Answer the following questions. Use your textbook and the ideas above.

1. Which is a plant's response to a stimulus? Circle the letter of the correct answer.
   a. light
   b. roots growing into soil
   c. pollination

Name _____ Date _____ Class _____

Plants

2. Read each word in the box. In each sentence below, fill in the correct word.

hormone	response	tropism

    a. A chemical made by a plant that controls how plants grow and develop is a

    _____.

    b. A plant's growth response toward or away from

    a stimulus is a _____.

3. Fill in the concept map about stimuli that plants respond to.

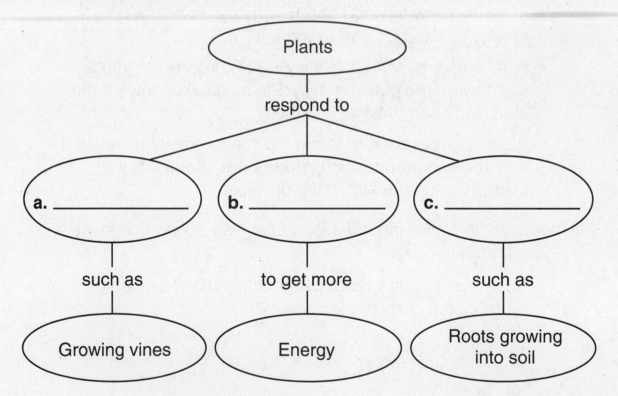

Seasonal Changes (page 286)

Key Concept: **Plant responses to seasonal changes include photoperiodism and dormancy.**

- A plant's response to changes in the length of night and day is called **photoperiodism**.

- Some plants flower when nights are longer. These plants usually bloom in the fall or winter. Poinsettias and chrysanthemums are two examples.

- Some plants flower when nights are shorter. These plants usually bloom in the spring or summer. Irises are an example.

- Other plants are not sensitive to the amount of darkness. Dandelions and tomatoes flower without being affected by the length of night.

- Many plants go into a state of dormancy when winter approaches. **Dormancy** is when an organism's growth or activity stops.

- A tree loses its leaves in fall. Sugars and water move into the tree's roots. Then the tree is dormant. It can survive freezing temperatures.

Answer the following questions. Use your textbook and the ideas above.

4. Circle the letter of each sentence that is true about seasonal changes.

   a. Plants that flower when nights are longer usually flower in fall or winter.

   b. All plants are sensitive to the amount of darkness.

   c. A plant stops growing during dormancy.

5. The picture shows two trees. Circle the letter of the tree that is dormant.

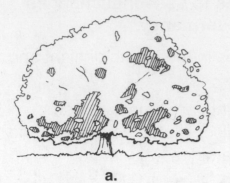

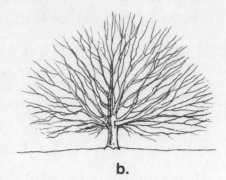

a.   b.

Life Spans of Angiosperms (page 287)

Key Concept: **Angiosperms are classified as annuals, biennials, or perennials based on the length of their life cycles.**

* **Annuals** complete a life cycle within one growing season. Marigolds and cucumbers are annuals.

* **Biennials** (by EN ee ulz) are flowering plants that complete their life cycle in two years. These plants do not flower and make seeds until the second year. Parsley is a biennial.

* **Perennials** live for more than two years. Most perennials have flowers every year. Maple trees and peonies are perennials.

Answer the following question. Use your textbook and the ideas above.

6. Draw a line from each kind of flowering plant to the length of its life cycle.

Kind of Plant	Length of Life Cycle
annual	**a.** two years
biennial	**b.** more than two years
perennial	**c.** one growing season

Sponges, Cnidarians, and Worms

What Is an Animal? (pages 294–299)

Structure of Animals (page 295)

Key Concept: **The cells of most animals are organized into higher levels of structure, including tissues, organs, and systems.**

- **Cells** are the building blocks of all living things. Cells are tiny. Cells do the jobs needed to keep an animal alive. Animals' bodies have many cells.

- A group of many cells that do one job is a called a **tissue**.

- A group of different tissues is an **organ**. A stomach is an organ. It has more than one kind of tissue.

- Systems are groups of organs. The digestive system is one kind of system. The parts of the digestive system break down food.

Answer the following questions. Use your textbook and the ideas above.

1. Use words from above to fill in the blanks in the flowchart.

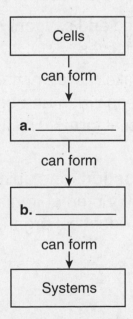

2. Circle the letter of the tiny unit that makes up the bodies of all animals.

   a. organ

   b. cell

   c. tissue

3. A stomach is an example of a(an)

   _____.

   a. tissue

   b. system

   c. organ

Functions of Animals (pages 296–297)

Key Concept: **The major functions of animals are to obtain food and oxygen, keep internal conditions stable, move, and reproduce.**

- **Adaptations** help animals meet their needs. Some adaptations are body parts. A bird uses its beak to get food. A beak is a body part that is an adaptation. Some adaptations are ways of behaving. A dog pants when it gets too hot. Panting is an adaptation.

- All animals need food and oxygen. All animals can move at some time in their lives.

- Animals need to make more animals like themselves. **Fertilization** happens when an egg cell and a sperm cell join. A new animal forms. This is called **sexual reproduction**.

- In **asexual reproduction**, one animal makes a new animal just like itself. Some animals split down the middle to make two identical organisms.

Sponges, Cnidarians, and Worms

Answer the following questions. Use your textbook and the ideas on page 136.

4. Circle the letter of each sentence that is true about animals.

   a. Animals need food.

   b. Most animals do not move.

   c. All animals need oxygen.

5. Is the following sentence true or false? Adaptations

   help animals meet their needs. _____

6. Read each word in the box. In each sentence below, fill in the correct word or words.

> adaptation   sexual reproduction
> asexual reproduction

   a. When one animal makes a new animal just like

   itself, it is called _____.

   b. A new animal forms when an egg cell and a sperm

   cell join during _____.

Classification of Animals (pages 298–299)

Key Concept: **Animals are classified according to how they are related to other animals. These relationships are determined by an animal's body structure, the way the animal develops, and its DNA.**

- Scientists sort animals into groups. A **phylum** (FY lum) is a group of animals that are alike in some ways.

Sponges, Cnidarians, and Worms

- **Vertebrates** are animals with a backbone. There is only one phylum of vertebrates. Birds and fishes are vertebrates.

- **Invertebrates** are animals without a backbone. There are many groups of invertebrates. Spiders and worms are invertebrates.

Answer the following questions. Use your textbook and the ideas on page 137 and above.

7. This picture shows two animals. One animal has a backbone. One animal does not have a backbone. Label the pictures using the words in the box.

vertebrate   invertebrate   phylum

 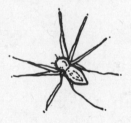

a. _____   b. _____

8. Circle the letter of the word that is used for an animal with a backbone.

   a. phylum

   b. vertebrate

   c. invertebrate

9. Is the following sentence true or false? A phylum is a group of animals that is alike in some ways.

_____

Sponges, Cnidarians, and Worms

Animal Symmetry (pages 300–302)

The Mathematics of Symmetry (pages 300–301)

Key Concept: **The balanced arrangement of parts, called symmetry, is characteristic of many animals.**

- Most animals have **bilateral symmetry**. If you draw a line down the middle of an animal's body, the line would make two equal halves. A butterfly has this kind of body.

- Some animals have **radial symmetry**. Their bodies have a middle point. There many ways you could draw a line to divide the body into equal halves. A starfish has this kind of body.

- Sponges' bodies have no symmetry. Sponges' bodies cannot be divided into equal halves.

Answer the following questions. Use your textbook and the ideas above.

1. Draw a line from each term to the correct picture.

   a. radial symmetry

   b. bilateral symmetry

   c. no symmetry

 Sponge

 Frog

 Sea Urchin

Sponges, Cnidarians, and Worms

2. Read each word in the box. In each sentence below, fill in the correct words.

```
radial symmetry    bilateral symmetry    no symmetry
```

a. An animal with _____ has a middle point in its body.

b. Butterflies are one kind of animal with

_____.

Symmetry and Daily Life (pages 301–302)

Key Concept: Depending on their symmetry, animals share some general characteristics.

• You can learn about how and where an animal lives by looking at its body.

• Animals with radial symmetry live in the water. Most of them move slowly. Some do not move at all.

• Animals with bilateral symmetry move more quickly. They have sense organs in the front end of their bodies. For example, a mouse has eyes, ears, a nose, and a mouth on its head.

• Most kinds of animals have bilateral symmetry. Some live in water. Some live on land.

Answer the following questions. Use your textbook and the ideas above.

3. Circle the letter of each sentence that is true about animals with bilateral symmetry.

a. They have sense organs in the front end.

b. Most of these animals move very slowly.

c. Some live on land.

Name _____ Date _____ Class _____

Sponges, Cnidarians, and Worms

4. Read each word in the box. In each sentence below, fill in the correct words.

radial symmetry   bilateral symmetry   no symmetry

a. Most kinds of animals have

_____.

b. Most animals with _____ live in the water and move slowly.

5. Complete the table below that tells about different kinds of animals and how they live.

Animal Body Plans		
Kind of Symmetry	**Where They Live**	**Body Characteristics**
Radial	a. _____	body has a middle point
b. _____	land and water	sense organs in the front of the body

Sponges and Cnidarians

(pages 303–311)

Sponges (pages 303–305)

Key Concept: **Sponges are invertebrate animals that usually have no body symmetry and never have tissues or organs.**

- A sponge has different kinds of cells. Sponges do not have tissues or organs. Sponges have no symmetry.

- Moving water carries food and oxygen into a sponge. Moving water takes away the sponge's wastes.

- Sponges can reproduce asexually. A new sponge can grow on the side of an adult sponge. This is called budding.

- Sponges can also reproduce sexually. An egg and sperm join to form a **larva**. A larva does not look like an adult sponge.

Answer the following questions. Use your textbook and the ideas above.

1. Circle the letter of the sentence that tells how a sponge gets food.

   a. Sponges hunt for food.

   b. Water carries food into a sponge.

   c. Sponges make food using sunlight.

2. Circle the letter of each sentence that is true about the how sponges reproduce.

   a. Sponges can reproduce asexually.

   b. Sponges can reproduce sexually.

   c. Sponges cannot reproduce.

Name _____ Date _____ Class _____

Cnidarians (pages 307–309)

Key Concept: **Cnidarians are invertebrate animals that use stinging cells to capture food and defend themselves.**

- **Cnidarians** (ny DEHR ee unz) are a group of animals that live in the water. Jellyfishes, corals, and sea anemones are all cnidarians.

- Cnidarians have stinging cells. They use stinging cells to catch food. They use stinging cells to defend themselves.

- Some cnidarians have bodies shaped like a vase. This kind of body is called a **polyp**. Some cnidarians have bodies shaped like a bowl. This kind of body is called a **medusa**.

- Some cnidarians reproduce sexually. Some reproduce asexually.

Answer the following questions. Use your textbook and the ideas above.

3. This picture shows two cnidarians. Label the pictures using the words in the box.

medusa   stinging cells   polyp

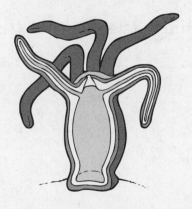 

a. _____   b. _____

4. Circle the letter of each sentence that is true about cnidarians.

    a. Cnidarians have only one kind of body shape.

    b. Cnidarians use stinging cells to catch food.

    c. Coral is one kind of cnidarian.

Life in a Colony (pages 310–311)

Key Concept: **Coral reefs are home to more species of fishes and invertebrates than any other environment on Earth.**

- Some cnidarians live in a colony. A **colony** is a group of many animals of the same kind. A Portuguese man-of-war is a colony. It is made up of many cnidarians.

- Some corals live in colonies. A coral reef is made of the skeletons of coral animals. Many different kinds of animals live in coral reefs.

Answer the following questions. Use your textbook and the ideas above.

5. Circle the letter of each sentence that is true about coral reefs.

    a. Many different kinds of animals live in coral reefs.

    b. Coral reefs are made of coral skeletons.

    c. The Portuguese-man-of-war makes coral reefs.

6. Is the following sentence true or false? A colony is made of one animal. _____

Sponges, Cnidarians, and Worms

Worms (pages 315–320)

Characteristics of Worms (pages 314–315)

Key Concept: **Biologists classify worms into three major phyla—flatworms, roundworms, and segmented worms.**

- The three main groups of worms are flatworms, roundworms, and segmented worms.

- Worms are invertebrates because they do not have a backbone. Worms have bilateral symmetry. Worms have cells, tissues, organs, and systems.

- Worms have a brain and sense organs.

- Some worms reproduce sexually. Some worms reproduce asexually.

Answer the following questions. Use your textbook and the ideas above.

1. Circle the letter of each sentence that is true about worms.
   a. There are three main groups of worms.
   b. Worms have radial symmetry.
   c. Worms have a brain.

2. Is the following sentence true or false? All worms reproduce asexually. _____

3. Circle the letter of each term that tells about worms.
   a. invertebrate
   b. bilateral symmetry
   c. vertebrate

Sponges, Cnidarians, and Worms

Flatworms (pages 316–317)

***Key Concept:* Flatworms are flat and as soft as jelly.**

- Flatworms are one of the three groups of worms.

- Some flatworms are parasites. **Parasites** live on or in another organism called a **host**. Parasites take food from the host. Tapeworms are flatworms that are parasites.

- Some flatworms are free-living. **Free-living organisms** do not live on or in a host. Free-living flatworms live in water or wet soil.

- Planarians are a kind of flatworm. They are free-living scavengers. **Scavengers** eat dead or decaying things. Planarians also eat other small animals.

Answer the following questions. Use your textbook and the ideas above.

4. Draw a line from each term to its meaning.

Term	Meaning
free-living	**a.** takes food from a host
parasite	**b.** eats dead and decaying things
	c. does not live in or on a host
scavenger	

5. Circle the letter of the word that tells what a parasite lives on.
- **a.** scavenger
- **b.** host
- **c.** larva

6. Organisms that do not live in or on a host are called _____.

Sponges, Cnidarians, and Worms

Roundworms (page 318)

Key Concept: **Unlike cnidarians or flatworms, roundworms have a digestive system that is like a tube, open at both ends.**

- Roundworms are one of the three groups of worms. Roundworms live in many places.

- Some roundworms are parasites. Other roundworms are free-living.

- Roundworms have a digestive system that is open on both ends. Food goes into the mouth and moves through the body. Waste leaves through the **anus**, an opening at the other end.

Answer the following questions. Use your textbook and the ideas above.

7. Circle the letter of each sentence that is true about roundworms.

    a. Some roundworms are parasites.

    b. Roundworms have a digestive system with two openings.

    c. Roundworms can live in only one place on Earth.

8. Read each word in the box. In the sentences below, fill in the correct words.

tube	mouth	anus

Food enters a worm's body through the

_____. The food moves through the body. Waste leaves the worm's body through the

_____.

Sponges, Cnidarians, and Worms

Segmented Worms (pages 319–320)

***Key Concept:* Segmented worms have bodies made up of many linked sections called segments.**

- Segmented worms are one of the three groups of worms. Segmented worms have bodies made of many parts joined in a row. Earthworms are one kind of segmented worm.

- Segmented worms have a digestive system that is open on both ends. They have a mouth and an anus.

- Segmented worms have a **closed circulatory system**. Blood stays inside tubes in their bodies.

- Earthworms make tunnels in soil. The tunnels make the soil better for plants. Earthworm wastes also make soil better for plants.

Answer the following questions. Use your textbook and the ideas above.

9. Circle the letter of each sentence that is true about segmented worms.

   a. Segmented worms do not have a mouth.

   b. Segmented worms have a closed circulatory system.

   c. An earthworm is a segmented worm.

10. Look at the pictures. Circle the picture that shows a segmented worm.

Mollusks, Arthropods, and Echinoderms

Mollusks (pages 328–333)

Characteristics of Mollusks (page 329)

Key Concept: **In addition to a soft body often covered by a shell, a mollusk has a thin layer of tissue called a mantle that covers its internal organs, and an organ called a foot.**

- **Mollusks** are invertebrate animals with soft bodies. Clams, snails, and squids are mollusks.

- Mollusks have an organ called a foot. The foot is used for digging, moving, or catching prey.

- Mollusks have a tissue called the mantle. The mantle covers the organs in the body. In some mollusks, the mantle makes a hard shell.

- Mollusks that live in water have gills. **Gills** are organs that absorb oxygen from water.

Answer the following questions. Use your textbook and the ideas above.

1. Read each word in the box. In each sentence below, fill in one of the words.

mantle	foot	gills

a. An organ that mollusks use to move, dig, or catch food is called the _____.

b. A tissue that covers a mollusk's organs and sometimes makes a hard shell is the

_____.

2. Organs that absorb oxygen from water are called

_____.

Mollusks, Arthropods, and Echinoderms

3. Circle the letter of each sentence that is true about mollusks.

   a. Mollusks have a foot.

   b. Mollusks are vertebrates.

   c. Mollusks have a mantle.

Snails and Slugs (page 330)

Key Concept: **The three major groups of mollusks are gastropods, bivalves, and cephalopods. Gastropods have a single external shell or no shell at all.**

- **Gastropods** are one kind of mollusk. Gastropods have one shell or no shell. Snails and slugs are gastropods.

- Some gastropods live in water. Other gastropods live on land.

- Gastropods use a **radula** (RAJ oo luh) to get food. The radula has tiny teeth that tear and scrape up food.

- Some gastropods are **herbivores**. They eat plants. Some gastropods are **carnivores**. They eat animals.

Answer the following questions. Use your textbook and the ideas above.

4. The picture shows some body parts of a gastropod. One body part is not labeled. It is the body part that gastropods use to get food. Fill in the blank with the name of that body part.

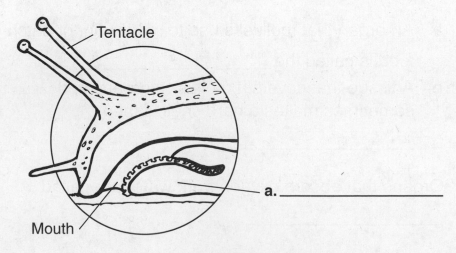

Tentacle

a. _____

Mouth

Mollusks, Arthropods, and Echinoderms

5. Circle the letter of each sentence that is true about gastropods.

    a. Gastropods have two shells.

    b. Gastropods are mollusks.

    c. Gastropods use a radula to get food.

6. Read each word in the box. In each sentence below, fill in one of the words.

> herbivore   radula   carnivore

    a. An animal that eats plants is a

    _____.

    b. An animal that eats other animals is a

    _____.

Two-Shelled Mollusks (page 331)

Key Concept: **Bivalves are mollusks that have two shells held together by hinges and strong muscles.**

- **Bivalves** are mollusks with two shells. Oysters and clams are bivalves.

- Bivalves are filter feeders. A filter feeder strains tiny plants and animals from the water.

- Most bivalves are **omnivores**. They eat both plants and animals.

- Most adult bivalves move slowly or not at all.

Answer the following questions. Use your textbook and the ideas above.

7. Is the following sentence true or false? Bivalves have

    two shells. _____

Mollusks, Arthropods, and Echinoderms

8. Circle the letter of the sentence that tells how filter feeders get food.

   a. Filter feeders hunt for food.

   b. Filter feeders are parasites that live in hosts.

   c. Filter feeders strain plants and animals from the water.

Octopuses and Their Relatives

(pages 332–333)

Key Concept: **A cephalopod is an ocean-dwelling mollusk whose foot is adapted to form tentacles around its mouth.**

- **Cephalopods** are a kind of mollusk. They live in the ocean. Octopuses and squids are cephalopods.

- Not all cephalopods have shells.

- Cephalopods are carnivores. They eat other animals.

- Cephalopods have tentacles that can move and bend. They use the tentacles to catch food.

Answer the following questions. Use your textbook and the ideas above.

9. Circle the letter of each sentence that is true about cephalopods.

   a. Cephalopods eat plants.

   b. Cephalopods live in the ocean.

   c. Cephalopods have tentacles.

10. Is the following sentence true or false? Cephalopods do not have a foot. _____

Mollusks, Arthropods, and Echinoderms

Arthropods (pages 335–342)

Characteristics of Arthropods (pages 48–49)

Key Concept: **Arthropods are invertebrates that have an external skeleton, a segmented body, and jointed attachments called appendages.**

- **Arthropods** are invertebrates. Arthropods have a body covering called an **exoskeleton**. The exoskeleton keeps the arthropod from drying out.

- Arthropods' bodies are made up of segments.

- Arthropods have body parts called appendages that can bend. Legs are one kind of appendage.

- **Antennae** are another kind of appendage. Arthropods use antennae to find food.

- Different kinds of arthropods have different numbers of legs, antennae, and body segments.

Answer the following questions. Use your textbook and the ideas above.

1. Circle the letter of each sentence that is true about arthropods.
   a. They are invertebrates.
   b. All arthropods have the same number of body segments.
   c. Arthropods have body parts that can bend.

2. A covering that helps keep an arthropod from drying out is a(an) _____.

Mollusks, Arthropods, and Echinoderms

Crustaceans (pages 338–339)

Key Concept: **Crustaceans are arthropods with two or three body sections, five or more pairs of legs, and two pairs of antennae.**

- **Crustaceans** (krus TAY shunz) are one kind of arthropod. Shrimp and lobsters are crustaceans.

- Crustaceans have two or three body sections. Crustaceans have five or more pairs of legs. They have two pairs of antennae.

- Most crustaceans live in water. Some crustaceans live in damp places on land.

- Crustaceans start life as larvae. The larvae do not look like adults. The larvae undergo metamorphosis. **Metamorphosis** (met uh MAWR fuh sis) is when an animal's body goes through a big change in a short time. After the larva's body changes, the larva becomes an adult.

Answer the following questions. Use your textbook and the ideas above.

3. Fill in the table below about crustaceans.

Crustaceans		
Number of Body Segments	**Number of Pairs of Antennae**	**Number of Pairs of Legs**
a. _____	2	b. _____

4. Is the following sentence true or false? All crustaceans live on land. _____

Mollusks, Arthropods, and Echinoderms

Arachnids (pages 340–341)

***Key Concept:* Arachnids are arthropods with two body sections, four pairs of legs, and no antennae.**

- **Arachnids** (uh RAK nidz) are one kind of arthropod. Spiders, mites, ticks, and scorpions are four groups of arachnids.

- Arachnids have two body sections. The first body section has the head and midsection. The second body section is called the **abdomen**.

- Arachnids have four pairs of legs. Arachnids have no antennae.

Answer the following questions. Use your textbook and the ideas above.

5. Circle the letter of each sentence that is true about arachnids.

   a. Arachnids have two pairs of legs.

   b. Arachnids have a body section called an abdomen.

   c. Arachnids have no antennae.

6. Complete the concept map about groups of arachnids.

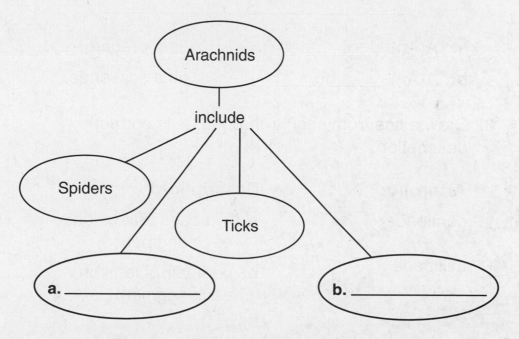

Mollusks, Arthropods, and Echinoderms

Centipedes and Millipedes (page 342)

Key Concept: **Centipedes and millipedes are arthropods with two body sections and many pairs of legs.**

- Centipedes and millipedes are arthropods. Their bodies have two sections. One body section is the head. There is one pair of antennae on the head. The other body section has many parts called segments. The legs are attached to the segments.

- Centipedes have one pair of legs on each segment. Centipedes are predators. They catch and eat other animals.

- Millipedes have two pairs of legs on each segment. Millipedes are scavengers. They eat dead leaves

Answer the following questions. Use your textbook and the ideas above.

7. Read each word in the box. In each sentence below, fill in one of the words.

centipede	anthropod	millipede

a. A(An) _____ is a predator.

b. A(An) _____ is a scavenger.

8. Draw a line from each arthropod to its correct description.

Arthropod

centipede

millipede

Description

a. two pairs of legs on each segment

b. one pair of legs on each segment

Mollusks, Arthropods, and Echinoderms

Insects (pages 343–347)

Body Structure (page 344)

Key Concept: **Insects are arthropods with three body sections, six legs, one pair of antennae, and usually one or two pairs of wings.**

- Insects are arthropods. Insect have three body sections. Insects have one pair of antennae. Insects have one or two pairs of wings. Insects have six legs.

- The front section of an insect is the head. The eyes and antennae are on the head.

- The middle section of an insect is the **thorax**. The wings and legs are attached to the thorax.

- The abdomen is the back section of an insect. Air enters the insect's body through holes in the abdomen.

Answer the following questions. Use your textbook and the ideas above.

1. This picture shows an insect. Label the picture using the words in the box.

thorax	head	abdomen

b. _____

a. _____   c. _____

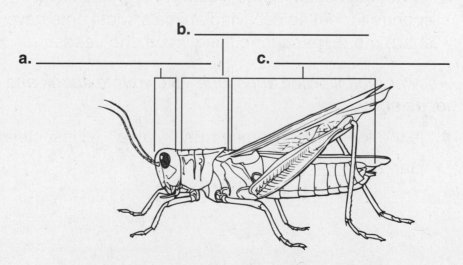

Mollusks, Arthropods, and Echinoderms

2. Fill in the blanks in the table about insects' bodies.

Insects			
Number of Body Sections	**Number of Pairs of Antennae**	**Number of Pairs of Wings**	**Number of Legs**
a. _____	b. _____	1 or 2	c. _____

3. Is the following sentence true or false? Insects get oxygen through holes in the thorax. _____

Obtaining Food (page 345)

Key Concept: **An insect's mouthparts are adapted for a highly specific way of getting food.**

- Some insects eat plants. Some insects eat the blood of other animals. Some insects eat dead animals and decaying leaves.

- You can tell what an insect eats by looking at its mouth. A butterfly's mouth is like a long tube. The tube is used for getting nectar. Some flies have a mouth like a sponge for eating decaying animals. Most ants have sharp mouth parts for cutting wood and seeds.

Answer the following questions. Use your textbook and the ideas above.

4. Is the following sentence true or false? All insects eat plants. _____

Mollusks, Arthropods, and Echinoderms

5. Read each word in the box. In each sentence below, fill in one of the words.

fly	butterfly	ant

a. A(An) _____ has a mouth like a long tube.

b. A(An) _____ has a mouth with parts like a sponge.

Life Cycle (pages 345–347)

Key Concept: **Each insect species undergoes either complete metamorphosis or gradual metamorphosis.**

*   Insects have two kinds of life cycles: complete metamorphosis and gradual metamorphosis.

*   **Complete metamorphosis** has four different stages. The first stage is the egg. The egg hatches into a larva. A larva looks like a worm. The larva changes into a **pupa**. A pupa does not eat or move much. After the pupa stage, the insect becomes an adult.

*   **Gradual metamorphosis** also begins with an egg. A nymph hatches from the egg. A **nymph** (nimf) looks like a small adult with no wings. The nymph grows and becomes an adult.

Answer the following questions. Use your textbook and the ideas above.

6. Circle the letter of each sentence that is true about the life cycle of an insect.

a. All insects start as an egg.

b. Some insects have complete metamorphosis.

c. A larva is one kind of egg.

Mollusks, Arthropods, and Echinoderms

7. Read each word in the box. In each sentence below, fill in one of the words.

nymph	pupa	larva

a. A _____ looks like a small adult insect with no wings.

b. A _____ does not eat or move much.

8. Read the words in the box. Use the words to fill in the steps of gradual metamorphosis.

Nymph	Egg	Larva

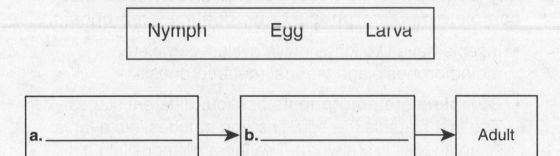

a. _____ → **b.** _____ → Adult

9. Read the words in the box. Use the words to fill in the steps of complete metamorphosis.

Pupa	Larva	Nymph

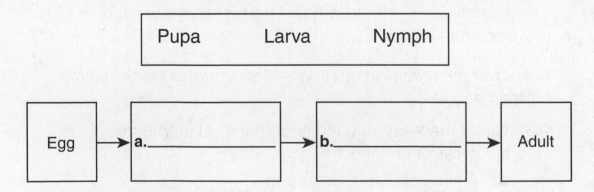

Egg → **a.** _____ → **b.** _____ → Adult

Insect Ecology (pages 350–355)

Insects and the Food Chain (pages 350–353)

Key Concept: Insects play key roles in food chains because of the many different ways that they obtain food and then become food for other animals.

- Animals get energy by eating plants or other animals. A **food chain** shows how energy moves from one living thing to another. Insects are a part of many food chains.

- Many insects eat plants. When an insect eats a plant, it gets energy. Many animals eat insects. They get energy by eating insects.

- Some insects are decomposers. A **decomposer** eats wastes and dead organisms.

- Insects are used for food by some people. Insects make other products that people use. Silk and honey are two products made by insects.

Answer the following questions. Use your textbook and the ideas above.

1. Draw a line from each term to its meaning.

Term	Meaning
decomposer	**a.** eats wastes and dead organisms
food chain	**b.** shows how energy moves from one living thing to another

Mollusks, Arthropods, and Echinoderms

2. Circle the letter of the sentence that tells what is happening in this picture.

a. The bird is getting energy from the caterpillar.

b. The caterpillar is getting energy from the bird.

c. The caterpillar is getting energy by being a decomposer.

3. Circle the letter of the sentence that tells about an insect being a decomposer.

a. An insect eats a leaf on a tree.

b. An insect is eaten by a bird.

c. An insect eats a dead bird.

Mollusks, Arthropods, and Echinoderms

Other Interactions (page 354)

Key Concept: **Two ways insects interact with other living things are by moving pollen among plants and by spreading disease-causing organisms.**

- Some insects help other living things. Some insects harm other living things.

- Some insects are pollinators. A **pollinator** carries pollen from plant to plant. This helps plants to reproduce.

- Some insects spread diseases to people and other animals. Fleas are one example of insects that spread disease.

Answer the following questions. Use your textbook and the ideas above.

4. Circle the letter that best describes a pollinator.
   a. spreads disease
   b. carries pollen
   c. eats dead organisms

5. Read each word in the box. In each sentence below, fill in one of the words.

disease   pollinator   decomposer

   a. An insect that carries _____ harms other living things.

   b. A _____ helps plants reproduce.

Mollusks, Arthropods, and Echinoderms

Controlling Pests (page 355)

Key Concept: **To try to control pests, people use chemicals, traps, and living things, including other insects.**

- **Pesticides** are chemicals that kill harmful insects. Pesticides also kill helpful insects. Pesticides are not always the best way to control insects.

- Scientists look for other ways to control harmful insects. One way is by using predators. The predators eat the harmful insects. Helpful insects are not harmed. Ladybug beetles are one example of a predator that eats harmful insects.

Answer the following questions. Use your textbook and the ideas above.

6. Circle the letter of each sentence that is true about pesticides.
   a. Pesticides are chemicals.
   b. Pesticides kill insects.
   c. Pesticides are always the best choice to control insects.

7. Circle the letter of each sentence that is true about using predators to control harmful insects.
   a. Predators eat only helpful insects.
   b. Ladybug beetles are one kind of predator.
   c. Predators eat harmful insects.

Echinoderms (pages 358–361)

Characteristics of Echinoderms (pages 358–359)

Key Concept: **Echinoderms are invertebrates with an internal skeleton and a system of fluid-filled tubes called a water vascular system.**

- **Echinoderms** (ee KY noh durmz) are invertebrates. All echinoderms live in salt water. Sea stars are echinoderms.

- Echinoderms have a skeleton inside their bodies.

- Echinoderms have tubes of water in their bodies. This is a **water vascular system**. The water vascular system is used for movement.

- Echinoderms have **tube feet** on the bottom of their bodies. Tube feet help echinoderms move and catch food. Tube feet are part of the water vascular system.

Answer the following questions. Use your textbook and the ideas above.

1. Circle the letter of each sentence that is true about echinoderms.
   a. They live on land.
   b. They have tube feet.
   c. They are invertebrates.

2. Is the following sentence true or false? Echinoderms have a water vascular system. _____

Mollusks, Arthropods, and Echinoderms

3. This picture shows a sea star. It is one kind of echinoderm. Fill in the blank to label the body part.

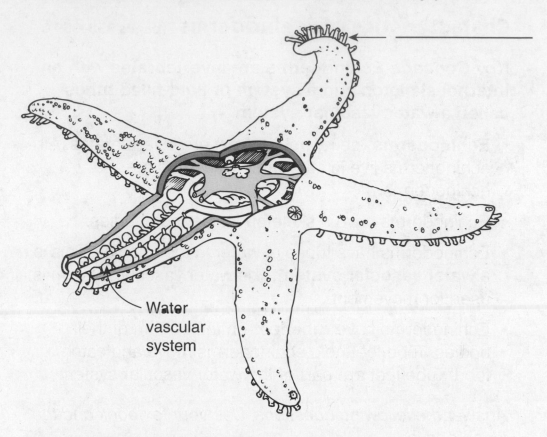

Water vascular system

Diversity of Echinoderms (pages 360–361)

Key Concept: **There are four major groups of echinoderms: sea stars, brittle stars, sea urchins, and sea cucumbers.**

- Sea stars have five arms. They attack and eat animals like clams. They use tube feet to move.

- Brittle stars use tube feet to catch food but not to move. Brittle stars wave their long arms to move.

- Sea urchins eat seaweed. They move using their tube feet.

- Sea cucumbers have soft bodies. They use tube feet to crawl on the ocean floor.

Name _____ Date _____ Class _____

Mollusks, Arthropods, and Echinoderms

Answer the following question. Use your textbook and the ideas on page 166.

4. Read the words in the box. Use the words to fill in the blanks in the table about the four different kinds of echinoderms.

Sea stars   Sea cucumbers   Brittle stars

Echinoderm Group	Description
Sea urchins	They move using tube feet. They eat seaweed.
a. _____ _____	They move using tube feet. They eat clams.
b. _____ _____	They move by waving their arms. They catch food using their tube feet.
c. _____ _____	They use tube feet to crawl on the ocean floor. They have a soft body.

Fishes, Amphibians, and Reptiles

What Is a Vertebrate? (pages 368–371)

Characteristics of Chordates (pages 368–369)

Key Concept: **At some point in their lives, chordates will have a notochord, a nerve cord that runs down their back, and slits in their throat area.**

- A phylum is a group of animals that are alike in some ways. Vertebrates are a part of the phylum Chordata. Animals in the phylum Chordata are called **chordates** (KAWR dayts).

- Chordates have a bendable rod in their backs called a **notochord**. Chordates have a nerve cord in their backs. The nerve cord connects the brain to the nerves in the body.

- All chordates have gill slits at some time in their lives. Some chordates have gill slits their whole lives.

- There are five main groups of vertebrates: fishes, amphibians, reptiles, birds, and mammals.

Answer the following questions. Use your textbook and the ideas above.

1. Circle the letter of each sentence that is true about chordates.
   a. Chordates have a nerve cord in their backs.
   b. Vertebrates are chordates.
   c. Chordates belong to the phylum Chordata.

2. Is the following sentence true or false? All chordates have gill slits for their whole lives.

   _____

Fishes, Amphibians, and Reptiles

3. Read the words in the box. Use the words to fill in the blanks in the table about parts of vertebrates' bodies.

Notochord	Nerve cord	Gill slits

Body Part	What the Body Part Does
a. _____ _____	A flexible rod that supports the back
b. _____ _____	Connects the brain and the nerves in the body

Characteristics of Vertebrates (pages 369–370)

Key Concept: **A vertebrate has a backbone that is part of an internal skeletal system.**

- A vertebrate is an animal with a backbone. Cats, fishes, and dogs are all vertebrates.

- A backbone is made of many little bones called **vertebrae**.

- Vertebrates have a skeleton inside their bodies. The skeleton protects the body. It gives the body shape. It gives the muscles a place to attach.

- Animals with skeletons inside their bodies can move easily. They can grow bigger than animals that do not have skeletons inside their bodies.

Fishes, Amphibians, and Reptiles

Fishes, Amphibians, and Reptiles

Answer the following questions. Use your textbook and the ideas on page 169.

4. Vertebrates have a skeleton inside their bodies. Fill in the concept map to tell the functions of the skeleton.

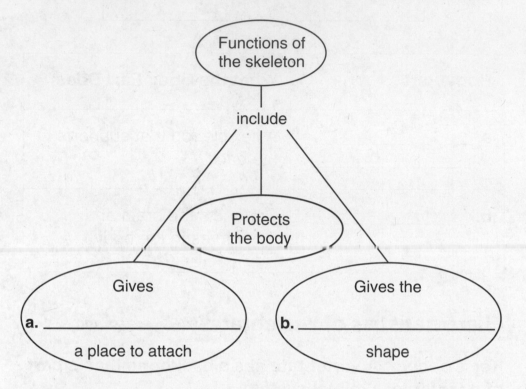

Functions of the skeleton

include

Protects the body

Gives
a. _____
a place to attach

Gives the
b. _____
shape

5. Circle the letter of the small bones that make up a backbone.

   a. chordates

   b. vertebrae

   c. endoskeletons

6. Circle the letter of the kind of animals that usually grow to be the biggest.

   a. animals with no skeleton

   b. animals with a skeleton outside of their body

   c. animals with a skeleton inside of their body

Name _____ Date _____ Class _____

Fishes, Amphibians, and Reptiles

Keeping Conditions Stable (pages 370–371)

Key Concept: **The body temperature of most fishes, amphibians, and reptiles is close to the temperature of their environment. In contrast, birds and mammals keep a stable body temperature that is often warmer than their environment.**

- Some animals have a body temperature that changes. If they sit in the sun, their bodies get warm. If they swim in cool water, their bodies get cool. They are called **ectotherms**. Fishes, amphibians, and reptiles are ectotherms.

- Some animals have a body temperature that stays the same. They are called **endotherms**. Birds and mammals are endotherms.

- Endotherms sweat or pant to keep from getting too hot. Endotherms have fur, hair, or feathers to keep from getting too cold.

Answer the following questions. Use your textbook and the ideas above.

7. Look at the pictures of animals. Use the words *endotherm* and *ectotherm* to label the pictures. You will use one word twice.

a. _____   b. _____   c. _____

8. Is the following sentence true or false? Ectotherms have a body temperature that stays the same.

_____

Fishes, Amphibians, and Reptiles

Fishes (pages 374–380)

Characteristics of Fishes (pages 375–377)

Key Concept: **In addition to living in water and having fins, most fishes are ectotherms, obtain oxygen through gills, and have scales.**

- **Fishes** are vertebrates because they have a backbone. Fishes bodies are covered with scales. Fishes are ectotherms.

- Fishes get oxygen from water. As water moves over the gills, oxygen enters a fish's body.

- Fishes move using fins.

- Fishes have a nervous system and sense organs. Fishes use their sense organs to find food and avoid predators.

Answer the following questions. Use your textbook and the ideas above.

1. This picture shows a fish. Use two of the words in the box to label the picture.

gills	fin	scales

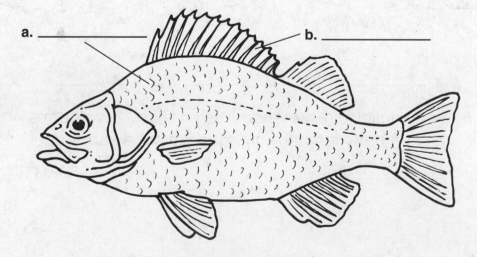

Fishes, Amphibians, and Reptiles

2. Circle the letter of each sentence that is true about fishes.

   a. Fishes have gills.

   b. Fishes are Invertebrates.

   c. Fishes have scales.

3. Fishes are ectotherms. Circle the letter of the sentence that tells about ectotherms.

   a. Their body stays one temperature.

   b. Their body temperature changes.

   c. Their body is always cold.

Jawless Fishes (page 377)

Key Concept: **Jawless fishes are unlike other fishes in that they have no jaws and no scales.**

- There are three groups of fishes. Jawless fishes are one group of fishes. Lampreys are one kind of jawless fishes.

- Jawless fishes have no jaws. They have no scales.

- Jawless fishes have a skeleton made of cartilage **Cartilage** is a tissue that is more flexible than bone.

- Some jawless fishes eat dead or dying animals. Other jawless fishes are parasites.

Answer the following questions. Use your textbook and the ideas above.

4. Circle the the letter of each body part that jawless fishes have.

   a. scales   b. skeleton   c. jaw

Fishes, Amphibians, and Reptiles

5. Jawless fishes have skeletons made of

_____.

Cartilaginous Fishes (page 378)

Key Concept: **Cartilaginous fishes have jaws, scales, and skeletons made of cartilage.**

- Cartilaginous (kahr tuh LAJ uh nuhs) fishes have jaws and rough scales. Their skeletons are made of cartilage. Sharks are one kind of cartilaginous fishes.

- Most cartilaginous fishes eat other animals. They are carnivores.

Answer the following questions. Use your textbook and the ideas above.

6. Circle the letter of each sentence that is true about cartilaginous fishes.
   a. They have scales.
   b. They do not have jaws.
   c. Most eat animals.

7. One kind of cartilaginous fishes is

_____.

Bony Fishes (pages 379–380)

Key Concept: **A bony fish has jaws, scales, a pocket on each side of the head that holds the gills, and a skeleton made of hard bones.**

- Bony fishes have jaws and scales. Bony fishes have a skeleton made of bone. Trout and tuna are two kinds of bony fishes.

- Bony fishes have a pocket on each side of their heads. The pocket holds their gills.

Fishes, Amphibians, and Reptiles

- Bony fishes have a swim bladder. A **swim bladder** is a sac filled with gas. The swim bladder helps a fish float under water. The swim bladder helps a fish move higher or lower in the water.

- Most fishes are bony fishes. There are many kinds of bony fishes.

Answer the following questions. Use your textbook and the ideas on page 174 and above.

8. Circle the letter of each sentence that is true about bony fishes.
   a. Bony fishes do not have jaws.
   b. Bony fishes have scales.
   c. Bony fishes have swim bladders.

9. A bony fish has a pocket on the side of its head that holds its _____.

10. Complete the concept map about groups of fishes.

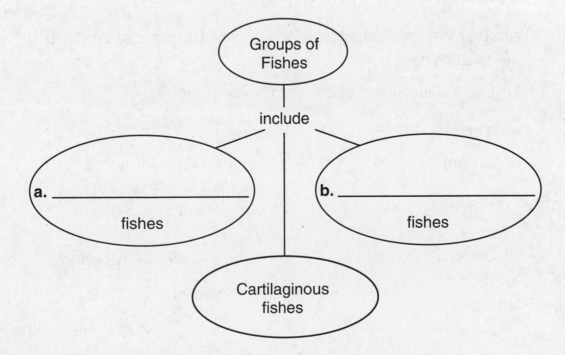

Amphibians (pages 382–386)

What Is an Amphibian? (pages 382–383)

Key Concept: **After beginning their lives in water, most amphibians spend their adulthood on land, returning to water to reproduce.**

- Frogs, salamanders, and toads are **amphibians**. Amphibians are ectotherms. Amphibian larvae live in water. Most adult amphibians live on land.

- Some amphibians, like salamanders, keep their tails when they are adults. Other amphibians, like frogs, do not have a tail when they are an adult.

- Amphibians undergo metamorphosis—big changes in their bodies—as they grow.

- A frog's life cycle starts with an egg. The larva that comes out of the egg is called a **tadpole**. The tadpole grows hind legs. Then the tadpole grows front legs. The tail then disappears, and the frog is an adult.

Answer the following questions. Use your textbook and the ideas above.

1. Draw a line from each term to its meaning.

Term	Meaning
amphibian	**a.** lives on land for some parts of its life and in water for some parts of its life
tadpole	
metamorphosis	**b.** a big change in the body
	c. a frog larva

Name _____ Date _____ Class _____

Fishes, Amphibians, and Reptiles

2. Read the words in the box. Use the words to fill in the blanks in the cycle diagram of how a frog changes during its life.

Tadpoles hatch	Hind legs grow	Tail disappears

Frog Metamorphosis

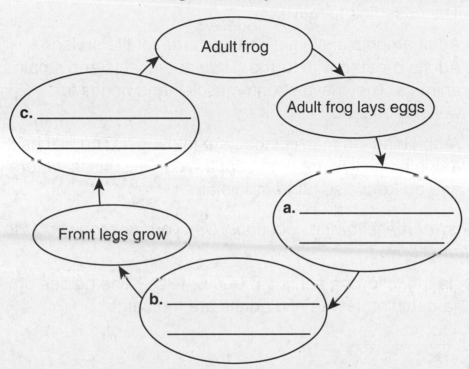

3. Read each word in the box. In each sentence below, fill in one of the words.

frog	salamander	larva

a. A _____ keeps its tail when it is an adult.

b. A _____ does not have a tail when it is an adult.

Fishes, Amphibians, and Reptiles

Living on Land (pages 384–386)

Key Concept: **The respiratory and circulatory systems of adult amphibians are adapted for life on land. In addition, adult amphibians have adaptations for obtaining food and moving.**

- Amphibian larvae have bodies made for life in the water. Larvae have gills for breathing. They eat pond plants. They use fins to move.

- Adult amphibians have bodies made for life on land. Adults breathe with **lungs**. They eat insects and small animals. They have strong muscles and bones for walking on land.

- Amphibians in many places are in danger. The places amphibians live are being destroyed. Poisons in water and on land also hurt amphibians.

Answer the following questions. Use your textbook and the ideas above.

4. Is the following sentence true or false? The bodies of amphibian larvae and adults are the same.

   _____

5. Circle the letter of each sentence that is true about amphibian larvae.
   a. They have strong bones.
   b. They have gills.
   c. They use fins to move.

6. Circle the letter of each sentence that is true about amphibian adults.
   a. They have lungs.
   b. They eat pond plants.
   c. They walk on land.

Fishes, Amphibians, and Reptiles

7. Read the words in the box. Use the words to fill in the blanks in the table about how amphibian larvae and adults are different.

plants	lungs	insects	fins	gills

Amphibians			
Life Stage	**What They Eat**	**How They Move**	**How They Breathe**
Larva	a. _____	b. _____	c. _____
Adult	d. _____	strong bones and muscles	e. _____

Fishes, Amphibians, and Reptiles

Reptiles (pages 387–394)

Adaptations for Life on Land (pages 388–389)

Key Concept: **The skin, kidneys, and eggs of reptiles are adapted to conserve water.**

- **Reptiles** are vertebrates. Most reptiles live on land their whole lives. Turtles, snakes, alligators, and crocodiles are reptiles.

- Reptiles' bodies are made to keep from losing water. Reptiles have thick scaly skin to keep water inside the body.

- **Kidneys** are the body parts that take waste out of the blood. Kidneys make urine. A reptile's kidneys do not use much water to make urine.

- Reptiles have **amniotic eggs**. These eggs have a shell. The shell keeps the eggs from drying out.

Answer the following question. Use your textbook and the ideas above.

1. This picture shows a turtle egg. Circle the letter of the sentence that tells what the egg shell does.

   a. It feeds the turtle.

   b. It keeps the turtle from drying out.

   c. It makes the turtle's urine.

Amniotic Egg

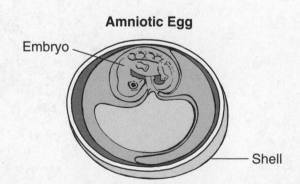

Embryo

Shell

Fishes, Amphibians, and Reptiles

Lizards and Snakes (pages 390–391)

Key Concept: Both lizards and snakes are reptiles that have skin covered with overlapping scales.

- Lizards and snakes are reptiles. In some ways they are the same. Most snakes and lizards eat other animals. Most snakes and lizards live in warm places.

- Snakes and lizards are different in some ways. Lizards have four legs. They walk and run on land. Snakes do not have legs. They slither on the ground.

- Lizards have eyelids. Snakes do not have eyelids.

- Lizards have two lungs. Most snakes have one lung.

Answer the following questions. Use your textbook and the ideas above.

2. Is the following sentence true or false? Lizards and snakes have skin covered with scales. _____

3. Complete the Venn diagram by labeling which side describes lizards and which side describes snakes.

a. _____   b. _____

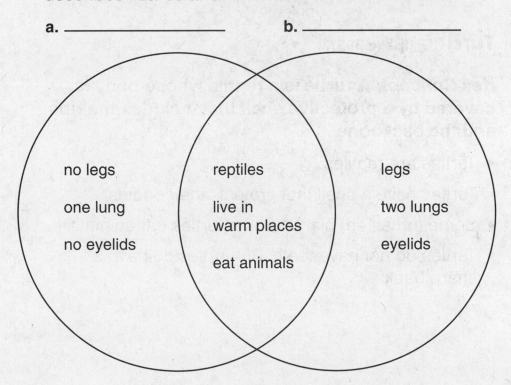

no legs

one lung

no eyelids

reptiles

live in warm places

eat animals

legs

two lungs

eyelids

Fishes, Amphibians, and Reptiles

Alligators and Crocodiles (page 392)

Key Concept: **Both alligators and crocodiles are large, carnivorous reptiles that care for their young.**

- Alligators and crocodiles are reptiles.

- Alligators and crocodiles take care of their young. After the eggs hatch, the female takes the babies to the water. She takes care of them until they can feed themselves.

- Alligators and crocodiles hunt for prey. They swim quickly. They have strong jaws and sharp teeth to catch and eat animals.

Answer the following question. Use your textbook and the ideas above.

4. Circle the letter of each sentence that is true about alligators and crocodiles.

   a. Alligators and crocodiles eat plants.
   b. Alligators and crocodiles take care of their young.
   c. Alligators and crocodiles are reptiles.

Turtles (page 393)

Key Concept: **A turtle is a reptile whose body is covered by a protective shell that includes the ribs and the backbone.**

- Turtles are reptiles.

- Turtles have a shell that protects their bodies.

- Some turtles eat plants. Some turtles eat animals.

- Turtles do not have teeth. But turtles do have a sharp beak.

Fishes, Amphibians, and Reptiles

Answer the following question. Use your textbook and the ideas on page 182.

5. Is the following sentence true or false? Turtles use their sharp teeth to catch food. _____

Extinct Reptiles—The Dinosaurs (page 394)

Key Concept: **Dinosaurs were the earliest vertebrates that had legs positioned directly beneath their bodies.**

- Dinosaurs were reptiles. Dinosaurs are extinct because there are no more living dinosaurs.

- Some dinosaurs ate plants. Most of these dinosaurs walked on four legs.

- Some dinosaurs ate animals. Most of those dinosaurs walked on two legs.

Answer the following questions. Use your textbook and the ideas above.

6. What does it mean if a kind of animal is extinct? Circle the letter of the correct answer.
   a. They eat animals.
   b. They have a backbone.
   c. They are not living anymore.

7. Circle the letter of each sentence that is true about dinosaurs.
   a. Some dinosaurs walked on two legs.
   b. All dinosaurs ate plants.
   c. Dinosaurs were reptiles.

Name _____ Date _____ Class _____

Vertebrate History in Rocks

(pages 395–399)

What Are Fossils? (pages 396–397)

Key Concept: **Fossils are found most frequently in sedimentary rock.**

- A **fossil** is the hard remains of a plant or animal that lived long ago.

- Fossils are usually found in sedimentary rock. **Sedimentary rock** is rock made of hardened layers of mud, sand, or clay.

- Parts of dead plants and animals can get trapped in mud, sand, or clay. Over a long time, the plant or animal parts become fossils.

- Some fossils are imprints. These are fossils of footprints or leaves. Other fossils are bones, shells, or other hard parts of plants or animals.

Answer the following questions. Use your textbook and the ideas above.

1. Read each word in the box. In each sentence below, fill in the correct word.

    ┌─────────────────────────────────────┐
    │ fossil   sedimentary   imprint   │
    └─────────────────────────────────────┘

    a. Rock formed from hardened layers of mud, sand, and clay is called _____ rock.

    b. The remains of a plant or animal that lived long ago is a(an) _____.

Fishes, Amphibians, and Reptiles

2. Read each word the box. Use the words to fill in the blanks in the concept map about fossils.

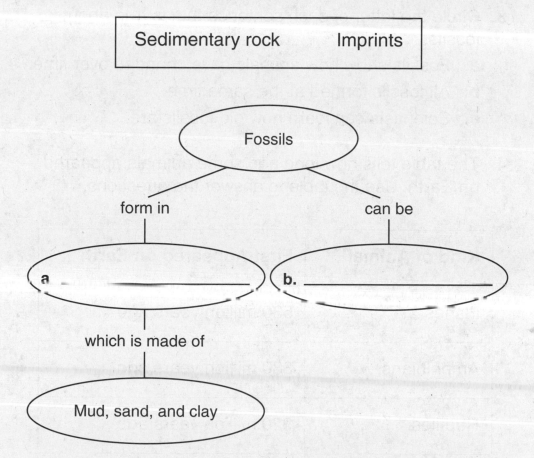

Sedimentary rock   Imprints

Fossils

form in   can be

a. _____   b. _____

which is made of

Mud, sand, and clay

Interpretation of Fossils (pages 398–399)

Key Concept: **By studying fossils, paleontologists can infer how animals changed over time.**

- **Paleontologists** (pay lee un TAHL uh jists) are scientists who study fossils.

- Fossils show when different animals first appeared on Earth.

- Fossils show how animals have changed over time.

- Fossils show how animals are related.

- Scientists can find out how old fossils are. Fossils form in layers. The older fossils are in the bottom layers. The younger fossils are in the top layers.

Fishes, Amphibians, and Reptiles

Answer the following questions. Use your textbook and the ideas on page 185.

3. Circle the letter of each sentence that is true about fossils.

    a. Fossils show how animals have changed over time.

    b. All fossils formed at the same time.

    c. Scientists can learn how old fossils are.

4. The table tells how long ago some animals appeared on Earth. Use the table to answer the questions.

Kind of Animal	First Appeared on Earth
Fishes	530 million years ago
Amphibians	380 million years ago
Reptiles	320 million years ago
Mammals	220 million years ago
Birds	150 million years ago

    a. Which animals appeared on Earth *first*?

    _____

    b. Name two kinds of animals that appeared on Earth *after* amphibians. _____

Name _____ Date _____ Class _____

Fishes, Amphibians, and Reptiles

5. This picture shows fossils in layers of rock. Use the picture to answer the questions.

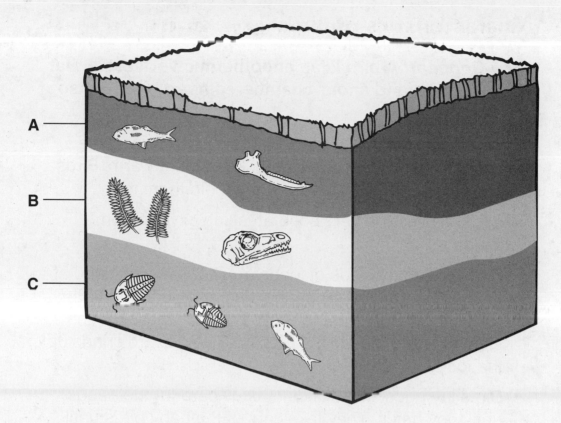

a. Which layer has the oldest fossils? _____

b. Which layer has the youngest fossils? _____

Birds (pages 406–413)

Characteristics of Birds (pages 407–411)

Key Concept: **A bird is an endothermic vertebrate that has feathers and a four-chambered heart. A bird also lays eggs.**

- **Birds** are vertebrates. Most birds can fly. Birds have short fluffy **down feathers** that keep them warm. Birds have large **contour feathers** that help them fly.

- Birds' bodies are very good at taking oxygen from the air.

- Birds eat many kinds of foods. You can tell what kind of food a bird eats by the shape of its bill. Food the bird swallows is stored in the **crop**. The food moves to the stomach, and then to the **gizzard**. The gizzard grinds up the food.

- Birds lay eggs. Most kinds of birds care for their eggs until they hatch. They take care of the baby birds until they can fly and feed themselves.

Answer the following questions. Use your textbook and the ideas above.

1. Circle the letter of each sentence that is true about birds.
    a. Birds lay eggs.
    b. Most birds can fly.
    c. Birds eat only one kind of food.

2. Circle the letter of each way feathers help birds.
    a. They help birds fly.
    b. They keep birds warm.
    c. They provide food for birds.

Name _____ Date _____ Class _____

Birds and Mammals

3. Read the words in the box. Use the words to fill in the blanks in the table about feathers.

| Contour feather   Down feather |

Kind of Feather	What It Looks Like	What It is Used For
a. _____ _____		keeps the bird warm
b. _____ _____		used for flying

Birds and Mammals

4. Read the words in the box. Use the words to fill in the blanks in the flowchart about how food moves through a bird's body.

| Crop   Heart   Gizzard   Eggs |

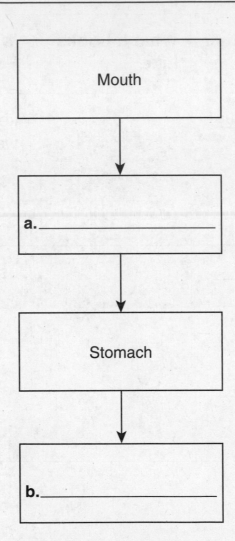

Mouth

a. _____

Stomach

b. _____

5. Is the following sentence true or false? Most birds care for their eggs and their young. _____

Birds and Mammals

Birds in the Environment (pages 412–413)

Key Concept: **Birds are adapted for living in diverse environments. You can see some of these adaptations in the shapes of their legs, claws, and bills.**

- There are many different kinds of birds. Birds live in many places on Earth.

- You can tell what a bird eats by the shape of its bill. You can tell where a bird lives by the shape of its legs and claws.

- Some birds help plants by carrying pollen from flower to flower. Other birds eat berries and spread seeds in their wastes. Some birds are predators that eat animals that are pests, such as rats and mice.

Answer the following questions. Use your textbook and the ideas above.

6. Circle the letter of each sentence that is true about birds.

   a. Some birds eat mice and rats.

   b. All birds have the same kind of claws.

   c. Birds live in many places on Earth.

7. If you want to learn what a bird eats, which body part would it be most helpful to look at? Circle the letter of the correct answer.

   a. claws

   b. legs

   c. bill

Birds and Mammals

The Physics of Bird Flight

(pages 416–419)

Staying in the Air (pages 416–417)

Key Concept: **The difference in pressure above and below the wings as a bird moves through the air produces an upward force that causes the bird to rise.**

- Air is all around us. Air pushes on everything on Earth. The force of air pushing on things is called air pressure.

- Airs moves around birds' wings when they fly. Air moves above and below the wings.

- The shape of a wing makes the air above the wing move factor than tho air bolow tho wing.

- Air that moves faster has less air pressure than air that moves more slowly. So, there is less air pressure above the wing than below the wing. This makes a force that pushes the bird upward, called **lift**.

Answer the following questions. Use your textbook and the ideas above.

1. What is lift? Circle the letter of the correct answer.
   a. The shape of a bird's wing.
   b. A force that pushes upward.
   c. The speed that air moves.

2. Circle the letter of each sentence that is true about air and air pressure.
   a. Air is all around.
   b. Air moves under birds' wings but not over birds' wings.
   c. Air pushes on everything on Earth.

Birds and Mammals

3. Look at the picture that shows air moving around a bird's wing. Use the picture to answer the questions.

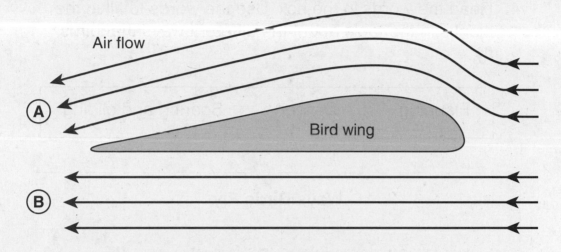

Air flow

Ⓐ

Bird wing

Ⓑ

a. Is the air moving faster at A or B?

_____

b. Is there more air pressure at A or at B?

_____

Birds in Flight (pages 418–419)

Key Concept: **Three types of bird flight are flapping, soaring and gliding, and diving.**

- All birds flap their wings when they fly. Some birds flap their wings to get off the ground. Flapping uses a lot of energy.

- Some birds soar and glide when they fly. Soaring means rising up on air currents. Gliding means moving downward on an air current. Birds do not move their wings much when they soar and glide. Soaring and gliding do not take much energy.

- Some birds dive from the sky to catch prey. When a bird dives, it pulls its wings close to its body so there is no lift at all. Then gravity pulls the bird downward at very fast speeds. Birds do not move their wings when they dive. Diving does not take much energy.

Name _____ Date _____ Class _____

Birds and Mammals

Answer the following questions. Use your textbook and the ideas on page 193.

4. Read the words in the box. Use the words to fill in the blanks in the table about the different ways that birds fly.

| Flapping | Diving | Soaring and gliding |

Ways Birds Fly	
Kind of Flight	**Description**
a. _____	The bird tucks in its wings. The bird moves downward very quickly.
b. _____	The bird moves its wings up and down.
c. _____ _____	The bird uses air currents to move up or down.

Birds and Mammals

5. Circle the box that tells about a kind of flying that uses a lot of energy.

```
┌─────────────────────────┐
│        Flapping         │
└─────────────────────────┘

┌─────────────────────────┐
│   Soaring and gliding   │
└─────────────────────────┘

┌─────────────────────────┐
│         Diving          │
└─────────────────────────┘
```

6. In which kind of flight do birds use air currents to move up or down? Circle the letter of the correct answer.
   a. flapping
   b. diving
   c. soaring and gliding

Birds and Mammals

Mammals (pages 420–428)

Characteristics of Mammals (pages 421–423)

Key Concept: **All mammals are endothermic vertebrates that have a four-chambered heart and skin covered with fur or hair. Most mammals are born alive, and every young mammal is fed with milk produced by organs in its mother's body.**

- Mammals are vertebrates. Mammals eat many different things. Mammals that eat animals have sharp, pointed teeth. Mammals that eat plants have wide, flat teeth.

- Mammals breathe with lungs. The **diaphragm** is a muscle that helps move air in and out of the lungs. In the lungs, oxygen moves into the blood.

- Mammals have hair or fur that helps keep their body at a steady temperature.

- Mammals move in different ways. Most mammals walk on four legs. Some walk on two legs. Some mammals, such as whales, swim in water.

- Mammals have large brains. They also have keen senses.

Answer the following questions. Use your textbook and the ideas above.

1. In each pair, circle the term that describes a mammal.
   a. exotherm   endotherm
   b. vertebrate   invertebrate
   c. four-chambered heart   three-chambered heart
   d. feathers   fur or hair

Birds and Mammals

2. Circle the letter of each sentence that is true about mammals.

   a. Mammals have lungs.

   b. All mammals walk on four legs.

   c. Mammals eat many different things.

3. Look at the two pictures of mammal skulls. Study the teeth. Which animal ate meat? Which animal ate plants?

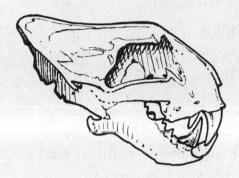

a. _____   b. _____

Birds and Mammals

Diversity of Mammals (pages 424–428)

Key Concept: **There are three main groups of mammals—monotremes, marsupials, and placental mammals. The groups differ in how their young develop.**

- There are three groups of mammals: monotremes, marsupials, and placental mammals.

- **Monotremes** are mammals that lay eggs. Milk seeps out of the mother's skin to feed the young.

- **Marsupials** are mammals that have a pouch. Young marsupials grow in their mothers' pouch after they are born. They stay in the pouch until they are fully developed.

- **Placental mammals** are not born until they are fully developed. The **placenta** is an organ in the mother that passes food and oxygen to the developing embryo. Most mammals are placental mammals.

- Baby mammals cannot take care of themselves. The mother or parents care for the young after they are born.

Answer the following questions. Use your textbook and the ideas above.

4. How are mammals divided into groups? Circle the letter of the correct answer.
   a. by what they eat
   b. by the way they move
   c. by the way their young develop

5. Is the following sentence true or false? The placenta passes food and oxygen to a developing embryo.

   _____

6. Read the words in the box. Use the words to fill in the blanks in the concept map about the three groups of mammals.

Marsupials   Monotremes   Placental mammals

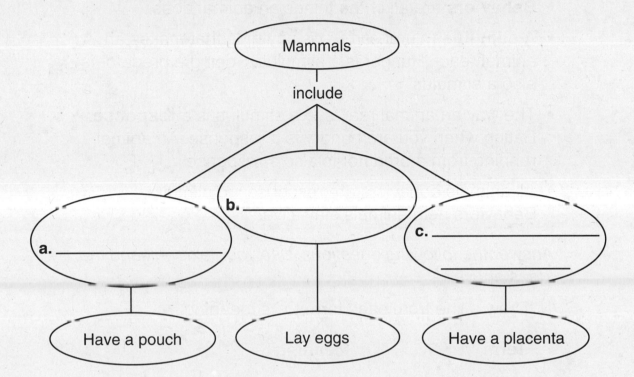

What Is Behavior? (pages 436–442)

The Behavior of Animals (page 437)

Key Concept: **All animal behaviors are caused by stimuli.**

- **Behaviors** are all of the things an animal does.

- A **stimulus** (plural *stimuli*) is anything that makes an animal react. Hunger is a stimulus. Seeing a predator is also a stimulus.

- The way an animal reacts to a stimulus is a **response**. Eating when you are hungry is a response. An animal running from a predator is also a response.

- All animals behaviors are responses to stimuli. Behaviors help animals stay alive.

Answer the following questions. Use your textbook and the ideas above.

1. Draw a line from each term to its meaning.

Term	Meaning
stimulus	**a.** the way an animal reacts to a stimulus
response	**b.** anything that makes an animal react

2. Circle the letter of each sentence that tells about a stimulus.

   a. An animal breathes oxygen.

   b. An animal feels thirsty.

   c. An animal sees a predator.

3. Read the words in the box. Use the words to fill in the blanks in the sentence below.

stimulus	behavior	predator

A _____ is a response to a

_____.

Behavior by Instinct (page 438)

Key Concept: **An instinct is a response to a stimulus that is inborn and that an animal performs correctly the first time.**

- Animals are born knowing how to respond to some stimuli.

- An **instinct** is a response that an animal does not have to learn. For example, a spider spins its web by instinct It does not need to learn how. Most birds build nests by instinct.

Answer the following questions. Use your textbook and the ideas above.

4. Circle the letter of each sentence that is true about instincts.
   a. An instinct is a response to a stimulus.
   b. Instincts need to be learned.
   c. An animal is born knowing how to do some things.

5. Circle the letter of each example of an instinct.
   a. a bird building a nest
   b. a spider spinning a web
   c. a child learning to read

Learned Behavior (pages 438–442)

Key Concept: **Learned behaviors include imprinting, conditioning, trial-and-error learning, and insight learning.**

- **Imprinting** is a kind of learning in which a young animal follows the first moving thing it sees. Most young animals imprint on their mothers. This keeps young animals safe.

- **Conditioning** is learning that a certain stimulus or response leads to something good or bad. Have you seen a cat run to the kitchen when it hears a can opener? This is an example of conditioning. The cat learned that the sound of a can opener means food.

- **Trial-and-error learning** is when an animal gets a reward for doing a certain thing. The animal learns to do that thing again to get the reward.

- When an animal uses what it already knows to solve a new problem, it is called **insight learning**.

Answer the following questions. Use your textbook and the ideas above.

6. A dog sees its leash. It jumps and wags its tail. Circle the letter of the kind of leaning this is.

   a. trial-and-error learning

   b. insight learning

   c. conditioning

Name _____ Date _____ Class _____

7. Read the words in the box. Use the words to fill in the blanks in the table about animal behavior.

| Instinct | Insight learning | Imprinting |
| Conditioning |

Behavior	Description
a. _____	A young animal follows the first thing it sees.
b. _____ _____	An animal uses what it already knows to solve a new problem.
c. _____	An animal learns that a particular stimulus has a good or bad outcome.
Trial-and error learning	An animal learns behavior by getting a reward for certain actions.

Patterns of Behavior (pages 444–451)

Communication (page 445)

Key Concept: **Animals use mostly sounds, scents, and body movements to communicate with one another.**

- Animals cannot talk, but they can tell each other things in different ways. Animals use sounds, smells, and body movements to send messages.

- Some animals use sounds or body movements to find mates.

- Animals use chemicals called **pheromones** (FEHR uh mohnz) to send messages.

- Some animals warn others about danger. Some animals help others find food.

Answer the following questions. Use your textbook and the ideas above.

1. What is a pheromone? Circle the letter of the correct answer.
   a. a body movement
   b. a sound
   c. a chemical that sends messages

2. Circle the letter of each sentence that is true about animal communication.
   a. Animals can send messages to each other.
   b. Some animals use sounds to send messages.
   c. Some animals warn others about danger.

Competitive Behavior (pages 446–447)

Key Concept: **Animals compete with one another for limited resources, such as food, water, space, shelter, and mates.**

- Animals compete with each other for the things they need to live.

- **Aggression** is a threatening behavior. Animals use aggression when they compete.

- A **territory** is a place an animal lives and looks for food. Animals compete for territory.

- Animals compete for mates. **Courtship behavior** is the way an animal acts to attract a mate.

Answer the following questions. Use your textbook and the ideas above.

3. Draw a line from each term to its meaning.

Term	Meaning
aggression	**a.** behavior used to find a mate
courtship behavior	**b.** threatening behavior
territory	**c.** the place an animals lives and looks for food

4. Use the terms in the box to fill in the blanks in the sentences.

> compete   aggression   territory

a. Animals use _____ when they compete.

b. Animals _____ for the things they need to live.

Animal Behavior

Group Behavior (pages 448–449)

Key Concept: **Living in groups enables animals to cooperate.**

- Living in a group helps animals stay safe from predators.

- Some animals work in a group to find food.

- Some animals live in a society. A **society** is a group of the same kind of animal that works together. Different animals do different jobs. Bees and ants live in societies.

Answer the following question. Use your textbook and the ideas above.

5. Circle the letter of each sentence that is true about animals that live in a group

   a. All animals live in groups.

   b. Living in a group can help animals stay safe.

   c. Living in a group can help animals find food.

Behavior Cycles (pages 450–451)

Key Concept: **Cyclic behaviors usually change over the course of a day or a season.**

- Cyclic behavior is behavior that always changes in a certain way.

- Behaviors that change in a certain way during a day are called **circadian** (sur KAY dee un) **rhythms**. For example, some animals hunt during the night and sleep during the day.

Animal Behavior

- Some behavior changes with the seasons. For example, some animals are not active when it is cold. This is called **hibernation**.

- Migration is a cyclic behavior. **Migration** is moving from one place to another and back again. Some animals migrate to find food. Some animals migrate to find a good place to mate.

Answer the following question. Use your textbook and the ideas on page 206 and above.

6. Read the words in the box. Use the words to fill in the blanks in the table about cyclic behavior.

Circadian rhythm   Hibernation   Migration

Cyclic Behavior	Description
a. _____	moving from one place to another and back again
b. _____	resting when the weather gets cold
c. _____ _____	patterns that are about a day long

Animal Behavior

Tracking Migrations (pages 454–457)

Technologies for Tracking (pages 455–456)

Key Concept: **Electronic tags give off repeating signals that are picked up by radio devices or satellites. Scientists can track the locations and movements of the tagged animals without recapturing them.**

- Scientists can learn about migrations by putting tags on animals.

- Scientists used to use metal bands to tag birds.

- Today scientists also use electronic tags. These tags have a **transmitter** that sends out radio waves. The scientist's **receiver** picks up the signal. Scientists can follow the tagged animal.

- Some animals are tracked using **satellites** that fly high above Earth.

Answer the following questions. Use your textbook and the ideas above.

1. Circle the letter of each sentence that is true about tracking migrations.
   a. There is only one way to track migrating animals.
   b. Scientists can learn about animals by tracking their migration.
   c. Some scientists use satellites to track animals' migrations.

2. Is the following sentence true or false? Scientists use only metal bands to track animal migrations.

   _____

Animal Behavior

3. Read the words in the box. Use the words to fill in the blanks in the table about tracking migrations.

| Transmitter | Receiver | Metal band |

Tool	Description
a. _____	A scientist uses this to pick up signals from tagged animals.
b. _____	It is attached to an animal and sends out a signal.
Satellite	A tool that orbits Earth.

Name _____ Date _____ Class _____

Animal Behavior

Why Tracking Is Important (pages 456–457)

Key Concept: **Tracking migrations is an important tool to better understand and protect species.**

- Tracking lets scientists learn about animal migrations.
- Tracking can be used to protect animals as they migrate.
- Tracking can be used to find out if the same number of animals migrates each year.
- Tracking can be used to find out what land to set aside for migrating animals.

Answer the following question. Use your textbook and the ideas above.

4. Read the words in the box. Use the words to fill in the blanks in the concept map about how scientists use tracking.

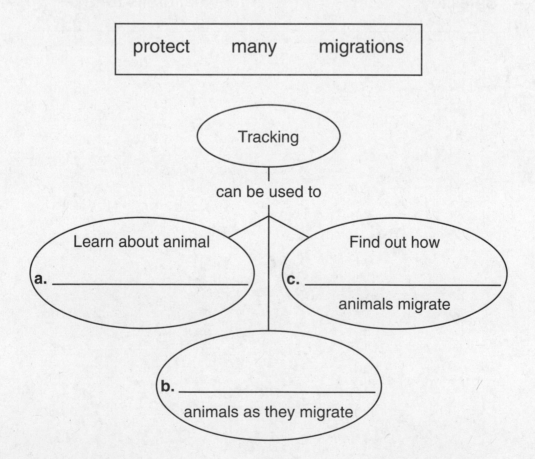

protect   many   migrations

Tracking

can be used to

Learn about animal
a. _____

Find out how
c. _____
animals migrate

b. _____
animals as they migrate

Bones, Muscles, and Skin

Body Organization and Homeostasis (pages 468–473)

Cells (page 469)

***Key Concept:* Cells are the smallest unit of organization in the human body.**

- The **cell** is the basic building block of living things. Most cells are too small to see, even with a microscope. Some living things, including you, are composed of trillions of cells.

- Each cell has many parts. The **cell membrane** is the outside covering of the cell. Inside the cell is a part called the nucleus. The **nucleus** controls everything the cell does.

- Cells do several jobs that help keep the body alive. For example, cells give the body energy for everything it does.

Answer the following questions. Use your textbook and the ideas above.

1. The basic building block of living things is the

   _____.

2. Is the following sentence true or false? The nucleus controls everything the cell does. _____

3. Circle the letter that describes the cell membrane.
   a. makes energy for the body
   b. outside covering of the cell
   c. controls everything the cell does

Bones, Muscles, and Skin

Tissues (page 470)

Key Concept: **After cells, tissues are the next unit of organization in the human body.**

- A **tissue** is a group of similar cells that do the same job. There are four main kinds of tissue in the human body. They are muscle tissue, nervous tissue, connective tissue, and epithelial tissue.

- **Muscle tissue** helps move body parts such as arms and legs.

- **Nervous tissue** carries messages back and forth between the brain and the rest of the body.

- **Connective tissue** supports the body and holds it together. Bone is one kind of connective tissue.

- **Epithelial** (ep uh THEE lee ul) **tissue** covers and protects body surfaces. Skin is one kind of epithelial tissue.

Answer the following question. Use your textbook and the ideas above.

4. Fill in the blanks in the table about types of tissue.

Types of Tissue	
Type of Tissue	**Job in the Body**
Muscle tissue	moves body parts
Nervous tissue	carries messages
a. _____	supports the body
b. _____	covers the body

Bones, Muscles, and Skin

Organs and Organ Systems (pages 470–471)

Key Concept: **After tissues, organs are the next unit of organization in the human body. Organs are combined into organ systems.**

- An **organ** is a body part that is made up of different kinds of tissue. Each organ does a certain job. The heart is an example of an organ. The heart's job is to keep blood moving through the body.

- An **organ system** is a group of organs that work together to do a major job. Your body has 11 organ systems. One is the circulatory system. It includes your heart. It also includes blood vessels. The job of the circulatory system is to carry materials to and from cells.

Answer the following questions. Use your textbook and the ideas above.

5. Is the following sentence true or false? An organ is made up of just one kind of tissue. _____

6. Circle the letter of an example of an organ system.
    a. heart
    b. circulatory system
    c. blood vessels

7. Draw a line from each term to its meaning.

Term	Meaning
organ	a. a group of organs that work together
organ system	b. body part made of different kinds of tissue

Bones, Muscles, and Skin

Homeostasis (pages 472–473)

Key Concept: **Homeostasis is the process by which an organism's internal environment is kept stable in spite of changes in the external environment.**

- **Homeostasis** (hoh mee oh STAY sis) is all of the ways the body tends to keep itself in balance. For example, when your body is too warm, you sweat. Sweating helps to cool your body.

- If something scares you or excites you, it can throw your body out of balance. Your heart races, and your breathing speeds up. These changes in your body are called **stress**. When the stress is over, your body becomes balanced again.

Answer the following questions. Use your textbook and the ideas above.

8. Read the words in the box. In each sentence below, fill in one of the words.

homeostasis   sweating   stress

    a. How your body reacts to something scary or exciting is called _____.

    b. All of the ways your body tends to keep itself in balance is _____.

9. Is the following sentence true or false? Sweating to cool your body is an example of homeostasis.

_____

Bones, Muscles, and Skin

The Skeletal System (pages 474–481)

What the Skeletal System Does (pages 474–476)

Key Concept: **Your skeleton has five major functions. It provides shape and support, enables you to move, protects your organs, produces blood cells, and stores minerals and other materials until your body needs them.**

- Your **skeleton** is made up of all the bones in your body. An adult has more than 200 bones.

- Your skeleton gives your body its shape. The center of your skeleton is your backbone. Your backbone is made up of many small bones called **vertebrae** (VUR tuh bray).

- The bones of your skeleton, along with your muscles, let you move. Bones also protect the organs inside your body. For example, bones in your head protect your brain.

- Some bones make things your body needs. For example, bones in your arms and legs make blood cells. Bones also store minerals, such as calcium, until your body needs them.

Answer the following questions. Use your textbook and the ideas above.

1. All the bones in your body make up your

   _____.

2. Is the following sentence true or false? The center of your skeleton is your backbone. _____

3. Which is a job of the skeletal system? Circle the letter of the correct answer.

   a. making blood cells

   b. carrying materials to and from cells

   c. covering the body

Joints of the Skeleton (pages 476–477)

Key Concept: **Joints allow bones to move in different ways.**

• A **joint** is where two bones meet. Most joints can move, but some cannot move.

• Joints that cannot move are called immovable joints. Examples of immovable joints are the joints that hold together the bones in your head.

• Joints that can move are called movable joints. Tough tissues called **ligaments** hold together the bones in movable joints.

• A tissue called **cartilage** (KAHR tuh lij) covers the ends of the bones. Cartilage keeps the bones from rubbing together at the joint.

• There are several kinds of movable joints. They include hinge joints and ball-and-socket joints.

• In hinge joints, bones move back and forth in two directions. Elbows and knees are hinge joints.

• In ball-and-socket joints, bones move in a circle. Shoulders and hips are ball-and-socket joints.

Bones, Muscles, and Skin

Answer the following questions. Use your textbook and the ideas on page 216.

4. Read the words in the box. In each sentence below, fill in one of the words.

┌───┐
│ ligaments   joint   vertebrae   cartilage   │
└───┘

a. A place where two bones meet is a

_____.

b. The bones in movable joints are held together by

_____.

c. The tissue that keeps the ends of bones from

rubbing together is called _____.

5. Is the following sentence true or false? All joints can

move. _____

6. Which diagram shows how a hinge joint works? Which diagram shows how a ball-and-socket joint works? Write the correct name of the joint by each example.

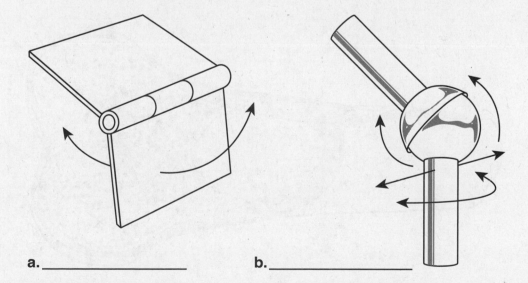

a. _____   b. _____

_____   _____

Bones, Muscles, and Skin

Bones—Strong and Living (pages 478–480)

Key Concept: **Bones are complex living structures that undergo growth and development.**

- Bones are living structures. Bones contain blood and nerves. Bones grow and develop as you do. Bones can also fix themselves if they break.

- The outside layers of bone are hard and strong. These layers contain mostly minerals, such as calcium. It takes a lot of force to break bones.

- The center of many bones contains soft tissue called **marrow.** Some marrow is red, and some marrow is yellow. Red marrow makes blood cells. Yellow marrow stores fat in case the body needs it for energy.

Answer the following questions. Use your textbook and the ideas above.

7. The picture shows the inside and outside of a bone. Circle the letter of the part of the bone that is labeled A.

   a. calcium

   b. marrow

   c. outside layer

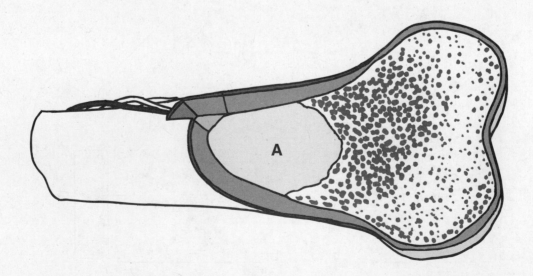

8. Is the following sentence true or false? Bones are not alive. _____

9. The Venn diagram compares red marrow and yellow marrow. Label the circle that describes red marrow. Label the circle that describes yellow marrow.

a. _____   **b.** _____

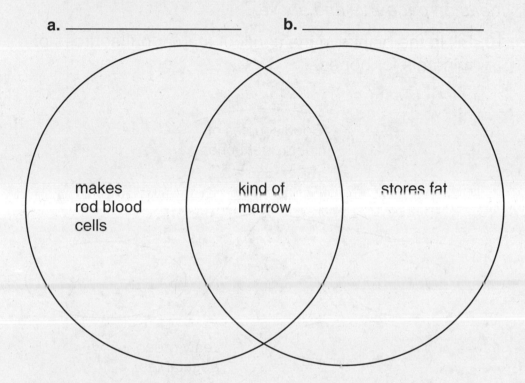

makes rod blood cells

kind of marrow

stores fat

Taking Care of Your Bones (pages 480–481)

Key Concept: **A combination of a balanced diet and regular exercise are important for a lifetime of healthy bones.**

• Bones are made mostly of minerals. You need to eat foods that contain minerals to have strong bones. Some of the best sources of minerals for your bones are meats, whole grains, leafy green vegetables, and milk.

• You also need exercise for healthy bones. Exercise helps your bones get stronger. Running and playing sports are good exercises for your bones.

Bones, Muscles, and Skin

- As people get older, their bones may lose minerals. Then the bones are weak and break easily. This condition is called **osteoporosis** (ahs tee oh puh ROH sis). A balanced diet and regular exercise when you are young may help prevent osteoporosis later in life.

Answer the following questions. Use your textbook and the ideas on page 219 and above.

10. Fill in the blanks in the concept map about sources of minerals for bones.

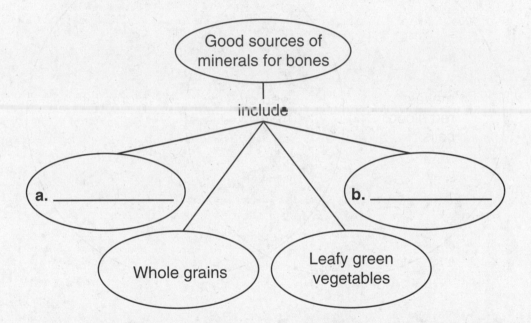

11. Is the following sentence true or false? Exercise helps bones get stronger. _____

12. Why do people with osteoporosis have bones that break easily? Circle the letter of the correct answer.

   a. Their bones have lost minerals.

   b. Their bones are still growing.

   c. Their bones contain too much calcium.

The Muscular System (pages 482–486)

Types of Muscle (pages 482–485)

Key Concept: **Your body has three types of muscle tissue—skeletal muscle, smooth muscle, and cardiac muscle. Some of these muscle tissues are involuntary, and some are voluntary.**

- **Skeletal muscles** are attached to bones. You use skeletal muscles every time you move.

- **Smooth muscles** are found in organs such as the stomach. In the stomach, smooth muscles squeeze and mix food.

- **Cardiac muscles** are found only in the heart. They keep your heart beating.

- Both smooth muscles and cardiac muscles are involuntary muscles. **Involuntary muscles** are muscles that you cannot control.

- Skeletal muscles are voluntary muscles. **Voluntary muscles** are muscles that you can control.

Answer the following questions. Use your textbook and the ideas above.

1. Draw a line from the type of muscle tissue to where it is found.

Muscle Tissue	Where It Is Found
skeletal muscle	a. in organs such as the stomach
smooth muscle	b. only in the heart
cardiac muscle	c. attached to bones

2. Muscles that you can control are _____ muscles.

Name _____ Date _____ Class _____

Bones, Muscles, and Skin

Muscles at Work (pages 485–486)

Key Concept: **Because muscle cells can only contract, not extend, skeletal muscles must work in pairs. While one muscle contracts, the other muscle in the pair relaxes to its original length.**

- Muscles work by contracting, or getting shorter. For example, when the muscle in the front of your upper arm contracts, it pulls on bones in your lower arm. This bends your elbow.

- Muscles cannot extend, or get longer. So, how do you straighten your elbow? The muscle in the back of your upper arm contracts and pulls on the bones in your lower arm. At the same time, the muscle in the front of your upper arm relaxes again.

- Exercise makes muscles stronger and more flexible. Muscles that are flexible can stretch easily. They are less likely to be hurt. If muscles do get hurt, resting the muscles helps them heal.

Answer the following questions. Use your textbook and the ideas above.

3. Is the following sentence true or false? Exercising muscles when they are hurt helps them heal.

_____

4. The drawing shows upper arm muscles. Which muscle, A or B, contracts to bend your elbow?

_____

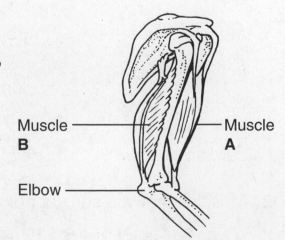

Muscle B

Muscle A

Elbow

The Skin (pages 488–493)

The Body's Tough Covering (pages 488–489)

Key Concept: **The skin covers and protects the body from injury, infection, and water loss. The skin also helps regulate body temperature, eliminate wastes, gather information about the environment, and produce vitamin D.**

- Skin is the largest organ in the human body. Skin does many important jobs. One job of the skin is to help keep germs and other harmful things out of the body. The skin also keeps the body from drying out.

- Skin helps the body stay cool. Skin makes sweat, which cools the skin. Sweating also gets rid of some body wastes.

- Skin can sense things like pain and temperature. This helps keep you from getting hurt. For example, sensing temperature can tell you when something is too hot to handle.

- In sunlight, skin can make vitamin D. You need vitamin D for strong bones.

Answer the following questions. Use your textbook and the ideas above.

1. How does your skin help to keep you cool? Circle the letter of the correct answer.
    a. by making vitamin D
    b. by sensing pain
    c. by making sweat

2. Is the following sentence true or false? Skin helps keep germs out of the body. _____

Bones, Muscles, and Skin

The Epidermis (pages 490–491)

Key Concept: **The skin is organized into two main layers, the epidermis and the dermis.**

- The **epidermis** is the top layer of the skin. The epidermis is a thin layer of cells. The epidermis does not have nerves or blood vessels.

- When cells of the epidermis die, new cells replace them. The dead cells move to the surface of the skin. They form a tough outside layer. This layer of dead cells helps keep germs out of the body.

- **Melanin** is a material in the epidermis that gives skin its color. Melanin helps protect skin from sunburn.

Answer the following questions. Use your textbook and the ideas above.

3. The top layer of skin is the _____.

4. Circle the letter of each sentence that is true about the epidermis.
    a. The epidermis is very thick.
    b. The epidermis has blood vessels.
    c. The epidermis contains melanin.

The Dermis (page 491)

Key Concept: **The dermis is the other main layer of the skin.**

- The **dermis** is the bottom layer of skin, below the epidermis. The dermis is much thicker than the epidermis.

- The dermis has nerves and blood vessels.

Bones, Muscles, and Skin

- The dermis has sweat glands, which make sweat. The sweat reaches the outside of the skin through openings in the skin called **pores**.

- Hairs grow in the dermis. They grow out of pockets called **follicles** (FAHL ih kulz).

Answer the following questions. Use your textbook and the ideas on page 224 and above.

5. The bottom layer of skin is the

 _____.

6. The diagram shows the layers of skin. Circle the letter of the structure labeled A.

   a. blood vessel

   b. sweat gland

   c. hair follicle

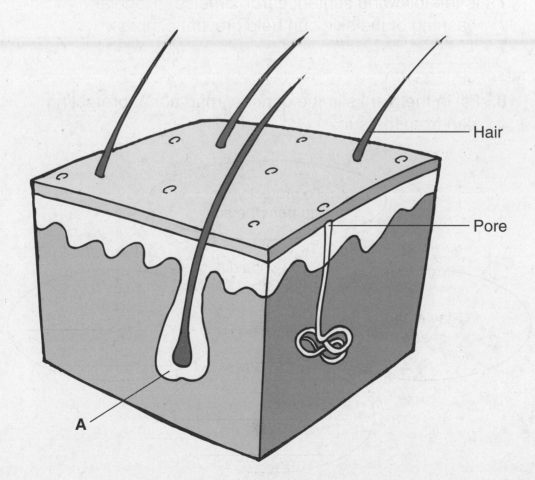

Hair

Pore

A

Bones, Muscles, and Skin

Caring for Your Skin (pages 492–493)

Key Concept: **Three simple habits can help you keep your skin healthy. Eat a healthful diet. Keep your skin clean and dry. Limit your exposure to the sun.**

- A healthy diet gives your skin cells what they need to grow and replace themselves.

- Washing your skin gets rid of dirt and germs. Regular washing can help prevent acne, or pimples.

- Too much sun can cause wrinkles and skin cancer. **Cancer** is a disease in which some cells get out of control and keep dividing. To protect your skin from the sun, stay in the shade, wear a hat, and use sunscreen.

Answer the following questions. Use your textbook and the ideas above.

7. Is the following sentence true or false? Regular washing of the skin can help prevent pimples.

_____

8. Fill in the blanks in the concept map about protecting skin from the sun.

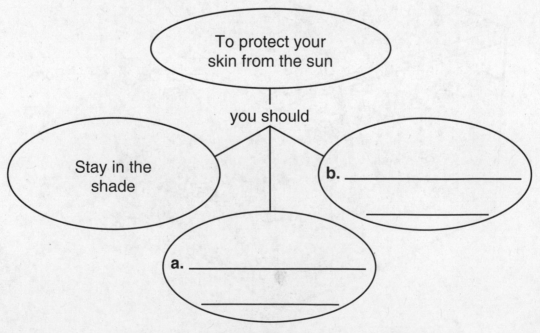

Food and Energy (pages 502–514)

Why You Need Food (pages 502–503)

Key Concept: **Food provides your body with materials for growing and for repairing tissues. Food also provides energy for everything you do.**

- Your body breaks down the food you eat into nutrients. **Nutrients** (NOO tree unts) are substances in food that your body needs.

- Humans need six groups of nutrients: carbohydrates, fats, proteins, vitamins, minerals, and water.

- Your body uses some kinds of nutrients for energy. The amount of energy in food is measured in units called Calories. For example, a serving of plain popcorn has about 60 Calories.

- The number of Calories you need each day depends on your age and how active you are.

Answer the following questions. Use your textbook and the ideas above.

1. Read the words in the box. In each sentence below, fill in one of the words.

Calories	carbohydrates	nutrients

   a. Six groups of substances in food that your body needs are _____.

   b. The amount of energy in food is measured in units called _____.

Name _____ Date _____ Class _____

Food and Digestion

2. Fill in the blanks in the concept map about nutrients.

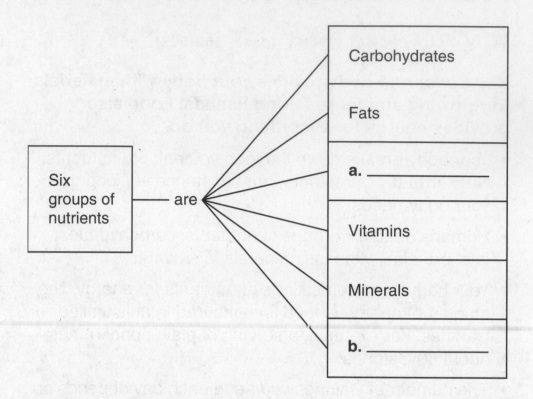

Carbohydrates (pages 504–505)

Key Concept: **In addition to providing energy, carbohydrates provide the raw materials to make cell parts.**

- **Carbohydrates** (kahr boh HY drayts) are nutrients that your body uses mainly for energy.

- Carbohydrates include sugars and starches. Oranges and bananas are good sources of sugars. Potatoes and corn are good sources of starches.

- Between 45 and 65 percent of the Calories that you eat each day should come from carbohydrates.

Food and Digestion

Answer the following questions. Use your textbook and the ideas on page 228.

3. Is the following sentence true or false? Bananas and corn are good sources of carbohydrates. _____

4. What percent of Calories that you eat each day should come from carbohydrates? Cirlce the letter of the correct answer.

    a. between 45 and 65 percent

    b. between 20 and 25 percent

    c. between 0 and 5 percent

Fats (pages 505–506)

Key Concept: In addition to providing energy, fats have other important functions. Fats form part of the cell membrane, the structure that forms the boundary of a cell. Fatty tissue protects and supports your internal organs and insulates your body.

- **Fats** are nutrients that your body uses for energy and other important jobs.

- Foods contain three different kinds of fats: saturated fats, unsaturated fats, and trans fats. Unsaturated fats are better for you than the other kinds of fats.

- Many animal foods also contain a fatlike material called cholesterol (kuh LES tur awl). Cholesterol is not a nutrient. Your body can make all the cholesterol it needs.

- No more than 30 percent of the Calories that you eat each day should come from fats.

Answer the following questions. Use your textbook and the ideas above.

5. Is the following sentence true or false? Saturated fats are better for you than other kinds of fat. _____

6. Fill in the blanks in the concept map about kinds of fats.

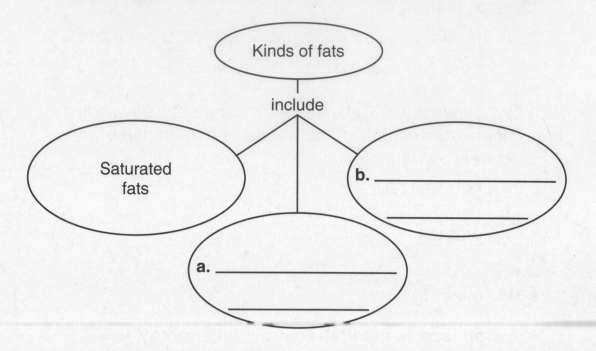

Proteins (page 507)

Key Concept: **Proteins are needed for tissue growth and repair. They also play an important part in chemical reactions within cells.**

- Proteins are nutrients that your body needs for the growth and repair of tissues. Proteins can also be used for energy.

- Proteins are made up of smaller parts called **amino** (uh MEE noh) **acids**. Your body can make some amino acids. You must get other amino acids—called essential amino acids—from foods.

- About 10 to 35 percent of the Calories that you eat each day should come from proteins.

Answer the following questions. Use your textbook and the ideas above.

7. Is the following sentence true or false? Your body can make all the amino acids it needs. _____

8. What percent of the Calories that you eat each day should come from proteins? Circle the letter of the correct answer.

   a. 15 to 65 percent

   b. 35 to 45 percent

   c. 10 to 35 percent

Vitamins and Minerals (pages 508–510)

Key Concept: **Both vitamins and minerals are needed by your body in small amounts to carry out chemical processes.**

- **Vitamins** and **minerals** are nutrients that you need in very small amounts. Your body does not use them for energy. Instead, vitamins and minerals help your body do many different jobs. For example, vitamin K is needed to help stop bleeding. The mineral calcium is needed for muscles and nerves to work well.

- You need different amounts of different vitamins and minerals. Good sources of many vitamins and minerals include leafy green vegetables and whole-grain breads and cereals.

Answer the following questions. Use your textbook and the ideas above.

9. Is the following sentence true or false? Vitamins and minerals help your body do many different jobs.

   _____

10. Circle the letter of each sentence that is true about vitamins and minerals.

 a. Your body uses vitamins and minerals mainly for energy.

 b. You need different amounts of different vitamins and minerals.

 c. Leafy green vegetables are good sources of many vitamins and minerals.

Water (page 511)

Key Concept: **Water is the most important nutrient because the body's vital processes—including chemical reactions such as the breakdown of nutrients—take place in water.**

• You could probably live for weeks without food. But you could live for only a few days without water.

• About 65 percent of your body is water. Water makes up most of body fluids, including blood and sweat. Many important materials—such as nutrients—are dissolved in body fluids.

• You should drink about 2 liters of water each day. You may need more water when the weather is hot.

Answer the following questions. Use your textbook and the ideas above.

11. The most important nutrient is

_____.

12. Circle the letter of about how much water you should drink each day.

 a. 0.5 L

 b. 1 L

 c. 2 L

Guidelines for a Healthy Diet (page 512)

Key Concept: **The USDA guidelines provide a personalized way to help people make healthy food choices based on their age, sex, and amount of physical activity.**

- The USDA is the United States Department of Agriculture. In 2005, the USDA introduced a new set of guidelines to promote healthy eating and physical activity.

- The new guidelines provide each person with a personalized nutrition plan. Each person's plan depends on the person's age, sex, and amount of physical activity.

- In a MyPyramid diagram, the pyramid is divided into six bands. Each band represents one of five food groups, plus oils.

- The five food groups are grains, vegetables, fruits, milk, and meat and beans.

- The different widths of the bands tell you how much of your diet should come from each group.

- Daily exercise is an important part of staying healthy.

Answer the following questions. Use your textbook and the ideas above.

13. Is the following sentence true or false? You should eat more oils than fruits. _____.

Food and Digestion

14. The diagram shows a food pyramid. Fill in the blanks with the names of the missing food groups.

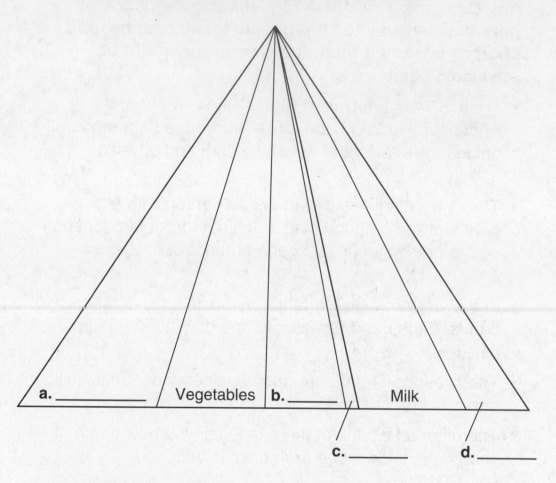

a. _____   Vegetables   b. _____   Milk

c. _____   d. _____

Food Labels (pages 513–514)

Key Concept: **Food labels allow you to evaluate a single food as well as to compare the nutritional value of two different foods.**

- Food labels can help you make healthy food choices. A food label tells you the amount in one serving of the food. It also tells you how many Calories and nutrients are in one serving of the food.

- A food label lists everything that is in the food. These are the ingredients. The ingredients are listed in order by weight. The main ingredient is always listed first.

Name _____ Date _____ Class _____

Food and Digestion

Answer the following question. Use your textbook and the ideas on page 234.

15. Read the food label below. Then answer the questions that follow.

Nutrition Facts

Serving Size 3 Crackers (13g)
Servings Per Container about 17

Amount Per Serving

Calories 60   Calories from Fat 25

                                       % Daily Value*

Total Fat 3g	5%
Saturated Fat 1.5g	8%
Cholesterol 0mg	0%
Sodium 140mg	6%
Total Carbohydrates 8g	3%
Dietary Fiber 0g	0%
Sugars 1g	
Protein 2g	

Vitamin A 0%   •   Vitamin C 0%

Calcium 0%   •   Iron 2%

*Percent Daily Values are based on a 2000 calorie diet. Your dail
values may be higher or lower depending on your calorie needs:

	Calories	2,000	2,500
Total Fat	Less than	65g	80g
Sat Fat	Less than	20g	25g
Cholesterol	Less than	300mg	300mg
Sodium	Less than	2,400mg	2,400mg
Total Carbohydrate		300g	375g
Dietary Fiber		25g	30g

INGREDIENTS: WHEAT FLOUR, WHEAT GERM,
COCONUT OIL, PARTIALLY HYDROGENATED
SOYBEAN AND/OR COTTONSEED OIL, SUGAR,
LEAVENING (AMMONIUM AND SODIUM BICARBONATE),
SALT, SKIM MILK POWDER, WHEAT BRAN,
HYDROLYZED SOY PROTEIN (CARAMEL COLOR,
NATURAL FLAVOR), PROTEASE, SODIUM
METABISULPHITE PRESERVATIVE.

a. How much is in one serving of this food?

_____

b. How many grams of protein are in one serving of

this food?_____

c. What is the main ingredient of this food?

_____

The Digestive Process Begins

(pages 516–521)

Functions of the Digestive System (pages 516–517)

Key Concept: **The digestive system has three main functions. First, it breaks down food into molecules the body can use. Then, the molecules are absorbed into the blood and carried throughout the body. Finally, wastes are eliminated from the body.**

- The digestive system includes the mouth, esophagus, stomach, small intestine, and large intestine.

- The digestive system breaks down food into tiny pieces called molecules. The process of breaking down food is called **digestion**.

- Digestion includes both mechanical digestion and chemical digestion. Mechanical digestion breaks chunks of food into smaller pieces. Chemical digestion breaks big food molecules into smaller, simpler food molecules.

- After food is digested, food molecules pass from the digestive system into the blood. This process is called **absorption** (ab SAWRP shun).

- Some materials in the digestive system cannot be absorbed. These materials pass out of the body as wastes. This process is called elimination.

Answer the following questions. Use your textbook and the ideas above.

1. _____ digestion breaks chunks of food into smaller pieces.

2. _____ digestion breaks big food molecules into smaller, simpler food molecules.

Food and Digestion

3. Draw a line from each term to its meaning.

Term	Meaning
digestion	**a.** food molecules pass into the blood
absorption	**b.** wastes pass out of the body
elimination	**c.** food is broken down into molecules

4. The picture shows organs of the digestive system. Fill in the blanks with the names of the organs shown.

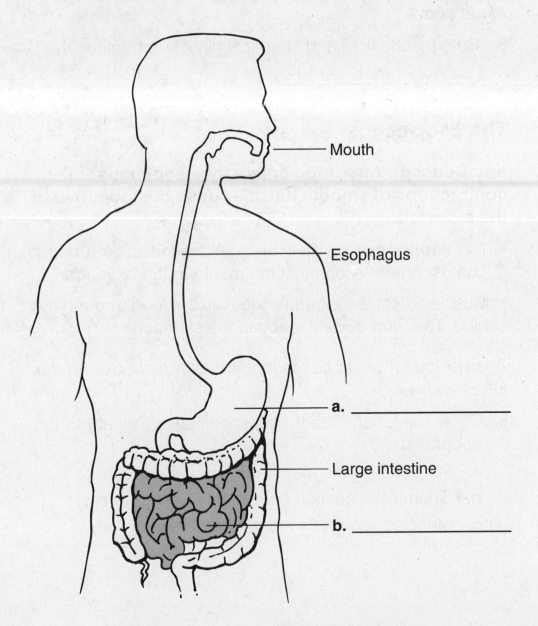

Mouth

Esophagus

a. _____

Large intestine

b. _____

Food and Digestion

The Mouth (pages 518–519)

Key Concept: **Both mechanical and chemical digestion begin in the mouth.**

- When you chew, your teeth tear and crush food into smaller pieces. Chewing starts mechanical digestion.

- Saliva starts chemical digestion. **Saliva** (suh LY vuh) is the fluid in your mouth. Saliva breaks big starch molecules into smaller sugar molecules.

Answer the following question. Use your textbook and the ideas above.

5. Both mechanical and chemical digestion begin in the

   _____ .

The Esophagus (page 519)

Key Concept: After food enters the esophagus, contractions of smooth muscles push the food toward the stomach.

- The **esophagus** (ih SAHF uh gus) is a muscular tube. The esophagus connects the mouth to the stomach.

- Muscles of the esophagus squeeze the food through the tube. The food quickly reaches the stomach.

Answer the following question. Use your textbook and the ideas above.

6. Circle the letter of each sentence that is true about the esophagus.
   a. Food enters the esophagus from the mouth.
   b. Chemical digestion begins in the esophagus.
   c. Muscles squeeze food through the esophagus.

Name _____ Date _____ Class _____

Food and Digestion

The Stomach (pages 520–521)

Key Concept: **Most mechanical digestion and some chemical digestion occur in the stomach.**

- The **stomach** is a muscular organ that looks like a pouch. Stomach muscles squeeze and mix the food in the stomach. The mixing finishes mechanical digestion.

- The stomach makes digestive juices. These juices continue chemical digestion.

- By the time food leaves the stomach, it is a thick fluid.

Answer the following questions. Use your textbook and the ideas above.

7. Is the following sentence true or false? Only chemical digestion takes place in the stomach. _____

8. What causes chemical digestion in the stomach? Circle the letter of the correct answer.
   a. saliva
   b. stomach muscles
   c. digestive juices

Food and Digestion

Final Digestion and Absorption (pages 524–527)

The Small Intestine (pages 524–526)

Key Concept: **Almost all chemical digestion and absorption of nutrients takes place in the small intestine.**

- When fluid leaves the stomach, it goes to the small intestine. The **small intestine** is the part of the digestive system where most chemical digestion takes place.

- Chemicals from the small intestine and other nearby organs break down the rest of the food molecules in the small intestine.

- The lining of the small intestine is covered with millions of tiny bumps called **villi** (VIL eye). When digestion is finished, food molecules pass through the villi into the blood.

Answer the following questions. Use your textbook and the ideas above.

1. The part of the digestive system where most chemical

   digestion takes place is the _____.

2. Is the following sentence true or false? Chemicals from other organs help break down food in the small

   intestine. _____

3. Circle the letter of the job of villi in the small intestine.
   a. digest food particles
   b. break down protein molecules
   c. absorb food molecules

Food and Digestion

The Large Intestine (page 527)

Key Concept: **As the material moves through the large intestine, water is absorbed into the bloodstream. The remaining material is readied for elimination from the body.**

- Any material that is not absorbed in the small intestine moves on to the large intestine. The **large intestine** is the last organ in the digestive system.

- The main job of the large intestine is to remove water from the material that passes through it. The waste material that is left leaves the body through the anus. The **anus** is an opening to the outside of the body.

Answer the following questions. Use your textbook and the ideas above.

4. The last organ in the digestive system is the

   _____.

5. Is the following sentence true or false? The main job of the large intestine is to remove nutrients from food.

   _____

The Body's Transport System

(pages 534–543)

The Cardiovascular System (pages 534–535)

Key Concept: **The cardiovascular system carries needed substances to cells and carries waste products away from cells. In addition, blood contains cells that fight disease.**

- The **cardiovascular system** is made up of the heart, blood vessels, and blood. The heart pumps blood through the blood vessels.

- Blood carries oxygen and other needed materials to all of the body's cells. Blood also picks up wastes, such as carbon dioxide, from the cells.

- Some cells in blood kill germs. The cells fight disease and help you get well.

Answer the following questions. Use your textbook and the ideas above.

1. The system that is made up of the heart, blood vessels, and blood is the _____ system.

2. Circle the letter of each job of the cardiovascular system.
   a. carries materials to cells
   b. fights disease
   c. picks up wastes from cells

Circulation

The Heart (pages 536–537)

Key Concept: **Each time the heart beats, it pushes blood through the blood vessels of the cardiovascular system. The right side of the heart is completely separated from the left side by a wall of tissue called the septum. Each side has two compartments, or chambers—an upper chamber and a lower chamber.**

- The **heart** is a hollow organ about the size of a fist. It is mostly made of muscle. The heart is in the center of the chest.

- The heart is separated into a left side and a right side. Each side of the heart is divided into an upper and lower "room," or chamber. The upper chamber on each side is called the **atrium** (AY tree um) (plural *atria*). The lower chamber on each side is called the **ventricle**.

- With each beat of the heart, muscles in the heart pump blood by contracting. First, both atria contract. This squeezes blood out of the atria and into the ventricles. Then, both ventricles contract. This squeezes blood out of the ventricles and into blood vessels.

- A **valve** is a flap of tissue over a hole that lets blood flow through the hole in just one direction. There are two valves in each side of the heart.

- How fast your heart beats is controlled by a group of cells in the heart called the **pacemaker**.

Answer the following questions. Use your textbook and the ideas above.

3. The organ that pumps blood throughout the body is the

   _____.

4. A group of cells in the heart that controls how fast the

   heart beats is called the _____.

Circulation

Name _____ Date _____ Class _____

Circulation

5. Fill in the blanks in the table comparing the upper chambers and the lower chambers of the heart.

Chambers of the Heart	
Name of Chamber	**What It Does**
a. _____	pumps blood into a ventricle
b. _____	pumps blood into a blood vessel

6. The diagram below shows the heart and its four chambers. When the heart beats, which two chambers contract first? Circle the letter of the correct answer.
   a. A and B
   b. C and D
   c. A and C

The Heart

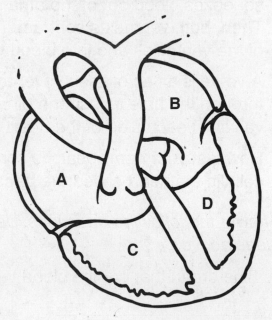

Circulation

Two Loops (pages 538–539)

Key Concept: **In the first loop, blood travels from the heart to the lungs and then back to the heart. In the second loop, blood is pumped from the heart throughout the body and then returns again to the heart.**

- After leaving the heart, blood travels through arteries. **Arteries** are blood vessels that carry blood away from the heart.

- From arteries, blood flows into capillaries. **Capillaries** are tiny blood vessels with very thin walls. In capillaries, materials are passed back and forth between the blood and body cells.

- From capillaries, blood flows into veins. **Veins** are blood vessels that carry blood back to the heart.

- The right ventricle of the heart pumps blood to the lungs. In the lungs, the blood drops off wastes and picks up oxygen. From the lungs, the blood returns to the heart. This path of the blood is called the first loop, or loop one.

- The left ventricle of the heart pumps blood to the rest of the body. The blood leaving the heart is full of oxygen. The blood drops off oxygen and picks up wastes at the body cells. Then the blood returns to the heart. This path of the blood is called the second loop, or loop two.

Answer the following questions. Use your textbook and the ideas above.

7. Is the following sentence true or false? Blood flows through the body in one large loop. _____

Name _____ Date _____ Class _____

Circulation

8. Fill in the blanks in the table comparing different kinds of blood vessels.

Kinds of Blood Vessels	
Kind of Blood Vessel	**What It Does**
Artery	carries blood away from the heart
a. _____	passes materials between blood and body cells
b. _____	carries blood back to the heart

9. The diagram shows how blood flows through the body. In which loop—loop one or loop two—does blood travel from the heart to the body and back to the heart again?

_____

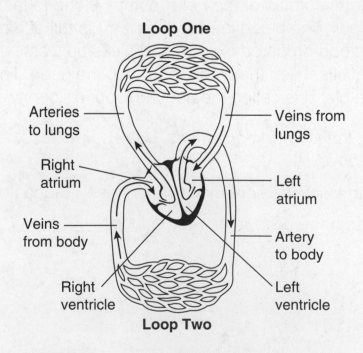

Loop One

Arteries to lungs

Veins from lungs

Right atrium

Left atrium

Veins from body

Artery to body

Right ventricle

Left ventricle

Loop Two

Circulation

Arteries (pages 540–541)

Key Concept: **When blood leaves the heart, it travels through arteries. The walls of arteries are generally very thick. In fact, artery walls consist of three cell layers.**

- Every time your heart beats, a spurt of blood is forced through the arteries. The spurt of blood pushes against the artery walls. The artery walls must be thick and strong to withstand the force of the spurting blood.

- The middle layer of artery walls is made of muscles. These muscles help control the flow of blood by changing the width of the arteries. When more blood is needed, the muscles relax and the arteries get wider. When less blood is needed, the muscles contract and the arteries get narrower.

Answer the following questions. Use your textbook and the ideas above.

10. Is the following sentence true or false? When blood

leaves the heart, it travels through veins. _____

11. The drawing shows the three layers of an artery wall. What is the layer labeled B made of?

_____

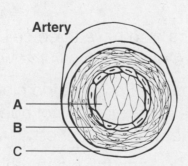

Artery

A

B

C

Circulation

Capillaries (page 541)

Key Concept: **In the capillaries, materials are exchanged between the blood and the body's cells. Capillary walls are only one cell thick.**

- Capillary walls are very thin. Many materials can pass easily through the thin capillary walls.

- Materials such as oxygen and nutrients pass from the blood into the body's cells. Waste materials travel in the opposite direction—from the body's cells into the blood.

Answer the following question. Use your textbook and the ideas above.

12. Circle the letter of each sentence that is true about capillary walls.
    a. The walls are very thick.
    b. The walls are one cell thick.
    c. The walls allow many materials to pass through.

Veins (page 542)

Key Concept: **After blood moves through capillaries, it enters larger blood vessels called veins, which carry blood back to the heart. The walls of veins, like those of arteries, have three layers, with muscle in the middle layer.**

- The walls of veins also have three cell layers. But, the walls of veins are not as thick as the walls of arteries.

- By the time blood enters veins, the blood has very little force. So, the walls of veins do not need to be as thick and strong as the walls of arteries.

- Veins need help to keep the blood moving. When leg muscles contract, they squeeze the veins in the legs. This helps push the blood along. Some veins also have valves. Valves in veins keep blood flowing in just one direction.

Answer the following questions. Use your textbook and the ideas on page 248.

13. Blood flows from capillaries into

_____.

14. Circle the letter of a reason why blood keeps flowing through veins.

   a. Blood in veins has a lot of force.

   b. Vein walls are one cell thick.

   c. Contraction of muscles helps push blood along.

Blood Pressure (pages 542–543)

Key Concept: **Blood pressure is caused by the force with which the ventricles contract.**

- When the ventricles contract, blood spurts out of the heart and into the arteries. The spurting blood pushes against the artery walls. The force of blood against the walls of the arteries is called **blood pressure**.

- An instrument can measure blood pressure. Blood pressure is given as two numbers, written like a fraction. For example, a normal blood pressure is 120/80.

Answer the following questions. Use your textbook and the ideas above.

15. Is the following sentence true or false? Blood pressure is the force of blood against artery walls. _____

16. Circle the letter of the numbers that show a normal blood pressure.

   a. 120/80

   b. 80/120

   c. 80/200

Blood and Lymph (pages 545–551)

Blood (pages 545–548)

Key Concept: Blood is made up of four components: plasma, red blood cells, white blood cells, and platelets.

- About 55 percent of blood is liquid. The liquid part of blood is called **plasma**. Plasma is mostly water, with materials such as nutrients dissolved in it.

- About 45 percent of blood is cells. There are three types blood cells: red blood cells, white blood cells, and platelets.

- **Red blood cells** carry oxygen. They pick up oxygen in the lungs and take it to cells throughout the body. Red blood cells look like tiny disks. There are more red blood cells than any other kind of blood cells.

- **White blood cells** fight disease. They find and kill germs. White blood cells are bigger than red blood cells.

- **Platelets** (PLAYT lits) are pieces of cells. They help blood clot and form a scab when a blood vessel is cut. Platelets gather around the cut and stick to the blood vessel.

Answer the following questions. Use your textbook and the ideas above.

1. The liquid part of blood is called

   _____.

2. Is the following sentence true or false? Red blood cells find and kill germs. _____

3. Fill in the blanks in the table about the kinds of blood cells.

Kinds of Blood Cells	
Kind of Blood Cell	**What It Does**
Red blood cells	carry oxygen
a. _____	fight disease
b. _____	help blood clot

Blood Types (pages 548–550)

Key Concept: **The marker molecules on your red blood cells determine your blood type and the type of blood that you can safely receive in transfusions.**

- Sometimes people bleed so much that they need a transfusion. A transfusion is taking some blood from one person and giving it to another person who needs it.

- People have different types of blood. For example, your blood can be type A, B, AB, or O. Your blood can also be Rh positive or Rh negative. Your blood type depends on certain molecules, called marker molecules, that are on your red blood cells.

- In a transfusion, you can receive only certain types of blood. For example, if you have type A blood, you can receive only type A or type O blood. If you have Rh-negative blood, you can receive only Rh-negative blood. Receiving the wrong type of blood in a transfusion can make you very sick or even kill you.

Circulation

Answer the following questions. Use your textbook and the ideas on page 251.

4. Circle the letter of what a transfusion is.

   a. bleeding a lot

   b. taking some blood from one person and giving it to another person who needs it

   c. finding out your blood type

5. Circle the letter of each sentence that is true about blood types.

   a. There are different types of blood.

   b. Everybody has the same blood type.

   c. Blood types are important for transfusions.

6. Is the following sentence true or false? In a blood transfusion, you can receive any type of blood.

   _____

The Lymphatic System (pages 550–551)

Key Concept: **The lymphatic system is a network of veinlike vessels that returns fluid to the bloodstream.**

- Some fluid leaks into tissues out of the blood through capillary walls. The fluid is called **lymph**.

- The **lymphatic** (lim FAT ik) **system** is a system of vessels that collect and carry lymph. Lymphatic vessels are like blood vessels. Lymphatic vessels pick up lymph from tissues all over the body. The vessels carry the lymph to veins in the chest. There, the lymph is returned to the blood.

- As lymph flows through the lymphatic system, it passes through small knobs of tissue called **lymph nodes**. Lymph nodes filter the lymph to remove germs from it.

Circulation

Answer the following questions. Use your textbook and the ideas on page 252.

7. Is the following sentence true or false? Lymph is fluid that leaks out of body cells. _____

8. Read the words in the box. In each sentence below, use the words to fill in the blank.

lymph node	lymph fluid	lymphatic system

   a. Vessels that carry lymph make up the

   _____.

   b. A knob of tissue that filters lymph is called a

   _____.

9. Is the following sentence true or false? The lymphatic system returns lymph to the blood. _____

Cardiovascular Health

(pages 552–556)

Cardiovascular Diseases (pages 553–555)

Key Concept: **Diseases of the cardiovascular system include atherosclerosis and hypertension.**

- Diseases of the cardiovascular system are the leading cause of death in the United States today.

- In **atherosclerosis** (ath uh roh skluh ROH sis), the walls of arteries get thicker because fatty materials build up inside the arteries.

- As artery walls get thicker, there is less room for blood to flow. Cells may die because too little blood and oxygen can flow through the narrow arteries. If cells in the heart die, it is called a **heart attack**.

- Atherosclerosis can cause hypertension. **Hypertension** (hy pur TEN shun) is high blood pressure. Remember, normal blood pressure is about 120/80. Hypertension is blood pressure higher than 140/90. High blood pressure can damage the heart and arteries.

Answer the following questions. Use your textbook and the ideas above.

1. Is the following sentence true or false? Atherosclerosis can lead to a heart attack. _____

2. Draw a line from each term to its meaning.

Term	Meaning
atherosclerosis	**a.** heart cells die
	b. high blood pressure
heart attack	**c.** artery walls get thicker
hypertension	

Keeping Healthy (page 556)

Key Concept: To help maintain cardiovascular health, people should exercise regularly; eat a balanced diet that is low in saturated fats and trans fats, cholesterol, and sodium; and avoid smoking.

- You should eat right and exercise to lower your chances of getting cardiovascular diseases.

- Regular exercise, such as biking or swimming, makes heart muscles stronger. Regular exercise also helps prevent atherosclerosis.

- Eating foods high in cholesterol, saturated fats, and trans fats can lead to atherosclerosis. Such foods include ice cream and potato chips. Eating less of these foods can help make the cardiovascular system healthier.

- Smoking can increase the risk of a heart attack. People who stop smoking can help improve their heart health.

Answer the following question. Use your textbook and the ideas above.

3. Fill in the blank in the concept map about cardiovascular health.

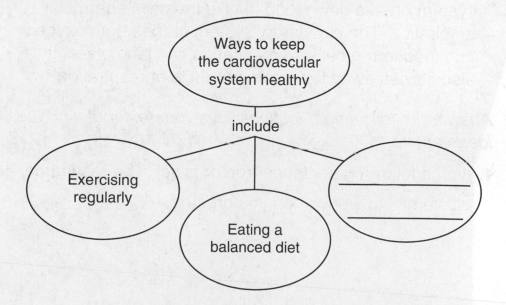

Respiration and Excretion

The Respiratory System

(pages 564–572)

Respiratory System Functions

(pages 565–566)

Key Concept: **The respiratory system moves oxygen from the outside environment into the body. It also removes carbon dioxide and water from the body.**

- **Respiration** is a process that takes place in your cells. It gives you energy. For respiration to take place, cells need oxygen.

- Cells produce carbon dioxide and water as waste products of respiration. Cells need to get rid of these wastes.

- The respiratory system provides oxygen for respiration. The respiratory system also gets rid of the waste products of respiration.

- The respiratory system is just one body system that makes respiration possible.

- Respiration could not take place without the digestive system and the circulatory system. The digestive system breaks down food to give the cells energy for respiration. The circulatory system carries both oxygen and food to the cells so respiration can take place. It also carries away the waste products of respiration.

Answer the following questions. Use your textbook and the ideas above.

Is the following sentence true or false? The respiratory system is at work when you breathe. _____

Respiration and Excretion

2. Fill in the blank in the concept map about the respiratory system.

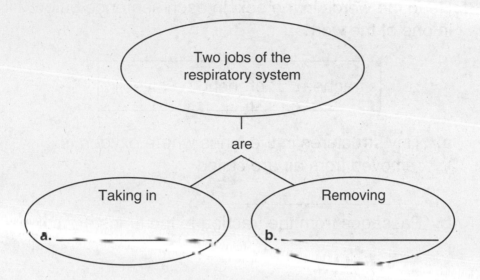

The Path of Air (pages 566–568)

Key Concept: **As air travels from the outside environment to the lungs, it passes through the following structures: nose, pharynx, trachea, and bronchi.**

- Air enters the respiratory system through the nose. From the nose, air moves to the **pharynx** (FAR ingks), or throat. Then, air goes into the **trachea** (TRAY kee uh), or windpipe. From the trachea, air passes into the bronchi. **Bronchi** (BRAHNG ky) are passages that go to the lungs.

- Most of these structures are lined with tiny hairs and a sticky material called mucus. The hairs and mucus clean and moisten the air before it reaches the lungs.

- The two **lungs** are the main organs of the respiratory system. The lungs are in the chest.

- The lungs are made up of tiny structures called **alveoli** (al VEE uh ly) (singular alveolus). Alveoli are hollow sacks. Air goes into the alveoli. In the alveoli, oxygen is removed from air and wastes are added to air.

Name _____ Date _____ Class _____

Respiration and Excretion

Answer the following questions. Use your textbook and the ideas on page 257.

3. Read the words in the box. In each sentence below, fill in one of the words.

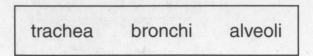

| trachea | bronchi | alveoli |

a. Tiny structures in the lungs where oxygen is removed from air are called

   _____.

b. Passages from the trachea to the lungs are called

   _____.

4. Fill in the blanks in the diagram of the respiratory system.

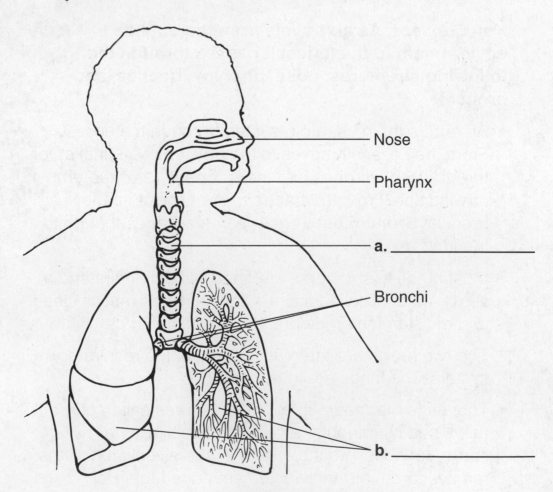

Nose

Pharynx

a. _____

Bronchi

b. _____

Respiration and Excretion

Gas Exchange (pages 569–570)

Key Concept: **After air enters the alveoli, oxygen passes through the walls of the alveoli and then through the capillary walls into the blood. Carbon dioxide and water pass from the blood into the alveoli. This whole process is known as gas exchange.**

• Gas exchange takes place in the alveoli. (Remember, alveoli are tiny hollow sacks in the lungs.) Alveoli are surrounded by capillaries.

• When you breathe in, air fills the tiny sacks of the alveoli. Oxygen in the air moves out of the sacks and into the capillaries. At the same time, carbon dioxide and water in the blood move out of the capillaries and into the sacks. When you breathe out, the air leaves the sacks, taking carbon dioxide and water with it.

• If you could spread out all the alveoli in your lungs, they would cover a very big area. Alveoli give the lungs a much bigger surface for gases to move across. With alveoli, a lot of gas can be exchanged quickly.

Answer the following questions. Use your textbook and the ideas above.

5. How do alveoli help the lungs exchange gases? Circle the letter of the correct answer.

   a. Alveoli give the lungs more energy to carry out gas exchange.

   b. Alveoli give the lungs a bigger surface for gases to move across.

   c. Alveoli help move air from the nose to the lungs.

Respiration and Excretion

6. What process does the picture show?

_____

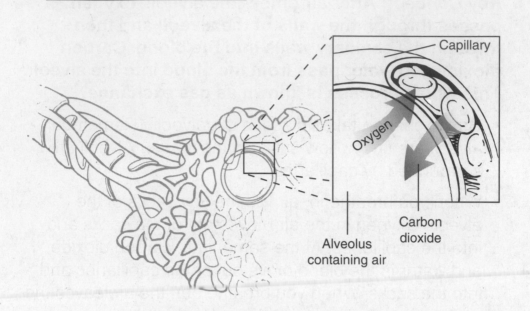

How You Breathe (pages 570–572)

Key Concept: **When you breathe, the actions of your rib muscles and diaphragm expand or contract your chest. As a result, air flows in or out.**

- Breathing is controlled by the diaphragm. The **diaphragm** (DY uh fram) is a large muscle just below the lungs.

- When you breathe in, the diaphragm contracts, or gets shorter. This makes the space inside the chest get bigger. Air rushes into the lungs to fill the extra space.

- When you breathe out, the diaphragm relaxes again. This makes the space inside the chest get smaller. Air is squeezed out of the lungs.

- **Vocal cords** are tissues at the top of the trachea. When you speak, outgoing breath passes over the vocal cords. The vocal cords vibrate, or move quickly back and forth. When the vocal cords vibrate, they make sounds.

Respiration and Excretion

Answer the following questions. Use your textbook and the ideas on page 260.

7. Fill in the blanks in the table about breathing.

How You Breathe		
What the Diaphragm Does	**How the Chest Changes**	**Which Way Air Moves**
Contracts	gets bigger	a. _____ _____
Relaxes	b. _____ _____	out of lungs

8. When air passes over the _____, they vibrate and make sounds.

Respiration and Excretion

Smoking and Your Health
(pages 574–578)

Chemicals in Tobacco Smoke (page 575)

Key Concept: **Some of the most deadly chemicals in tobacco smoke are tar, carbon monoxide, and nicotine.**

- **Tar** is a dark, sticky material that forms from burning tobacco. When people smoke, tar sticks to the tiny hairs lining the respiratory system. With tar on them, the hairs can no longer help clean the air. Tar also contains chemicals that can cause cancer.

- **Carbon monoxide** is a gas that you cannot see or smell. It comes from burning tobacco. When people smoke, carbon monoxide replaces oxygen in their blood. Their blood cannot carry enough oxygen for their cells.

- **Nicotine** is a chemical in tobacco that speeds up the heart and raises blood pressure. Over time, smokers become addicted to nicotine. Smokers find it very hard to quit smoking once they are addicted to nicotine.

Answer the following questions. Use your textbook and the ideas above.

1. Fill in the blanks in the concept map about dangerous chemicals in tobacco smoke.

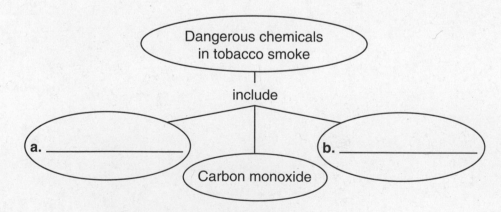

2. Is the following sentence true or false? Smokers become addicted to tar. _____

Health Problems and Smoking (pages 576–578)

Key Concept: **Over time, smokers can develop chronic bronchitis, emphysema, lung cancer, and atherosclerosis.**

- **Bronchitis** (brahng KY tis) is a disease of the breathing passages called bronchi. The passages get narrow and clogged with mucus. Chronic bronchitis is bronchitis that lasts a long time.

- **Emphysema** (em fuh SEE muh) is a disease of the lungs. The tissues of the lungs are destroyed, so there is less space for gas exchange. People with emphysema are always short of breath.

- Lung cancer is cancer of the lungs. Lumps of cancer tissue, or tumors, grow out of control. They take away space in the lungs for gas exchange.

- Some of the chemicals in tobacco smoke get into the blood. They help build up fatty materials in the arteries that cause of atherosclerosis.

Answer the following questions. Use your textbook and the ideas above.

3. List four health problems that can be caused by smoking.

a. _____   b. _____

c. _____   d. _____

4. Is the following sentence true or false? Chemicals in tobacco smoke can help cause atherosclerosis.

_____

Respiration and Excretion

The Excretory System (pages 579–583)

The Excretory System (page 580)

Key Concept: **The excretory system is the system in the body that collects wastes produced by cells and removes the wastes from the body. The structures of the excretory system that eliminate urea, water, and other wastes include the kidneys, ureters, urinary bladder, and urethra.**

- Wastes are produced when body cells use nutrients. For example, a waste called **urea** (yoo REE uh) is produced when cells break down proteins. **Excretion** is the process of removing wastes from the body.

- Wastes are removed from the body by the excretory system. The major organs of the excretory system are the two **kidneys**. Kidneys filter wastes out of the blood. The watery wastes are called **urine**.

- From the kidneys, urine travels through two tubes called **ureters** (yoo REE turz). The ureters carry urine to the **urinary bladder**. The bladder is a sack that stores the urine. Urine leaves the body through a tube called the **urethra** (yoo REE thruh).

Answer the following questions. Use your textbook and the ideas above.

1. Read the words in the box. In each sentence below, fill in one of the words.

urea	urine	urethra

   a. Wastes leave the kidneys as

   _____.

   b. A waste produced when cells break down proteins

   is _____.

Respiration and Excretion

2. The diagram shows the excretory system. Fill in the blanks with the missing labels.

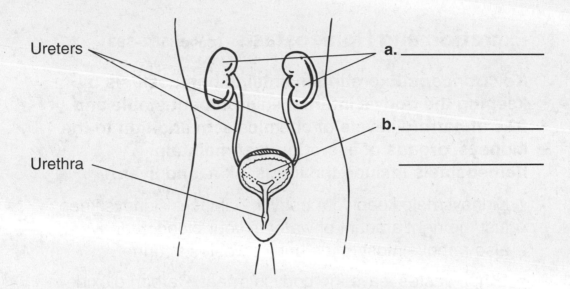

Ureters

a. _____

b. _____

_____

Urethra

Filtration of Wastes (pages 580–582)

Key Concept: **The nephrons filter wastes in stages. First, both wastes and needed materials, such as glucose, are filtered out of the blood. Then, much of the needed material is returned to the blood, and the wastes are eliminated from the body.**

- Kidneys contain millions of tiny structures called **nephrons**. Each nephron acts like a filter. It removes things from the fluid that passes through it.

- As blood flows through a nephron, urea, glucose, and some water are removed from the blood. Glucose is a simple sugar that cells need for energy.

- The materials filtered out of the blood form urine. Before urine leaves the nephron, all of the glucose and most of the water pass back into the blood.

Answer the following questions. Use your textbook and the ideas above.

3. Tiny structures in the kidneys that filter blood are called

_____.

4. Is the following sentence true or false? Nephrons remove only urea from blood. _____

Excretion and Homeostasis (pages 582–583)

Key Concept: **Excretion maintains homeostasis by keeping the body's internal environment stable and free of harmful levels of chemicals. In addition to the kidneys, organs of excretion that maintain homeostasis include the lungs, skin, and liver.**

- Kidneys help keep your body in balance. Kidneys keep just the right amount of water in your blood. Kidneys also remove most of the body's wastes in urine.

- Other wastes leave the body in sweat. Carbon dioxide and water leave the body in air that is breathed out.

- An organ called the liver produces urea and some other wastes.

Answer the following questions. Use your textbook and the ideas above.

5. Circle the letter of each way the kidneys help keep the body in balance.

    a. remove wastes

    b. produce sweat

    c. keep the right amount of water in the blood

6. Is the following sentence true or false? Urea is produced by the kidneys. _____

Infectious Disease (pages 592–596)

Understanding Infectious Disease
(page 593)

Key Concept: **When you have an infectious disease, pathogens have gotten inside your body and caused harm.**

- Many diseases are caused by tiny living things. Living things that cause disease are called **pathogens**.

- Diseases caused by pathogens are called **infectious diseases**.

- Pathogens make you sick by damaging cells. For example, when you have strep throat, pathogens have damaged cells in your throat.

Answer the following questions. Use your textbook and the ideas above.

1. Read the words in the box. In each sentence below, fill in one of the words.

pathogens	infectious	diseases

   a. Diseases caused by tiny living things are called
      _____ diseases.

   b. Living things that cause disease are called
      _____.

2. Is the following sentence true or false? Pathogens make you sick by damaging cells. _____

Fighting Disease

Kinds of Pathogens (page 594)

Key Concept: **The four major groups of human pathogens are bacteria, viruses, fungi, and protists.**

- Bacteria are living things made up of just one cell. Diseases caused by bacteria include strep throat and food poisoning.

- Viruses are tiny particles that are much smaller than bacteria. Diseases caused by viruses include colds and flu.

- Fungi are living things such as molds. Diseases caused by fungi include athlete's foot and ringworm.

- Protists are certain living things made up of one or more cells. One disease caused by protists is malaria. Malaria is common in warm parts of the world.

Answer the following questions. Use your textbook and the ideas above.

3. Fill in the blanks in the table about kinds of pathogens.

Kinds of Pathogens	
Pathogens	**What They Are**
Bacteria	living things made up of a single cell
a. _____	tiny particles much smaller than bacteria
b. _____	living things such as molds
Protists	living things made up of one or more cells

4. Circle the letter of each disease that is caused by viruses.

   a. food poisoning

   b. flu

   c. ringworm

5. Circle the letter of the kind of pathogen that causes strep throat.

   a. bacteria

   b. viruses

   c. protists

How Pathogens Are Spread (pages 595–596)

Key Concept: **Pathogens can spread through contact with either an infected person; soil, food, or water; a contaminated object; or an infected animal.**

- You can get pathogens that cause human diseases in four different ways.

- One way you can get pathogens is by direct contact with a sick person. For example, if you shake hands with a sick person, you may pick up pathogens on your hands. Cold viruses can spread this way.

- Another way you can get pathogens is by eating food or drinking water that has pathogens in it. Food poisoning can spread this way. You can also get pathogens from soil, because some pathogens live in soil.

- You can get pathogens by using objects—such as towels or silverware—that a sick person has used. Flu viruses can spread this way.

- Finally, you can get pathogens from animals. For example, you can get bacteria that cause Lyme disease from ticks. These tiny ticks pass the bacteria to people when they bite them.

Name _____ Date _____ Class _____

Fighting Disease

Answer the following question. Use your textbook and the ideas on page 269.

6. Fill in the blanks in the concept map about ways pathogens can spread.

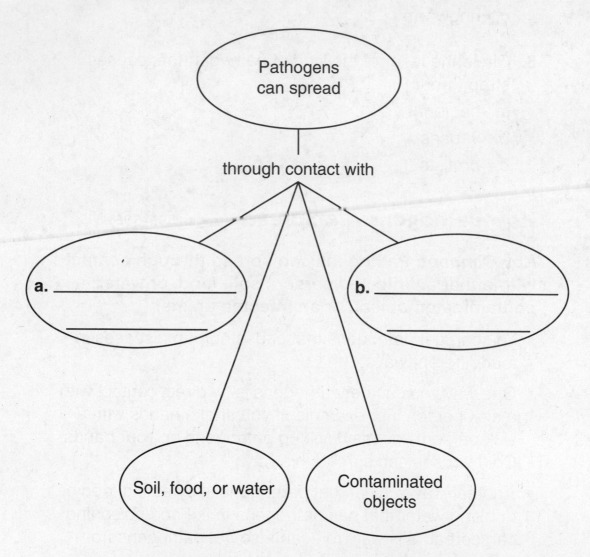

Fighting Disease

The Body's Defenses (pages 597–603)

Barriers That Keep Pathogens Out (page 598)

Key Concept: **In the first line of defense, the surfaces of the skin, breathing passages, mouth, and stomach function as barriers to pathogens. These barriers trap and kill most pathogens with which you come into contact.**

- Your body has three lines of defense against pathogens. The first line of defense keeps most pathogens from ever getting into your body. The first line of defense includes your skin

- Your skin acts like a wall, or barrier, between your body and pathogens. Most pathogens cannot get through skin. Sweat and oil on skin also kill most pathogens that land on the skin.

- The tiny hairs and mucus in your respiratory system are another barrier against pathogens. They trap most of the pathogens in the air you breathe in.

- Saliva in your mouth and acid in your stomach are another barrier against pathogens. They kill most of the pathogens that you swallow.

Answer the following questions. Use your textbook and the ideas above.

1. Is the following sentence true or false? Most pathogens can get through your skin. _____

2. Circle the letter of what happens to most pathogens that you breathe in.
   a. Oil and sweat kill them.
   b. Saliva and stomach acid kill them.
   c. Tiny hairs and mucus trap them.

Fighting Disease

3. Circle the letter of what happens to most pathogens that you swallow.

   a. Oil and sweat kill them.

   b. Saliva and stomach acid kill them.

   c. Tiny hairs and mucus trap them.

The Inflammatory Response (page 599)

Key Concept: **In the inflammatory response, fluid and white blood cells leak from blood vessels into nearby tissues. The white blood cells then fight the pathogens.**

• Sometimes pathogens get past the body's first line of defense. For example, bacteria might get into your body through a cut in the skin. Once pathogens get inside the body, they face the body's second line of defense, the **inflammatory response**.

• In the inflammatory response, extra blood flows to the area around the pathogens. The extra blood may make the area swollen, red, and warm.

• The blood brings white blood cells called **phagocytes** (FAG uh syts) to the area. Phagocytes destroy pathogens by swallowing them and then breaking them down.

• Sometimes the inflammatory response causes the body's temperature to rise. This is called a fever. The higher temperature of the body also kills some pathogens.

Answer the following questions. Use your textbook and the ideas above.

4. The body's second line of defense is the

   _____.

Fighting Disease

5. The drawing shows the part of the inflammatory response that involves white blood cells. What kind of white blood cell is shown in the drawing?

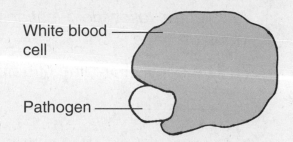

White blood cell

Pathogen

_____

6. Is the following sentence true or false? Sometimes the inflammatory response causes a fever. _____

The Immune System (pages 600–601)

Key Concept: **The cells of the immune system can distinguish between different kinds of pathogens. The immune system cells react to each kind of pathogen with a defense targeted specifically at that pathogen.**

- Sometimes pathogens survive the body's second line of defense. Then they face the body's third line of defense, the **immune system**.

- The immune system is the body's disease-fighting system. White blood cells called **lymphocytes** (LIM fuh syts) do most of the fighting for the immune system. Lymphocytes can tell one kind of pathogen from another. They base their attack on the kind of pathogen that enters the body. There are two kinds of lymphocytes: T cells and B cells.

- The job of most T cells is to attack and kill body cells that have pathogens inside them. This kills the pathogens inside the cells as well. The job of some T cells is to signal B cells to act.

- B cells make proteins called **antibodies**. Antibodies help kill pathogens. Antibodies stick to pathogens and make them clump together. Then the pathogens are swallowed by phagocytes.

Fighting Disease

Answer the following questions. Use your textbook and the ideas on page 273.

7. The body's third line of defense is the

_____.

8. The drawing shows proteins sticking to pathogens.

What are the proteins called? _____

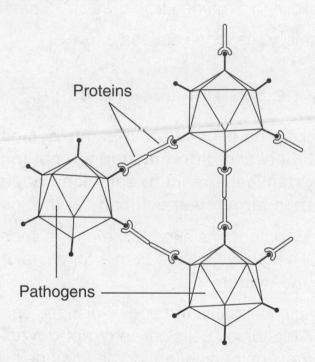

Proteins

Pathogens

9. Fill in the blanks in the table about kinds of lymphocytes.

Kinds of Lymphocytes	
Kind of Lymphocyte	**What It Does**
a. _____	attacks and kills cells that contain pathogens
b. _____	makes antibodies that help kill pathogens

Fighting Disease

AIDS (pages 602–603)

Key Concept: **HIV is the only kind of virus known to attack the human immune system directly and destroy T cells. HIV can spread from one person to another only if body fluids from an infected person come in contact with those of an uninfected person.**

- **AIDS** is a disease caused by a virus that attacks the immune system. The virus is called **HIV** (human immunodeficiency virus).

- HIV can pass from one person to another during sexual contact. It can also pass from a mother to her baby during childbirth or through breast milk. HIV can spread through blood as well.

- Once HIV gets into the body, it enters T cells. The virus multiplies inside the T cells. After a while, the T cells die. Without T cells, people with AIDS cannot fight off other diseases.

Answer the following questions. Use your textbook and the ideas above.

10. Is the following sentence true or false? HIV is a disease caused by a virus. _____

11. List the four ways that HIV can be spread.

a. _____   b. _____

c. _____   d. _____

12. Is the following sentence true or false? HIV destroys B cells. _____

Fighting Disease

Preventing Infectious Disease
(pages 606–610)

Active Immunity   (pages 606–609)

Key Concept: **A person acquires active immunity when their own immune system produces antibodies in response to the presence of a pathogen.**

- **Immunity** is the body's ability to kill pathogens before they can cause disease. There are two kinds of immunity: active immunity and passive immunity.

- With **active immunity**, your own immune system kills pathogens before they can cause disease. Active immunity to a disease often lasts a lifetime.

- You can get active immunity by having a disease or by getting a vaccination.

- When people have a disease, their immune system learns to recognize the pathogen that causes the disease. If the pathogen ever gets into their body again, their immune system kills it so quickly that they do not get sick.

- When people get a **vaccination** (vac suh NAY shun), harmless pathogens are put into their body. Then their immune system will learn to recognize those pathogens. Usually, the pathogens have been weakened or killed so they are harmless. A vaccination may be given with a needle.

- If you do get sick, medicines called **antibiotics** (an tih by AHT iks) can help kill bacteria in your body. However, medicines cannot kill viruses.

Answer the following questions. Use your textbook and the ideas above.

1. The body's ability to kill pathogens before they can

   cause disease is called _____.

Fighting Disease

2. Circle the letter of each sentence that is true about when you have active immunity to a disease.

   a. You must take antibiotics to kill pathogens.

   b. You need a vaccination to kill pathogens.

   c. Your own immune system kills pathogens.

3. The drawing shows one way a person can get active immunity. What is this way called?

   _____

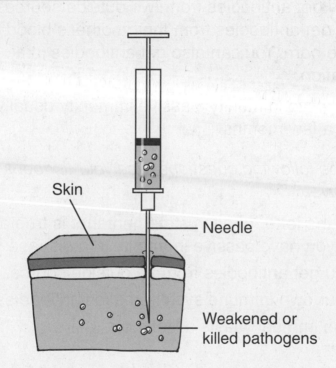

Skin

Needle

Weakened or killed pathogens

4. Medicines that can help kill bacteria in the body are called _____.

Fighting Disease

Passive Immunity (page 610)

Key Concept: **A person acquires passive immunity when the antibodies that fight the pathogen come from a source other than the person's body.**

- If you have **passive immunity**, you get antibodies from an outside source. Your own immune system does not make the antibodies. (Remember, antibodies are proteins that help fight pathogens.)

- You can get antibodies from two outside sources. Babies get antibodies from their mother's blood before they are born. You can also get antibodies in a vaccination.

- Unlike active immunity, passive immunity usually lasts for just a few months.

Answer the following questions. Use your textbook and the ideas above.

5. Circle the letter of each statement that is true about when you have passive immunity to a disease.

   a. You get antibodies from an outside source.

   b. Your own immune system makes antibodies.

   c. The immunity lasts a lifetime.

6. Fill in the blanks in the concept map about sources of antibodies that give you passive immunity.

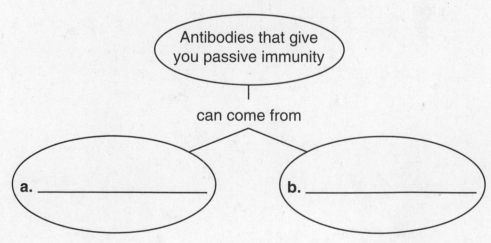

Noninfectious Disease

(pages 611–615)

Allergies (pages 612–613)

Key Concept: **An allergy develops in response to various foreign substances that set off a series of reactions in the body.**

- **Noninfectious diseases** are diseases that are not caused by pathogens. Allergies are one kind of noninfectious disease.

- An **allergy** is a disease in which the immune system reacts in a certain way to foreign materials. A foreign material is something not normally found in the body.

- Any material that causes an allergy is called an **allergen**. Dust and mold are common allergens.

- Certain white blood cells make antibodies when they find allergens in the body. These antibodies signal body cells to make a chemical called histamine. **Histamine** (HIS tuh meen) causes sneezing, watery eyes, and other allergy symptoms.

- In many people, allergies cause asthma. **Asthma** (AZ muh) is a disease in which air passages get narrower than normal. The narrow passages make it hard to breathe.

Answer the following questions. Use your textbook and the ideas above.

1. Circle the letter of the BEST description of what an allergy is.

  a. a disease involving the immune system

  b. something that makes you sneeze

  c. symptoms such as watery eyes

Name _____ Date _____ Class _____

Fighting Disease

2. Read the words in the box. In each sentence below, fill in one of the words.

> histamine   asthma   allergen

    a. Any material that causes an allergy is called a(an) _____.

    b. The chemical that causes allergy symptoms is called _____.

Diabetes (page 613)

Key Concept: **A person with diabetes has high levels of glucose in the blood and may even excrete glucose in the urine. The person's body cells, however, do not have enough glucose.**

- Glucose is the sugar that body cells use for energy. Cells take up glucose from the blood with the help of a chemical called **insulin** (IN suh lin).

- **Diabetes** (dy uh BEE tis) is a disease in which there is a problem with insulin. Sometimes, no insulin is made. Other times, body cells cannot use the insulin. In either case, body cells do not get enough glucose. Then the glucose builds up in the blood. The kidneys work hard to remove the extra glucose from the blood. Some of the extra glucose leaves the body in urine.

- There are two types of diabetes: Type I diabetes and Type II diabetes. Type I diabetes usually begins earlier in life and is more serious than Type II diabetes.

Name _____ Date _____ Class _____

Fighting Disease

Answer the following questions. Use your textbook and the ideas on page 280.

3. Why do people with diabetes have too much glucose in their blood? Circle the letter of the correct answer.

   a. They have a problem with insulin.

   b. They eat too many sweet snacks.

   c. Their kidneys do not work.

4. Is the following sentence true or false? Type II diabetes usually begins earlier in life than Type I diabetes.

_____

Cancer (pages 614–615)

Key Concept: **Cancer is a disease in which cells multiply uncontrollably, over and over, destroying healthy tissue in the process.**

- Normally, the body makes new cells at about the same rate that other cells die. In cancer, new cells are made too quickly. Cells keep dividing over and over again.

- Cancer cells may form a lump of tissue called a **tumor**. A tumor can spread and kill healthy tissues nearby. Tumor cells can also break away and travel in the blood. The cells may form new tumors in other parts of the body.

- Many things can cause cancer. Something that causes cancer is called a **carcinogen** (kahr SIN un jun). For example, tar in cigarette smoke is a carcinogen.

- Sometimes cancer can be treated with surgery to remove a tumor. Sometimes medicines are taken to kill cancer cells. X-rays can also be used to kill cancer cells.

- You will be less likely to get cancer if you avoid things that cause cancer. For example, you will be less likely to get cancer if you do not smoke.

Fighting Disease

Answer the following questions. Use your textbook and the ideas on page 281.

5. Is the following sentence true or false? In cancer, new cells are made too slowly. _____

6. Draw a line from each term to its meaning.

Term	Meaning
tumor	**a.** something that causes cancer
carcinogen	**b.** lump of tissue formed by cancer cells

7. Circle the letter of each sentence that is true about cancer.
   a. You are less likely to get cancer if you do not smoke.
   b. Surgery is the only way to treat cancer.
   c. X-rays can be used to kill cancer cells.

How the Nervous System
Works (pages 626–630)

Functions of the Nervous
System (pages 626–627)

Key Concept: **The nervous system receives information about what is happening both inside and outside your body. It also directs the way in which your body responds to this information. In addition, your nervous system helps maintain homeostasis.**

- The nervous system includes the brain, spinal cord, and nerves that run throughout the body. The nervous system also includes sense organs such as the eyes.

- The nervous system has three jobs:
  1. The nervous system receives information. For example, it tells you that a ball is zooming toward you.
  2. The nervous system responds to information. It makes you duck so the ball misses you.
  3. The nervous system also helps to keep the body in balance. For example, your nervous system makes you feel hungry when your body needs food.

Answer the following questions. Use your textbook and the ideas above.

1. Is the following sentence true or false? The nervous system includes the sense organs. _____

2. Circle the letter of each job of the nervous system.
   a. responds to information
   b. helps keep body in balance
   c. receives information

The Neuron (page 628)

Key Concept: **A neuron has a large cell body that contains the nucleus, threadlike extensions called dendrites, and an axon. Three kinds of neurons are found in the body—sensory neurons, interneurons, and motor neurons.**

- The cells of your nervous system are called nerve cells, or **neurons** (NOO rahnz). Neurons carry messages, called **nerve impulses**. A bundle of many neurons is called a **nerve**. Nerves can be very long.

- The main part of a neuron is the cell body. Threads called **dendrites** stick out from the cell body. Dendrites carry messages from outside the neuron to the cell body. A longer thread, called the **axon**, also sticks out from the cell body. The axon carries messages from the cell body to other cells.

- Three kinds of neurons work together in the body. **Sensory neurons** pick up information and change it to messages. **Interneurons** pass messages from neuron to neuron. Some interneurons pass messages to motor neurons. **Motor neurons** send messages to muscles.

Answer the following questions. Use your textbook and the ideas above.

3. Draw a line from the kind of neuron to what it does.

Neuron	What It Does
sensory neuron	**a.** passes messages from neuron to neuron
interneuron	**b.** picks up information and changes it to messages
motor neuron	**c.** sends messages to muscles

4. Is the following sentence true or false? Dendrites carry messages from the cell body to other cells. _____

How a Nerve Impulse Travels (pages 628–630)

***Key Concept:* For a nerve impulse to be carried along at a synapse, it must cross the gap between the axon and the next structure. The axon tips release chemicals that carry the impulse across the gap.**

- Nerve impulses travel from sensory neurons to interneurons and from interneurons to motor neurons.

- Suppose the phone rings. Sensory neurons in your ears send a message about the sound to interneurons in your brain. Your brain makes a decision about the sound and sends a message to motor neurons. Motor neurons pass the message to muscles. Muscles contract, and your hand picks up the phone.

- There is a space, or gap, between one neuron and the next. This gap is called a **synapse** (SIN aps). When messages reach a synapse, the axon produces certain chemicals. The chemicals carry messages across the gap, like a boat carries people across a river.

Answer the following questions. Use your textbook and the ideas above.

5. Fill in the blanks in the flowchart about how nerve impulses travel.

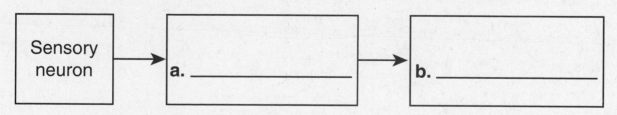

6. A gap between two neurons is a(an) _____.

Divisions of the Nervous System (pages 632–639)

Central Nervous System (page 633)

Key Concept: **The central nervous system is the control center of the body. It includes the brain and spinal cord.**

- The nervous system can be divided into two parts: the central nervous system and the peripheral nervous system.

- The **central nervous system** is made up of the brain and spinal cord. The **peripheral nervous system** (puh RIF uh rul) is made up of all the rest of the nerves in the body.

- The **brain** is inside the skull. The brain controls almost everything that goes on in the body. The **spinal cord** is a thick rope of nerves that runs down the center of the back. The spinal cord carries messages back and forth between the brain and peripheral nervous system.

Answer the following questions. Use your textbook and the ideas above.

1. Fill in the blanks in the concept map about the two parts of the nervous system.

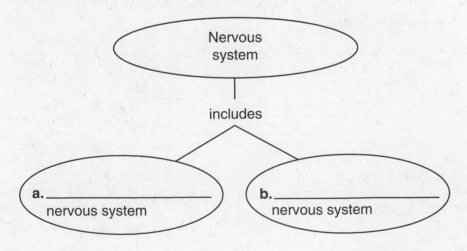

2. Is the following sentence true or false? The brain controls almost everything that goes on in the body.

_____

The Brain and Spinal Cord (pages 634–636)

Key Concept: **There are three main regions of the brain that receive and process information. These are the cerebrum, the cerebellum, and the brain stem. The spinal cord is the link between your brain and the peripheral nervous system.**

- The largest part of the brain is the cerebrum. The **cerebrum** (suh REE brum) controls movement, the senses, speech, and thinking. For example, you use your cerebrum to read.

- The second largest part of the brain is the cerebellum. The **cerebellum** (sehr uh BEL um) controls balance and muscles working together. For example, your cerebellum helps you walk.

- The smallest part of the brain is the brain stem. The **brain stem** controls involuntary actions. These are actions, such as breathing and heartbeat, that you cannot control.

- The spinal cord connects the brain with the nerves of the body. The spinal cord is surrounded by the backbone. The backbone helps to keep the spinal cord from getting hurt.

Answer the following questions. Use your textbook and the ideas above.

3. Is the following sentence true or false? The brain connects the spinal cord with the nerves of the body.

_____

4. Fill in the blanks in the table about parts of the brain.

Parts of the Brain	
Part of Brain	**What It Controls**
Cerebrum	movement, senses, speech, and thinking
a. _____	balance and muscles working together
b. _____	actions like breathing and heartbeat

Peripheral Nervous System (pages 636–637)

Key Concept: **The peripheral nervous system consists of a network of nerves that branch out from the central nervous system and connect it to the rest of the body. The peripheral nervous system is involved in both involuntary and voluntary actions.**

- All of the nerves of the peripheral nervous system start either in the brain or in the spinal cord. From there, the peripheral nerves branch out through the rest of the body.

- The peripheral nervous system can be divided into two parts: the somatic nervous system and the autonomic nervous system.

- Nerves of the **somatic** (soh MAT ik) **nervous system** control voluntary actions. For example, you use somatic nerves to control your fingers when you tie your shoes.

- Nerves of the **autonomic** (awt uh NAHM ik) **nervous system** control involuntary actions. For example, autonomic nerves control muscles in the walls of blood vessels.

Name _____ Date _____ Class _____

The Nervous System

Answer the following question. Use your textbook and the ideas on page 288.

5. Fill in the blanks in the table about the peripheral nervous system.

Parts of the Peripheral Nervous System	
Part of Peripheral Nervous System	**What It Controls**
a. _____ nervous system	voluntary actions
b. _____ nervous system	involuntary actions

Reflexes (pages 637–638)

Key Concept: **A reflex is an automatic response that occurs very rapidly and without conscious control. Reflexes help to protect the body.**

- A **reflex** is something you do automatically, without thinking about it. For example, if you touch a sharp object, you jerk your hand away from it. The rapid motion of your hand is a reflex. Like other reflexes, it helps to keep you from getting hurt.

- Remember, sensory neurons usually send messages that go to the brain. In some reflexes, sensory neurons send messages that go only as far as the spinal cord. These reflexes are very fast.

Answer the following questions. Use your textbook and the ideas above.

6. Something you do automatically is a(an) _____.

7. Is the following sentence true or false? Reflexes help to keep you from getting hurt. _____

Nervous System Injuries (page 639)

Key Concept: **Concussions and spinal cord injuries are two ways in which the central nervous system can be damaged.**

- A **concussion** is a bruise on the brain. It is caused by the brain knocking against the hard skull. This can happen when a person has an accident or plays a rough sport such as football.

- Concussions can cause headaches. Sometimes, people even pass out when they get a concussion. A concussion usually heals itself.

- Spinal cord injuries happen when the spinal cord is cut or crushed. Car crashes are the most common cause of spinal cord injuries.

- When the spinal cord is cut all the way through, messages cannot travel to and from the brain. Because the brain cannot send messages to muscles, parts of the body can no longer move.

Answer the following questions. Use your textbook and the ideas above.

8. A bruise on the brain is a(an) _____.

9. Why might a spinal cord injury make parts of the body unable to move? Circle the letter of the correct answer.

   a. because the brain cannot send messages to the muscles

   b. because the muscles are usually injured too

   c. because the muscles cannot send messages to the spinal cord

The Nervous System

The Senses (pages 642–650)

Vision (pages 643–645)

Key Concept: **Your eyes respond to the stimulus of light. They convert that stimulus into impulses that your brain interprets, enabling you to see.**

- Your eyes are the sense organs that let you see. You can see because your eyes sense light.

- Light enters the eye through a hole called the **pupil**. The pupil is the black part of the eye.

- From the pupil, light passes through the lens. The **lens** of the eye is something like a hand lens. It focuses light

- Light from the lens focuses on the inside surface at the back of the eye. This area is called the **retina** (RET 'n uh). The light hits cells in the retina that sense light. These cells send messages to the brain. The brain decides what you are looking at.

- If the eyeball is too short or too long, light from the lens does not focus on the retina. As a result, some objects look blurred or fuzzy. Eyeglasses or contact lenses can usually correct the problem.

Answer the following questions. Use your textbook and the ideas above.

1. Is the following sentence true or false? You can see

   because your eyes sense light. _____

The Nervous System

2. Read the words in the box. In each sentence below, fill in one of the words.

> lens   eyeball   retina   pupil

   a. The area at the back of the eye where light is focused is the _____.

   b. The hole where light enters the eye is the _____.

   c. The part of the eye that focuses light is the _____.

3. What happens if your eyeballs are too short or too long? Circle the letter of the correct answer.

   a. You can see more clearly than normal.

   b. Some objects look blurred or fuzzy.

   c. You cannot see anything.

Hearing and Balance (pages 646–648)

Key Concept: **Your ears are the sense organs that respond to the stimulus of sound. The ears convert the sound to nerve impulses that your brain interprets. Structures in your inner ear control your sense of balance.**

- Sound is caused by vibrations, or rapid back-and-forth movements. For example, when you hit the head of a drum, it vibrates back and forth. This sends waves of vibrations through the air. Your ears pick up the vibrations, and you hear the vibrations as sound.

- The ear has three main regions: the outer ear, the middle ear, and the inner ear.

The Nervous System

- The outer ear is the part of the ear that you can see. It gathers sound waves. Sound waves travel into the ear and hit a tissue called the **eardrum**. The eardrum is like the head of a drum. It vibrates when sound waves hit it.

- The middle ear contains three tiny bones. Vibrations in the eardrum pass through these bones to the inner ear.

- The inner ear contains fluid. The fluid picks up the vibrations from the middle ear. When the fluid vibrates, cells lining the inner ear send messages to the brain. The brain decides what the sound is.

- Your ears also help you keep your balance. The inner ears send messages to the brain about how your head is moving. The brain senses if you are losing your balance. If you are, the brain sends messages to muscles to move your body into balance again.

Answer the following questions. Use your textbook and the ideas on page 292 and above.

4. Circle the letter of each sentence that is true about the ears.
   a. Your ears let you hear sound.
   b. The outer ear has three tiny bones that vibrate.
   c. Your ears help you keep your balance.

5. Is the following sentence true or false? The eardrum sends messages about sounds to the brain.

   _____

6. Circle the letter of the region of the ear that sends messages to the brain about how your head is moving.
   a. outer ear
   b. middle ear
   c. inner ear

The Nervous System

Smell and Taste (page 649)

Key Concept: **The senses of smell and taste work closely together. Both depend on chemicals in food or in the air. The chemicals trigger responses in receptors in the nose and mouth.**

- When you smell or taste something, your body is sensing chemicals in food or in air.

- Cells in your nose sense chemicals in air. Cells in your tongue, called taste buds, sense chemicals in food. Both kinds of cells send messages to the brain about what they are sensing.

- Your nose can sense at least 50 different smells. Your taste buds can sense five main tastes: sweet, sour, salty, bitter, and meatlike tastes.

- Foods taste like they do because of both smell and taste. When you have a stuffy nose, you cannot smell as well as usual. So, food does not taste as good as it normally does.

Answer the following questions. Use your textbook and the ideas above.

7. Is the following sentence true or false? The senses of smell and taste work closely together.

_____

8. Circle the letter of each sentence that is true about the senses of smell and taste.

   a. Taste buds sense chemicals in the air.

   b. You can sense more different smells than tastes.

   c. The taste of food depends on both the sense of smell and the sense of taste.

The Nervous System

Touch (page 650)

Key Concept: **Your skin contains different kinds of touch receptors that respond to a number of stimuli.**

- The sense of touch is found in all areas of your skin. This makes your skin your largest sense organ. Sensory neurons in the skin send messages about touch to the brain.

- Skin can sense different kinds of touches. It can sense light touches, heavy pressure, pain, and temperature. Skin can also sense texture, or how smooth or rough objects are. For example, you can tell rough sandpaper from smooth writing paper with your eyes closed.

- Being able to feel pain and temperature helps keep you safe. For example, you can use your toe to feel how hot bath water is before you get into the tub. This can keep you from getting burned.

Answer the following questions. Use your textbook and the ideas above.

9. Your largest sense organ is your

_____.

10. Is the following sentence true or false? Skin can sense only pain and temperature. _____

The Nervous System

Alcohol and Other Drugs
(pages 651–657)

Drug Abuse (pages 651–653)

Key Concept: **Most commonly abused drugs, such as marijuana, alcohol, and cocaine, are especially dangerous because of their immediate effects on the brain and other parts of the nervous system. In addition, long-term abuse can lead to addiction and other health and social problems.**

- A **drug** is a chemical that changes your body or how you behave. **Drug abuse** means using a drug the wrong way on purpose. Abused drugs can be illegal or legal. Medicines can also be abused.

- Different drugs have different effects. For example, some drugs keep people awake; other drugs make people sleepy. Most abused drugs affect people's mood and feelings. They may make people feel better for a while, which is why most people start using them.

- If people take a drug for a long time, they may need to take more and more of it to get the same effect. This is called **tolerance**.

- Using some drugs for a long time can cause addiction. **Addiction** is a physical need for a drug. Without the drug, an addicted person suffers from physical problems, such as headaches and muscle cramps.

Answer the following questions. Use your textbook and the ideas above.

1. Is the following sentence true or false? Only illegal drugs can be abused. _____

The Nervous System

2. Read the words in the box. In each sentence below, fill in one of the words.

┌───┐
│   abuse   tolerance   addiction   │
└───┘

a. A physical need for a drug is called

_____.

b. Needing more and more of a drug to get the same

effect is called _____.

Kinds of Abused Drugs (pages 654–655)

Key Concept: **Commonly abused drugs include depressants, stimulants, inhalants, hallucinogens, anabolic steroids, and alcohol. Many drugs affect the central nervous system, while others affect the overall chemical balance in the body.**

- **Depressants** are drugs such as alcohol that make people relaxed and sleepy.

- **Stimulants** are drugs such as nicotine that speed up heartbeat and breathing.

- Inhalants are substances such as glue that people inhale, or breathe in, to change their mood.

- Hallucinogens are drugs such as LSD that can make people see or hear things that are not really there.

- **Anabolic steroids** (an uh BAH lik STEER oydz) are drugs that make muscles grow bigger. The drugs can also make people angry and violent and cause serious health problems.

- Most abused drugs do serious damage to the body when they are taken for a long time. For example, anabolic steroids and inhalants damage the kidneys and liver.

The Nervous System

Answer the following question. Use your textbook and the ideas on page 297.

3. Draw a line from each kind of drug to its effect.

Kind of Drug	Effect
depressant	**a.** speeds up heartbeat and breathing
stimulant	**b.** makes muscles grow bigger
anabolic steroid	**c.** makes people relaxed and sleepy

Alcohol (pages 656–657)

Key Concept: **Alcohol abuse can cause the destruction of cells in the brain and liver, and can lead to addiction and emotional dependence.**

- Alcohol is a drug found in drinks such as beer and wine. Teens abuse alcohol more than any other drug.

- Alcohol goes into the blood and affects most body systems. For example, alcohol makes blood pressure rise and vision get blurry.

- Over time, alcohol abuse can cause serious health problems such as brain damage. Alcohol abuse can also lead to alcoholism. **Alcoholism** is a disease in which people are physically and emotionally hooked on alcohol. Most alcoholics need help to stop drinking.

Answer the following questions. Use your textbook and the ideas above.

4. Is the following sentence true or false? Teens abuse alcohol more than any other drug. _____

5. A disease in which people are hooked on alcohol is

_____.

The Endocrine System
(pages 666–671)

Hormones and the Endocrine System
(pages 667–668)

Key Concept: **The endocrine system produces chemicals that control many of the body's daily activities. The endocrine system also regulates long-term changes such as growth and development.**

- The endocrine system is made up of glands. A gland is an organ that makes a chemical. Some glands release their chemicals into nearby tissues. **Endocrine** (EN duh krin) **glands** release their chemicals into the blood.

- Chemicals made by endocrine glands are called **hormones**. Hormones control activities in the body. Hormones turn on, turn off, speed up, or slow down body activities.

- Endocrine glands release hormones when the brain sends them messages. For example, the brain can trigger the release of adrenaline. This hormone helps the body respond to emergencies.

- Hormones affect only certain cells. The cells affected by hormones are called **target cells**.

Answer the following questions. Use your textbook and the ideas above.

1. Glands that release hormones into the blood are called

   _____ glands.

2. Circle the letter of what hormones do.
   a. make glands
   b. control activities in the body
   c. send messages to the brain

The Endocrine System and Reproduction

3. Is the following sentence true or false? Endocrine glands are controlled by the brain. _____

4. Circle the letter of the cells that hormones affect.

   a. cells of the stomach

   b. cells of the heart

   c. target cells

Functions of Endocrine Glands

(pages 668–670)

Key Concept: **The endocrine glands include the hypothalamus, pituitary, thyroid, parathyroid, adrenal, thymus, and pancreas. They also include the ovaries in females and testes in males.**

- Each endocrine gland makes different hormones. So, each gland controls different body activities.

- The **hypothalamus** (hy poh THAL uh mus) is in the brain. It controls all the other endocrine glands. The brain controls the endocrine system by controlling the hypothalamus.

- The **pituitary** (pih TOO ih tehr ee) **gland** is just below the hypothalamus. It is controlled by the hypothalamus. Most pituitary hormones control other endocrine glands. A few pituitary hormones control body activities directly. For example, the pituitary gland makes growth hormone, which controls growth in children.

Answer the following questions. Use your textbook and the ideas above.

5. Is the following sentence true or false? All endocrine glands make the same hormones. _____

The Endocrine System and Reproduction

6. Read the words in the box. In each sentence below, fill in one of the words.

hypothalamus   pituitary   endocrine

a. The gland that makes growth hormone is the

_____ gland.

b. The brain controls the endocrine system by

controlling the _____.

Negative Feedback (pages 670–671)

Key Concept: **Through negative feedback, when the amount of a particular hormone in the blood reaches a certain level, the endocrine system sends signals that stop the release of that hormone.**

- The endocrine system works like a furnace and thermostat. When a house is cold, the thermostat signals the furnace to make heat. Once the house is warm, the thermostat signals the furnace to stop making heat. This is an example of negative feedback. In **negative feedback**, a system is turned on or off by the conditions that it produces.

- Negative feedback controls the endocrine glands. The thyroid gland in the neck is a good example. One of the thyroid's hormones controls how much energy cells have. When cells have too little energy, the thyroid gland releases its hormone. Once cells have enough energy, the thyroid stops releasing its hormone.

- If the thyroid gland were a furnace, the hypothalamus would be the thermostat. The hypothalamus senses when cells need more or less energy. The hypothalamus then signals the pituitary gland to release, or to stop releasing, a hormone that controls the thyroid gland.

The Endocrine System and Reproduction

Answer the following questions. Use your textbook and the ideas on page 301.

7. How is the endocrine system like a furnace and thermostat? Circle the letter of the correct answer.

   a. Endocrine glands are turned on and off by their own hormones.

   b. Endocrine glands are controlled by body heat.

   c. Endocrine glands cannot work if they run out of fuel from the hypothalamus.

8. The flowchart shows the negative feedback loop that controls the thyroid gland. Fill in the blank with the name of the missing gland.

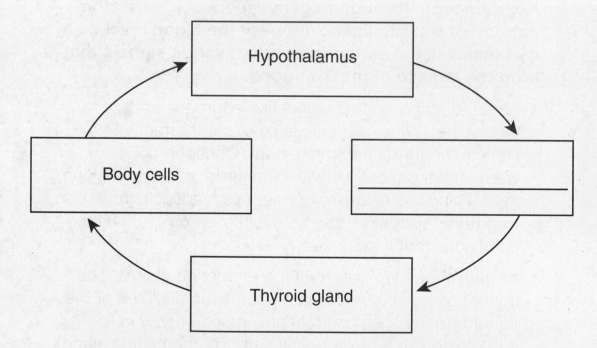

The Endocrine System and Reproduction

The Male and Female Reproductive Systems (pages 674–681)

Sexual Reproduction (page 675)

Key Concept: **Sexual reproduction involves the production of eggs by the female and sperm by the male. The egg and sperm join together during fertilization.**

- Each person begins life as a single cell. That single cell forms when an egg and a sperm join.

- Eggs and sperms are called sex cells. An **egg** is a sex cell produced by the mother. A **sperm** is a sex cell produced by the father.

- When an egg and a sperm join, it is called **fertilization**. The cell that is formed is a fertilized egg, called a **zygote**.

Answer the following questions. Use your textbook and the ideas above.

1. Is the following sentence true or false? A sex cell produced by a female is a sperm. _____

2. What process does the diagram show?
   _____

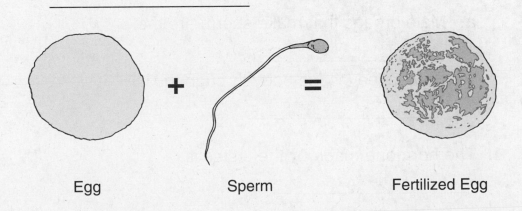

Egg   Sperm   Fertilized Egg

The Endocrine System and Reproduction

Male Reproductive System (pages 676–677)

Key Concept: The male reproductive system is specialized to produce sperm and the hormone testosterone. The structures of the male reproductive system include the testes, scrotum, and penis.

- The **testes** (TES teez) are male organs that make sperm. The testes are outside the body in a pouch of skin called the **scrotum** (SKROH tum).

- The testes also make testosterone. **Testosterone** (tes TAHS tuh rohn) is a hormone. It controls the growth of hair on the face and other physical traits of adult males.

- From the testes, sperm cells travel to other male organs inside the body. They pick up fluids in these other organs. The mixture of sperm cells and fluids is called **semen** (SEE mun). Semen leaves the body through an organ called the **penis**.

Answer the following questions. Use your textbook and the ideas above.

3. Read the words in the box. In each sentence below, fill in one of the words.

        +--+
        | scrotum   penis   testes |
        +--+

    a. Male organs that make sperm are the

        _____.

    b. Semen leaves the body through the

        _____.

4. The hormone made by the testes is

    _____.

The Endocrine System and Reproduction

5. Circle the letter of each sentence that is true about testosterone.

    a. Testosterone is a hormone that controls physical traits of adult males.

    b. Testosterone is made by the testes.

    c. Testosterone is the fluid in semen.

Female Reproductive System

(pages 678–679)

Key Concept: **The role of the female reproductive system is to produce eggs and, if an egg is fertilized, to nourish a developing baby until birth. The organs of the female reproductive system include the ovaries, fallopian tubes, uterus, and vagina.**

- The **ovaries** (OH vuh reez) are female organs that make eggs. The two ovaries are inside the body, just below the waist.

- The ovaries also make estrogen. **Estrogen** (ES truh jun) is a hormone. It controls breast development and other physical traits of adult females.

- From the ovaries, eggs enter tubes called **fallopian tubes**. If an egg is fertilized by a sperm, it usually happens inside a fallopian tube.

- The fallopian tubes lead to the uterus. The **uterus** (YOO tur us) is a hollow organ about as big as a pear.

- If an egg is fertilized, it sticks to the inside lining of the uterus. If the egg is not fertilized, it passes through the uterus and leaves the body through the vagina. The **vagina** (vuh JY nuh) is a wide tube that connects the uterus to the outside of the body.

The Endocrine System and Reproduction

Answer the following questions. Use your textbook and the ideas on page 305.

6. Is the following sentence true or false? Fertilization usually takes place inside the ovaries. _____

7. Fill in the missing labels in the diagram of the female reproductive system.

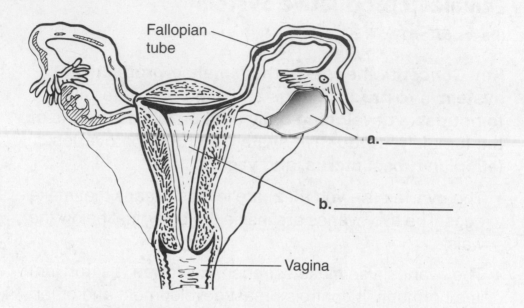

Fallopian tube

a. _____

b. _____

Vagina

The Menstrual Cycle (pages 679–681)

Key Concept: **During the menstrual cycle, an egg develops in an ovary. At the same time, the uterus prepares for the arrival of an embryo.**

- Certain changes happen in a woman's body month after month. These monthly changes are called the **menstrual** (MEN stroo ul) **cycle**.

- In the first half of the menstrual cycle, an egg develops in one of the ovaries. The lining of the uterus also gets thicker.

The Endocrine System and Reproduction

- About halfway through the menstrual cycle, the ovary releases the egg. This is called **ovulation** (ahv yuh LAY shun).

- If the egg is not fertilized, both the egg and the lining of the uterus start to break down.

- The next cycle begins when the egg and the lining of the uterus pass out of the body through the vagina. This is called **menstruation** (men stroo AY shun).

- Endocrine hormones control the menstrual cycle. The cycle begins in girls when they are about 10 to 14 years old. The cycle keeps repeating until women are about 50 years old.

Answer the following questions. Use your textbook and the ideas on page 306 and above.

8. Fill in the missing step of the menstrual cycle.

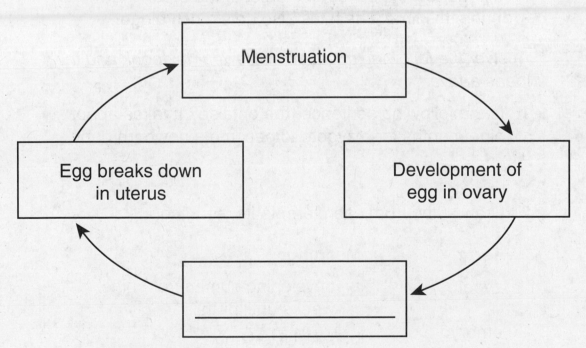

Menstruation

Development of egg in ovary

Egg breaks down in uterus

_____

9. Circle the letter of what controls the menstrual cycle.

    a. menstruation

    b. ovulation

    c. endocrine hormones

The Endocrine System and Reproduction

The Human Life Cycle (pages 682–690)

Development Before Birth (pages 682–683)

Key Concept: **The zygote develops first into an embryo and then into a fetus.**

- A zygote is a fertilized egg. It is about as big as the period at the end of this sentence. It takes about nine months for a tiny zygote to become a newborn baby.

- After the zygote forms, it begins to divide right away. Once the zygote begins to divide, the developing human is called an **embryo** (EM bree oh). It is called an embryo for the next eight weeks. During this time, the heart, eyes, and some other organs form.

- From nine weeks until birth, the developing human is called a **fetus** (FEE tus). The rest of the organs form during this time. The fetus also gets much bigger.

Answer the following questions. Use your textbook and the ideas above.

1. Is the following sentence true or false? It takes about nine months for a zygote to become a newborn baby.

   _____

2. Draw a line from each term to its meaning.

Term	Meaning
zygote	a. developing human from nine weeks until birth
embryo	b. a fertilized egg
fetus	c. developing human for first eight weeks

The Endocrine System and Reproduction

Protection and Nourishment (pages 684–685)

Key Concept. **The membranes and other structures that form during development protect and nourish the developing embryo, and later the fetus.**

- A baby grows in its mother's uterus. Inside the uterus, two layers surround the developing baby: the amniotic sac and the placenta.

- The **amniotic** (am NEE aht ik) **sac** is a bag filled with fluid. The fluid acts like a pillow. It helps keep the developing baby from getting hurt.

- The **placenta** (pluh SEN tuh) has many small blood vessels that connect mother and baby. Materials pass through the blood vessel walls. For example, oxygen and nutrients pass from the mother's blood to the baby's blood. Wastes pass from the baby's blood to the mother's blood.

Answer the following questions. Use your textbook and the ideas above.

3. The structure that lets a developing baby get oxygen and nutrients from its mother is the

   _____.

4. A bag filled with fluid that protects a developing baby is

   the _____.

Birth (pages 685–687)

Key Concept: **The birth of a baby takes place in three stages—labor, delivery, and afterbirth.**

- The first stage of birth is called labor. This stage may last many hours. During this stage, muscles of the uterus contract. The muscles push the baby out of the uterus.

The Endocrine System and Reproduction

- The second stage of birth is called delivery. It usually lasts less than an hour. During this stage, the baby is pushed all the way out of the uterus. The baby passes through the vagina and out of the body.

- The third stage of birth is called afterbirth. It usually lasts less than an hour. During this stage, the placenta and amniotic sac are pushed out of the uterus. They pass through the vagina and out of the body.

- Sometimes a mother has more than one baby at the same time. Two babies at a time are called twins.

Answer the following question. Use your textbook and the ideas on page 309 and above.

5. Fill in the blanks in the flowchart showing the stages of birth.

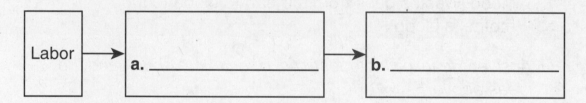

Labor → a. _____ → b. _____

Growth and Development (pages 688–690)

Key Concept: **The changes that take place between infancy and adulthood include physical changes, such as an increase in size and coordination. They also include mental changes, such as the ability to communicate and solve complex problems.**

- Infancy begins at birth and ends at age two years. Many changes take place during infancy. Most kids learn to walk and start to talk in infancy. Kids also grow very quickly in infancy.

The Endocrine System and Reproduction

- Childhood starts at age two years and ends between the ages of 9 and 15 years. During childhood, kids keep growing, but not as quickly as they grew in infancy. They also learn new skills, such as how to read and ride a bike.

- **Adolescence** (ad ul ES uns) begins between the ages of 9 and 15 years. During adolescence, children change into adults. They start to think and look like adults. For example, girls develop breasts and boys develop hair on their face.

- There are no clear markers for the end of adolescence and the start of adulthood. People stop growing taller in adulthood, but they still keep changing. For example, their skin gets wrinkled, their muscles get weaker, and their hair turns gray.

Answer the following questions. Use your textbook and the ideas on page 310 and above

6. Is the following sentence true or false? Most kids learn to walk in infancy. _____

7. Children change into adults during

_____.

8. Circle the letter of each sentence that is true about adulthood.
   a. People keep changing in adulthood.
   b. Adulthood begins between the ages of 9 and 15 years.
   c. There are no clear markers for the start of adulthood.

Living Things and the Environment

(pages 704–709)

Habitats (page 705)

Key Concept: **An organism obtains food, water, shelter, and other things it needs to live, grow, and reproduce from its environment.**

- An **organism** is a living thing. You are an organism.

- A **habitat** is a place that an organism needs to live, grow, and reproduce. A pond is a frog's habitat.

- Different organisms live in different habitats. They live in different habitats because they have different needs.

Answer the following questions. Use your textbook and the ideas above.

1. Read each word in the box. In each sentence below, fill in one of the words.

organism   environment   habitat

   a. A living thing is also called a(an)

   _____.

   b. A place that a living thing needs to live, grow, and

   reproduce is called a(an) _____.

2. Circle the letter of each sentence that is true about habitats.

   a. One area may contain many habitats.

   b. Different organisms live in different habitats.

   c. Each area has only one habitat.

Populations and Communities

Biotic Factors (page 705)

Key Concept: **An organism interacts with the living parts of its habitat.**

- Each organism affects all the other organisms in its habitat. All the other organisms also affect it.

- The living parts of a habitat include all the living things in it. The living things include all the different plants and animals, for example.

- The living parts of a habitat are called **biotic** (by AHT ik) **factors**. Biotic factors include animals, plants, and other organisms.

Answer the following questions. Use your textbook and the ideas above.

3. Is the following sentence true or false? Each organism affects all the other organisms in its habitat. _____

4. The living parts of a habitat are called _____ factors.

Abiotic Factors (page 706)

Key Concept: **An organism interacts with the nonliving parts of its habitat.**

- Each organism affects all the nonliving parts of its habitat. The nonliving parts also affect it.

- The nonliving parts of a habitat are called **abiotic factors**. Abiotic factors include water, sunlight, oxygen, temperature, and soil.

- Plants and algae need certain abiotic factors to make their own food. The food-making process is called **photosynthesis** (foh toh SIN thuh sis). To carry out photosynthesis, plants and algae need water, carbon dioxide, and sunlight.

Populations and Communities

- Most living things need oxygen to carry out the processes that keep them alive. You get oxygen from the air you breathe.

Answer the following questions. Use your textbook and the ideas on page 313 and above.

5. Complete the concept map about abiotic factors by filling in the blanks in the circles.

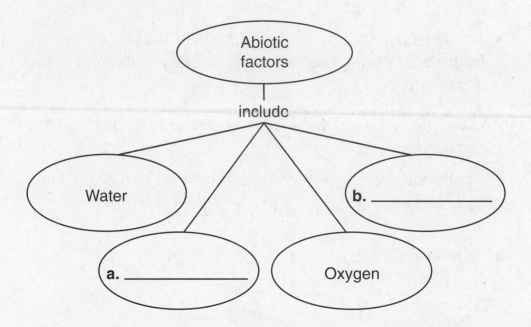

Abiotic
factors

include

Water

b. _____

a. _____

Oxygen

6. Read each word in the box. In each sentence below, fill in the correct word or words.

abiotic factors	photosynthesis	biotic factors

a. Plants make their own food in a process

   called _____.

b. The nonliving parts of a habitat are

   called _____.

Levels of Organization (pages 707–709)

Key Concept: The smallest level of organization is a single organism, which belongs to a population that includes other members of its species. The population belongs to a community of different species. The community and abiotic factors together form an ecosystem.

- A **species** (SPEE sheez) is a group of organisms that look alike and can mate with one another. For example, all lions are of the same species.

- A **population** includes all the members of the same species that live in an area.

- All the different populations in an area make up a **community**. All the plants and animals that live in the same forest are a community.

- An **ecosystem** is the community of organisms in an area and the nonliving parts of the area.

- **Ecology** is the study of how living things affect one another. Ecology also is the study of how living things affect the environment and how the environment affects living things. Scientists who study ecology are called ecologists.

Answer the following questions. Use your textbook and the ideas above.

7. Complete the diagram below. The diagram shows levels of organization in an ecosystem. The diagram begins at the left with the smallest level of organization.

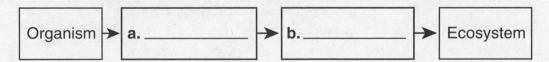

Organism → a. _____ → b. _____ → Ecosystem

Populations and Communities

8. Draw a line from each term to its meaning.

Term	Meaning
community	**a.** group of organisms that look alike and can mate with one another
ecosystem	**b.** all the members of the same species that live in an area
ecology	**c.** the study of how living things affect each other and the environment
population	**d.** all the different populations in an area
species	**e.** the community of organisms in an area and the nonliving parts of the area

Populations and Communities

Studying Populations (pages 711–718)

Determining Population Size

(pages 712–713)

Key Concept: **Some methods of determining the size of a population are direct and indirect observations, sampling, and mark-and-recapture studies.**

- You can find the size of a population by counting all the members of the population. This method is called direct observation.

- You can find the size of a population by looking for signs of organisms, such as nests. This method is called indirect observation.

- You can find the size of a population by sampling. In sampling, you count the number of organisms that live in a small area called a sample area. Then, you use that number to make an estimate of the total population. An **estimate** is a careful guess.

- You can find the size of a population by a method called "mark and recapture." First, you capture organisms and mark them. Later, you recapture the same kind of organisms and see how many are marked. Then, you use a mathematical formula to make an estimate of the total population.

Answer the following questions. Use your textbook and the ideas above.

1. Is the following sentence true or false? An estimate is an exact amount. _____

Name _____ Date _____ Class _____

Populations and Communities

2. Complete the table about methods used to determine the size of a population.

Methods Used to Determine Population Size	
Method	**Description of Method**
a. _____ _____	Count the number of organisms that live in a small area and use that number to make an estimate.
b. _____ _____	Count all the members of a population.
c. _____ _____	Look for signs of organisms.
d. _____ _____	Capture organisms and mark them. Later, recapture organisms and see how many are marked.

Populations and Communities

Changes in Population Size (pages 714–716)

Key Concept: **Populations can change in size when new members join the population or when members leave the population.**

- The main way new organisms join a population is by being born into it.

- New organisms also join a population by moving into it. **Immigration** (im ih GRAY shun) means moving into a population.

- The main way organisms leave a population is by dying.

- Organisms also leave a population by moving away. **Emigration** (em ih GRAY shun) means leaving a population.

- The number of individuals of a population that live in a certain area is called the area's **population density**.

Answer the following questions. Use your textbook and the ideas above.

3. Read each word in the box. In each sentence below, fill in the correct word or words.

emigration	population density	immigration

   a. Moving into a population is called

   _____.

   b. Leaving a population is called

   _____.

4. The two pictures show two different populations of birds. Each population lives in an area that is 8 square meters. Circle the area that has the greater population density.

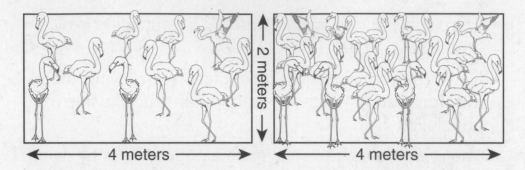

Limiting Factors (pages 716–718)

Key Concept: **Some limiting factors for populations are food and water, space, and weather conditions.**

- A **limiting factor** causes a population to get smaller.

- The amount of food and water can limit the size of a population. All organisms need food and water to live. Food and water are limiting factors.

- The amount of space can limit the size of a population. Space is a limiting factor.

- Weather conditions that are bad for a population can limit the size of the population. Bad weather is a limiting factor.

- The largest population an area can support is called the area's **carrying capacity**.

Answer the following questions. Use your textbook and the ideas above.

5. Is the following sentence true or false? Only some organisms need food and water to survive.

_____

Populations and Communities

6. Read each word in the box. In each sentence below, fill in the correct words.

population density   carrying capacity   limiting factor

   a. A _____ causes a population to get smaller.

   b. The largest population an area can support is

    called the area's _____.

7. Circle the letter of each sentence that is true about limiting factors.

   a. Weather conditions can limit the size of a population.

   b. The amount of food and water does not limit the size of a population.

   c. The amount of space can limit the size of a population.

Interactions Among Living Things (pages 722–729)

Adapting to the Environment (page 723)

Key Concept: **Every organism has a variety of adaptations that are suited to its specific living conditions.**

- **Natural selection** is the way that characteristics become common in a species. Individual organisms with helpful characteristics survive. These organisms reproduce. Their offspring inherit the helpful characteristics.

- Natural selection results in adaptations. An **adaptation** is a behavior or physical characteristic that helps an organism to live in an environment. For example, the green coloring of a frog helps the frog hide from its enemies.

- The way that an organism "makes its living" is called its **niche**. A niche includes the types of food an organism eats. It also includes how the organism gets its food and when it reproduces.

Answer the following questions. Use your textbook and the ideas above.

1. Read each word in the box. In each sentence below, fill in the correct word or words.

natural selection   adaptation   niche

   a. The way that an organism "makes its living" is

     called its _____.

   b. The way that characteristics become common in a

     species is called _____.

Populations and Communities

2. Is the following sentence true or false? A hawk's sharp claws are an adaptation because the sharp claws help the hawk catch animals for food. _____

Competition (page 724)

Key Concept: **Competition is one of the three major types of interactions among organisms.**

- **Competition** is the struggle between organisms to stay alive. For example, birds that live in the same part of a tree compete with one another to stay alive.

- Organisms struggle with one another for food, water, and space to live.

Answer the following questions. Use your textbook and the ideas above.

3. The struggle between organisms to keep alive is called

    _____.

4. Is the following sentence true or false? Organisms struggle with one another for space to live. _____

Predation (pages 725–727)

Key Concept: **Predation is one of the three major types of interactions among organisms.**

- **Predation** is when one organism kills another for food. For example, a hawk catches a mouse.

- An organism that kills another organism is called a **predator**. A hawk is a predator.

- An organism that is killed and eaten is called the **prey**. A mouse is a hawk's prey.

- Predators have adaptations to help them kill prey. For example, a cheetah can run fast to catch prey.

Populations and Communities

Answer the following question. Use your textbook and the ideas on page 323.

5. The picture shows a python eating a mouse. Label the predator and the prey.

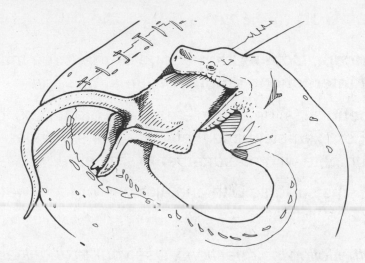

Symbiosis (pages 728–729)

Key Concept: **The three types of symbiotic relationships are mutualism, commensalism, and parasitism.**

- A close relationship between two species is called **symbiosis** (sim bee OH sis). At least one species is helped by the relationship.

- Symbiosis is called **mutualism** (MYOO choo uh liz um) when both species help each other. An example of mutualism is a bee and a flower.

- Symbiosis is called **commensalism** (kuh MEN suh liz um) when one species is helped and the other species is not harmed. An example of commensalisms is a bird building its nest in a tree.

- Symbiosis is called **parasitism** (PA ruh sit iz um) when one of the species is harmed. The organism that is helped is called a **parasite**. The organism that is harmed is called the **host**. A flea is a parasite on a dog, which is the host.

Populations and Communities

Answer the following questions. Use your textbook and the ideas on page 324.

6. Draw a line from each term to its meaning.

Term	Meaning
commensalism	**a.** relationship in which both species help each other
mutualism	**b.** relationship in which one species is helped and the other is not harmed
parasitism	**c.** a relationship in which one species is helped and the other is harmed

7. Read each word in the box. In each sentence below, fill in one of the words.

parasite	host	prey

a. The organism that is harmed in parasitism is called

the _____.

b. The organism that is helped in parasitism is called

the _____.

Populations and Communities

Changes in Communities (pages 730–733)

Primary Succession (page 731)

Key Concept: **Primary succession is the series of changes that occur in an area where no soil or organisms exist.**

- The series of changes that occur in a community over time is called **succession**.

- **Primary succession** occurs when succession starts where almost no organisms exist. There is no soil at the beginning of primary succession.

- The series of changes that occur after a volcano forms an island is an example of primary succession. The changes are primary succession because no organisms or soil exist on the new island.

Answer the following questions. Use your textbook and the ideas above.

1. The series of changes that occur in a community over time is called _____.

2. Circle the letter of each sentence that is true about primary succession.

   a. There are many organisms at the beginning of primary succession.

   b. Primary succession occurs when succession starts where almost no organisms exist.

   c. When a volcano forms an island, primary succession begins.

Populations and Communities

Secondary Succession (pages 732–733)

Key Concept: **Unlike primary succession, secondary succession occurs in a place where an ecosystem currently exists.**

- **Secondary succession** occurs where an ecosystem has been changed in some way.

- An ecosystem is already in place at the beginning of secondary succession.

- The changes in an area after a forest fire are an example of secondary succession. An ecosystem already exists, but the ecosystem was changed by the fire.

Answer the following questions. Use your textbook and the ideas above. Use the pictures below to answer questions 3 and 4.

3. In picture 1, are there any organisms or soil?

   _____

4. Which do these series of three pictures show, primary succession or secondary succession?

   _____

Energy Flow in Ecosystems (pages 740–745)

Energy Roles (pages 740–741)

Key Concept: Each of the organisms in an ecosystem fills the energy role of producer, consumer, or decomposer.

- Energy enters most ecosystems as sunlight.

- Energy moves through an ecosystem. Each organism in an ecosystem plays a part in the movement of energy.

- An organism that can make its own food is called a **producer**.

- An organism that gets energy by eating other organisms is called a **consumer**. **Herbivores** are consumers that eat only plants. **Carnivores** are consumers that eat only animals. **Omnivores** are consumers that eat both plants and animals.

- An organism that gets energy by eating wastes and dead organisms is called a **decomposer**. Mushrooms and bacteria are decomposers.

Answer the following questions. Use your textbook and the ideas above.

1. Energy enters most ecosystems as

   _____.

2. Draw a line from each term to its meaning.

Term	Meaning
decomposer	**a.** an organism that makes its own food
producer	**b.** an organism that gets energy by eating other organisms
consumer	**c.** an organism that gets energy by eating wastes and dead organisms

3. Draw a line from each type of consumer to its description.

Type of Consumers	Description
carnivore	**a.** consumer that eats only animals
herbivore	**b.** consumer that eats both plants and animals
omnivore	**c.** consumer that eats only plants

Food Chains and Food Webs (pages 742–743)

Key Concept: The movement of energy through an ecosystem can be shown in diagrams called food chains and food webs.

- Food chains and food webs are diagrams. They show how energy moves through an ecosystem.

- A **food chain** shows a series of organisms that eat other organisms.

- The first organism in a food chain is always a producer. The organism that eats the producer is called a first-level consumer. The organism that eats the first-level consumer is called a second-level consumer.

- A **food web** is made up of many food chains in an ecosystem. The food chains overlap and connect with one another.

Answer the following questions. Use your textbook and the ideas above.

4. A diagram that shows a series of organisms that eat other organisms is called a(an)

_____.

Ecosystems and Biomes

5. A diagram that is made up of many food chains is called a(an) _____.

6. The picture below shows a food chain. In this food chain, there is a producer, a first-level consumer, and a second-level consumer. Circle the organism that is the first-level consumer.

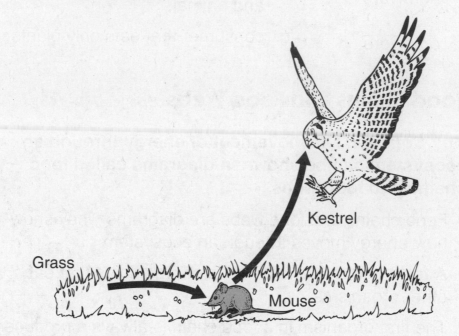

Kestrel

Grass

Mouse

Ecosystems and Biomes

Energy Pyramids (pages 744–745)

Key Concept: **In an energy pyramid, the most energy is available at the producer level of the pyramid. As you move up the pyramid, each level has less energy available than the level below.**

- An **energy pyramid** is a diagram in the shape of a pyramid. It shows how much energy moves from one feeding level to another. Energy moves from the bottom level up to the top level.

- The first level of an energy pyramid always has the most energy.

- Each level of an energy pyramid has less energy than the level below it.

Answer the following questions. Use your textbook and the ideas above.

7. Circle the letter of the name of a diagram that shows how much energy moves from one feeding level to another.

   a. food web

   b. energy pyramid

   c. food chain

8. Circle the letter of each sentence that is true about energy pyramids.

   a. Energy moves from the bottom level to the top level.

   b. The first level always has the most energy.

   c. Each level has more energy than the level below it.

Cycles of Matter (pages 746–751)

The Water Cycle (pages 746–747)

Key Concept: The processes of evaporation, condensation, and precipitation make up the water cycle.

- Matter cycles over and over through ecosystems. Cycles of matter include the water cycle, the carbon and oxygen cycles, and the nitrogen cycle.

- Water moves from Earth's surface to the air and back again through the **water cycle**.

- **Evaporation** is when a liquid changes into a gas. In the water cycle, liquid water evaporates from oceans, lakes, and other bodies of water. The liquid water evaporates to form water vapor, a gas, in the atmosphere.

- **Condensation** is when a gas changes into a liquid. In the water cycle, water vapor condenses in the atmosphere into water droplets. The water droplets then collect into clouds.

- In the water cycle, the droplets of water in clouds fall back to Earth as precipitation. **Precipitation** includes rain, snow, sleet, and hail.

Answer the following questions. Use your textbook and the ideas above.

1. Circle the letter of each sentence that is true about the water cycle
   a. The water cycle is the only cycle of matter on Earth.
   b. Water moves from Earth's surface to the air and back again.
   c. The water cycle includes snow and hail.

Ecosystems and Biomes

2. Complete the diagram of the water cycle by filling in the blanks.

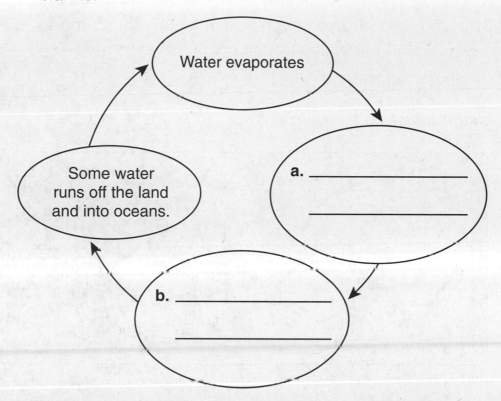

The Carbon and Oxygen Cycles (pages 748–749)

Key Concept: **In ecosystems, the processes by which carbon and oxygen are recycled are linked. Producers, consumers, and decomposers play roles in recycling carbon and oxygen.**

- Living things need both carbon and oxygen to live.

- In ecosystems, the carbon cycle and the oxygen cycle are closely linked together.

- In the carbon cycle, producers take in carbon dioxide from the air to use in photosynthesis. Producers, consumers, and decomposers all release carbon dioxide back into the air as a waste product.

- In the oxygen cycle, most organisms take in oxygen from the air to carry out life processes. Producers release oxygen into the air as a waste product of photosynthesis.

Ecosystems and Biomes

Answer the following questions. Use your textbook and the ideas on page 333.

3. Is the following sentence true or false? The carbon cycle and the oxygen cycle are closely linked in ecosystems. _____

Use the picture below to answer questions 4 and 5.

4. Circle the letter of what the tree releases into the air as a waste product of photosynthesis.

    a. carbon dioxide

    b. nitrogen

    c. oxygen

5. Circle the letter of what the horse releases back into the air as a waste product.

    a. carbon dioxide

    b. nitrogen

    c. oxygen

Ecosystems and Biomes

The Nitrogen Cycle (pages 750–751)

Key Concept: **In the nitrogen cycle, nitrogen moves from the air to the soil, into living things, and back into the air.**

- Air is about 78 percent nitrogen gas.

- Most organisms can use nitrogen only after it has been "fixed." Fixing nitrogen means combining it with other substances.

- Certain kinds of bacteria carry out nitrogen fixation. **Nitrogen fixation** is the process of combining nitrogen with other substances. Once nitrogen fixation occurs, organisms can use nitrogen to make compounds in their cells.

- Decomposers break apart dead organisms and animal wastes. This adds nitrogen compounds to the soil. In soil, certain bacteria break down nitrogen compounds and release nitrogen gas into the air.

Answer the following questions. Use your textbook and the ideas above.

6. The process of combining nitrogen with other

   substances is called nitrogen _____.

7. Circle the letter of each sentence that is true about the nitrogen cycle.

   a. Decomposers add nitrogen compounds to the soil.

   b. There is almost no nitrogen gas in the air.

   c. Most organisms can use nitrogen before it has been "fixed."

Biogeography (pages 752–755)

Continental Drift (page 753)

Key Concept: **One factor that has affected how species are distributed is the motion of Earth's continents.**

- The study of where organisms live is called **biogeography**.

- Biogeographers describe where living things live on Earth. They also study how species spread out on Earth.

- Earth's continents are on huge plates of Earth's crust. The plates move.

- As Earth's plates move, the continents move with them. The movement of continents with their plates is called **continental drift**.

- Continental drift affected where different species live on Earth.

Answer the following questions. Use your textbook and the ideas above.

1. Read each word in the box. In each sentence below, fill in the correct word or words.

continental drift   biogeography
Earth's continents

   a. The movement of continents with their plates is

   called _____.

   b. The study of where organisms live is called

   _____.

2. Circle the letter of each sentence that is true about continental drift.

    a. The continents are on plates that move.

    b. Continental drift affected where species live on Earth.

    c. The continents are now where they have always been.

Means of Dispersal (pages 753–754)

Key Concept: **Dispersal can be caused by wind, water, or living things, including humans.**

- The movement of organisms from one place to another is called **dispersal**. Organisms can be moved around in several ways.

- Wind can move around plant seeds, fungus spores, tiny spiders, and other small living things.

- Water can move around objects that float, such as leaves. Tiny animals can ride to a new home on top of a leaf.

- Organisms can be moved around by other living things. For example, birds can eat berries and then drop the seeds far away.

- Humans can move organisms around. For example, people can carry insects from place to place when flying on planes. An organism carried by people into a new area is called an **exotic species**.

Answer the following questions. Use your textbook and the ideas above.

3. An organism carried by people into a new area is

    called a(an) _____.

4. The movement of organisms from one place to

    another is called _____.

Ecosystems and Biomes

5. Complete the concept map about means of dispersal.

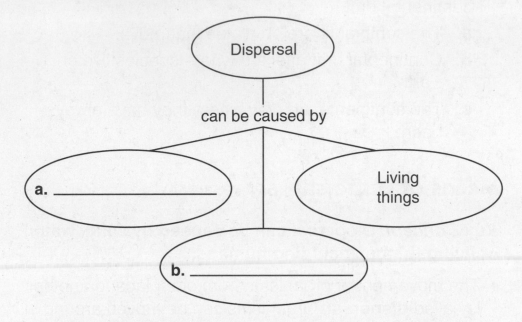

6. Is the following sentence true or false? Humans are
   never a cause of dispersal. _____

Limits to Dispersal (pages 754–755)

Key Concept: **Three factors that limit dispersal of a
species are physical barriers, competition, and
climate.**

- Barriers, competition, and climate limit how far species
  spread out. As a result, the same species are not found
  everyplace on Earth.

- Barriers can limit the spread of species. Barriers include
  oceans, lakes, mountains, and deserts.

- Competition can limit the spread of species. For
  example, when organisms first come to a new place,
  they must compete for food with organisms already
  living there.

- Climate can limit the spread of species. For example,
  plants that grow well in moist soil cannot spread into
  desert areas with little rainfall.

Ecosystems and Biomes

Answer the following questions. Use your textbook and the ideas on page 338.

7. Circle each sentence that is true about limits to dispersal.

   a. The same species are found everyplace on Earth.

   b. Competition can limit the spread of species.

   c. An ocean is a barrier that can limit dispersal.

8. A plant grows well in an area that gets a lot of rainfall. This plant never spreads into a nearby desert. Circle the letter of the factor that *most likely* limits the plant's dispersal.

   a. physical barrier

   b. competition

   c. climate

Biomes and Aquatic Ecosystems (pages 758–769)

Introduction (page 758)

Key Concept: **It is mostly the climate—temperature and precipitation—in an area that determines its biome.**

- A **biome** is a group of land ecosystems.

- All the ecosystems in a biome have climates and organisms that are similar.

- The climate of an area determines what plants grow there. The plants determine what animals live there. As a result, it's mostly the climate of an area that determines what the biome is.

Answer the following questions. Use your textbook and the ideas above.

1. A group of land ecosystems is called a(an)

   _____.

2. Is the following sentence true or false? All ecosystems in a biome have climates that are alike. _____

Rain Forest Biomes (pages 759–760)

Key Concept: **One of the six major biomes that most ecologists study is the rain forest biome.**

- Rain forest biomes include two types of rain forests. One type of rain forest is a temperate rain forest. Another type of rain forest is a tropical rain forest.

- A rain forest receives a lot of rain.

- Temperate rain forests are found in areas with moderate temperatures. Huge trees grow in temperate rain forests, including cedars and redwoods.

Ecosystems and Biomes

- Tropical rain forests are found in regions near the equator. Many different plants grow in a tropical rain forest.

- In a tropical rain forest, tall trees form a leafy roof called a **canopy**. Shorter trees underneath the canopy form an **understory**.

Answer the following questions. Use your textbook and the ideas on page 340 and above.

3. Complete the table below about types of rain forests.

Types of Rain Forests	
Type of Rain Forest	**Location on Earth**
a. _____ rain forest	Areas with moderate temperatures
b. _____ rain forest	Regions near the equator

4. Shorter trees in a tropical rain forest form a(an)

_____.

5. Tall trees in a tropical rain forest form a leafy roof

called a(an) _____.

Ecosystems and Biomes

Desert Biomes (page 761)

Key Concept: **One of the six major biomes that most ecologists study is the desert biome.**

- A **desert** is an area that receives very little rainfall. A desert receives less than 25 centimeters of rain per year.

- Deserts often have very hot days and very cold nights.

- Organisms that live in deserts must be adapted to a lack of rain and extreme temperatures. The saguaro cactus and Gila monster can live in such conditions.

Answer the following questions. Use your textbook and the ideas above.

6. Circle the letter of the name of an area that receives less than 25 centimeters of rain per year.
   a. desert
   b. forest
   c. grassland

7. Is the following sentence true or false? Deserts often have very hot days and very cold nights. _____

Grassland Biomes (page 762)

Key Concept: **One of the six major biomes that most ecologists study is the grassland biome.**

- A **grassland** is an area where mostly grasses grow. Plants without woody trunks and stems also grow in grasslands.

- A prairie is a grassland found in the middle latitudes. The middle latitudes are regions midway between the equator and the North and South poles.

- A **savanna** is a grassland in a region close to the equator. Shrubs and small trees can grow in a savanna.

- Many large grass-eating animals live in grasslands. Examples are elephants, bison (buffaloes), giraffes, and kangaroos.

Answer the following question. Use your textbook and the ideas on page 342 and above.

8. Draw a line from each term to its meaning.

Term	Meaning
grassland	**a.** a grassland found in a region close to the equator
prairie	**b.** an area where mostly grasses grow
savanna	**c.** a grassland found in the middle latitudes

Deciduous Forest Biomes (page 763)

Key Concept: **One of the six major biomes that most ecologists study is the deciduous forest biome.**

- A deciduous forest is a woods area made up mostly of deciduous trees.

- A **deciduous** (dee SIJ oo us) **tree** is a tree that loses its leaves in the fall and grows new leaves in the spring. Oaks and maples are deciduous trees.

- Temperatures in deciduous forests vary greatly during a year, with hot summers and cold winters.

- Animals that live in deciduous forests include wood thrushes, chipmunks, squirrels, foxes, deer, and black bears.

Ecosystems and Biomes

Answer the following questions. Use your textbook and the ideas on page 343.

9. Circle the letter of each sentence that is true about a deciduous forest biome.

   a. A deciduous forest is made up mostly of deciduous trees.

   b. A deciduous forest has hot summers and cold winters.

   c. Deer and black bears live in deciduous forests.

10. Is the following sentence true or false? A deciduous tree loses its leaves in the fall and grows new leaves in the spring. _____

Boreal Forest Biomes (page 764)

***Key Concept:* One of the six major biomes that most ecologists study is the boreal forest biome.**

• Most of the trees in a boreal forest are coniferous trees.

• A **coniferous** (koh NIF ur us) **tree** is a tree that has seeds in cones and leaves shaped like needles. Pine, fir, spruce, and hemlock are coniferous trees.

• Winter is very cold in a boreal forest. Summers are warm and rainy.

• Animals that live in boreal forests include snowshoe hares, moose, great horned owls, bears, wolves, and lynxes.

Answer the following questions. Use your textbook and the ideas above.

11. Is the following sentence true or false? Most of the trees in a boreal forest are coniferous trees.

_____

12. Circle an animal that you might see in a boreal forest.

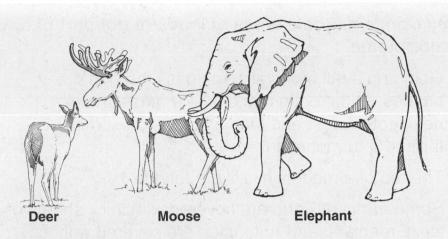

Deer   **Moose**   **Elephant**

Tundra Biomes (page 765)

Key Concept: One of the six major biomes that most ecologists study is the tundra biome.

- A **tundra** is an extremely cold and dry biome.

- Most of the soil in the tundra is frozen all year. Soil that is frozen all year round is called **permafrost**.

- Tundra plants include mosses, grasses, shrubs, and very small trees.

- Tundra animals include insects, birds, caribou, foxes, wolves, and Arctic hares.

Answer the following question. Use your textbook and the ideas above.

13. Read each word in the box. In each sentence below, fill in the correct word or words.

boreal forest   tundra   permafrost

a. A _____ is an extremely cold and dry biome.

b. Soil that is frozen all year round is called

_____.

Ecosystems and Biomes

Mountains and Ice (page 766)

Key Concept: **Some areas of land are not part of any major biome.**

- Going up a tall mountain, you pass through many biomes. At the bottom might be a grassland. A deciduous forest and then a boreal forest might be farther up a mountain.

- The top of a mountain is like a tundra.

- Some areas of Earth are covered with thick sheets of ice. Greenland and Antarctica are covered with ice year-round.

- Animals that live in areas covered with ice include penguins, polar bears, and seals.

Answer the following questions. Use your textbook and the ideas above.

14. Circle the letter of each sentence that is true about mountains.

    a. A mountain has the same biome from top to bottom.

    b. The top of a mountain is like a tundra.

    c. As you climb a mountain, you might pass through a deciduous forest.

15. Is the following sentence true or false? No animals live in areas that are covered with ice.

_____

Freshwater Ecosystems (page 767)

Key Concept: **Freshwater ecosystems include streams, rivers, ponds, and lakes.**

- Freshwater ecosystems include streams, rivers, ponds, and lakes.

- Streams and rivers contain flowing water. Plants and algae are the producers that grow in rivers. Consumers that live in or by rivers include insects, fishes, and frogs.

- Ponds and lakes are bodies of fresh water. The water in a pond or lake is still water, which is also called standing water.

- Algae are major producers in lakes. Lake animals include fishes, dragonflies, turtles, snails, and frogs.

Answer the following questions. Use your textbook and the ideas above.

16. Complete the concept map about freshwater ecosystems.

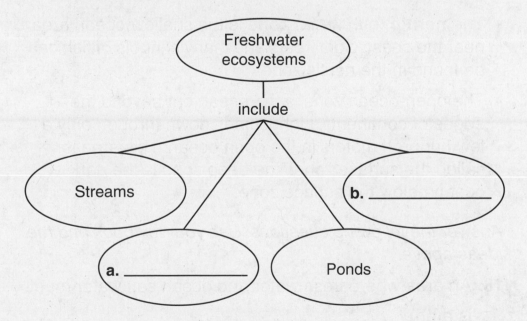

17. Circle the letter of each sentence that is true about freshwater ecosystems.

    a. Frogs are consumers that live by rivers.

    b. Algae are major producers in lakes.

    c. The water in a river is standing water.

Marine Ecosystems (pages 768–769)

Key Concept: **Marine ecosystems include estuaries, intertidal zones, neritic zones, and the open ocean.**

- Estuaries are found near ocean coasts. An **estuary** (ES choo ehr ee) is an area where fresh water and ocean salt water meet. Many animals use estuaries as places to breed and raise young.

- The ocean is home to a number of different ecosystems. They include the intertidal zone, the neritic zone, and the open-ocean zone.

- The **intertidal zone** is the area between the highest high-tide line and the lowest low-tide line. Clams and crabs are two kinds of organisms that live there.

- The **neritic** (nuh RIT ik) **zone** is the shallow ocean area near the coast. Coral reefs and many schools of fish can be found in the neritic zone.

- The open-ocean zone is the ocean out beyond the edges of continents. Light shines down through only a few hundred meters in the open ocean. This area is called the surface zone. The deep zone is the dark ocean below the surface zone.

Answer the following questions. Use your textbook and the ideas above.

18. An area where fresh water and ocean salt water meet is a(an) _____.

Ecosystems and Biomes

19. Circle the letter of each zone in the open ocean.

    a. surface zone

    b. neritic zone

    c. deep zone

20. Complete the table below about types of marine ecosystems.

Types of Marine Ecosystems	
Type of Marine Ecosystem	**Description**
a. _____ zone	The area between the highest high-tide line and the lowest low-tide line
b. _____ zone	The shallow ocean area near the coast
c. _____ zone	The ocean out beyond the edges of continents

Environmental Issues

(pages 778–782)

Types of Environmental Issues (pages 778–779)

Key Concept: **Environmental issues fall into three general categories: resource use, population growth, and pollution.**

- A **natural resource** is anything in the environment that is used by people.

- A natural resource that is always available is a **renewable resource**. Examples are sunlight and wind. A natural resource that is naturally replaced in a short time is also a renewable resource. Trees are a renewable resource.

- A **nonrenewable resource** is a natural resource that cannot be replaced in a useful time period. Coal and oil are two nonrenewable resources.

- The human population has been growing faster and faster since the 1600s. This population growth increases demands for natural resources.

- **Pollution** is when harmful substances are put into the land, water, or air.

Answer the following questions. Use your textbook and the ideas above.

1. Circle the letter of each sentence that is true about population growth.

   a. The human population has been growing faster and faster since the 1600s.

   b. Population growth decreases demands for natural resources.

   c. Population growth increases demands for natural resources.

2. Complete the table about Earth's resources.

Earth's Resources	
Type of Resource	**Description**
a. _____	Anything in the environment that is used by people
b. _____	A natural resource that is always available
c. _____	A natural resource that cannot be replaced

3. Putting harmful substances into the land, water, or air is called _____.

Name _____ Date _____ Class _____

Living Resources

Making Environmental Decisions
(pages 780–782)

Key Concept: To help balance the different opinions on an environmental issue, decision makers weigh the costs and benefits of a proposal.

- **Environmental science** is the study of the environment and how humans affect the environment. Environmental scientists advise decision makers.

- Decisions about the environment involve comparing the needs of the environment with the needs of people. For example, cutting down a forest may hurt the environment, but it may help people who build houses.

- Costs and benefits are often economic. That is, they involve money matters. Costs and benefits also may not be economic. For example, one cost of driving cars is air pollution. A benefit is being able to drive where you want to.

- A decision maker weighs the costs and benefits of a decision. In other words, the people who make decisions consider how much a proposal will cost compared to how much good it will do.

Answer the following questions. Use your textbook and the ideas above.

4. The study of the environment and how humans affect the environment is called _____ science.

5. Circle the letter of each sentence that is true about costs and benefits.
   a. Costs and benefits are always economic.
   b. A decision maker weighs the costs and benefits of a decision.
   c. Costs and benefits may not be economic.

Forests and Fisheries (pages 784–788)

Forest Resources (page 784)

Key Concept: **Forests contain many valuable resources.**

- Lumber comes from cutting down forest trees. Wood pulp also comes from cutting down trees. Wood pulp is used to make paper.

- Some forest products come from live trees. These products include maple syrup, rubber, and nuts.

- Forest trees and other plants are necessary for a healthy environment. They produce oxygen that most organisms need. Their roots hold soil in place and absorb rainwater.

Answer the following questions. Use your textbook and the ideas above.

1. Circle the letter of each product that comes from cutting down forest trees.
   a. wood pulp
   b. lumber
   c. maple syrup

2. Is the following sentence true or false? Forest trees and other plants produce oxygen that most organisms need.

   _____

Living Resources

Managing Forests (pages 785–786)

Key Concept: **Because new trees can be planted to replace trees that are cut down, forests can be renewable resources.**

- The two major methods of logging are: clear-cutting and selective cutting.

- **Clear-cutting** is a method of cutting forests in which all trees in an area are cut down at the same time. Clear-cutting is usually quicker and cheaper than selective cutting.

- **Selective cutting** is a method of cutting forests in which only some trees are cut down. A mix of trees is left standing. Selective cutting is usually less damaging to the environment than clear-cutting.

- People manage forests to provide a sustainable yield. A **sustainable yield** is an amount taken from a resource that does not harm the future supply of the resource. For example, you do not want to cut down so many trees that the health of the forest suffers.

Answer the following questions. Use your textbook and the ideas above.

3. Circle the letter of the picture that shows clear-cutting.

a.   b.

Living Resources

4. Complete the table about major methods of logging.

Major Methods of Logging	
Logging Method	**Description**
a. _____	All trees in an area are cut down at the same time
b. _____	Only some trees are cut down

5. Circle the letter of the sentence that describes what a sustainable yield is.

  a. an amount taken from a resource that causes harm to the future supply of the resource

  b. an amount taken from a resource that does not harm the future supply of the resource

  c. an amount taken from a resource that leaves more of the resource than was there before

Living Resources

Fisheries (pages 787–788)

Key Concept: **Managing fisheries for a sustainable yield includes strategies such as setting fishing limits, changing fishing methods, developing aquaculture techniques, and finding new resources.**

- A **fishery** is an ocean area that has a large population of valuable fishes and other living things. A fishery is a valuable natural resource.

- People manage a fishery in a way that provides a sustainable yield. For example, a fishery stays healthy when the fishery is not overfished. Overfishing is when fish are caught faster than they can breed. The result of overfishing is a smaller fish population.

- Setting fishing limits means passing laws about fishing. Laws sometimes ban the fishing of certain kinds of fish. Laws may also limit the number of fish that may be caught.

- **Aquaculture** is raising fish and other aquatic organisms for food. Raising salmon or catfish in a pond is an example of aquaculture.

Answer the following questions. Use your textbook and the ideas above.

6. Circle the letter of each sentence that is true about fisheries.

    a. Fisheries can be overfished.

    b. A fishery can be a valuable natural resource.

    c. Fisheries are places where fish are raised in a pond.

7. Is the following sentence true or false? Laws sometimes ban the fishing of certain kinds of fish.

_____

Name _____ Date _____ Class _____

Biodiversity (pages 792–801)

The Value of Biodiversity (pages 792–793)

Key Concept: **Biodiversity has both economic value and ecological value within an ecosystem.**

- The **biodiversity** of an area is the number of different species that live there. Protecting biodiversity is important for two main reasons: biodiversity has money value, and biodiversity is important for the health of ecosystems.

- Many plants, animals, and other living things have economic value. Having economic value means having worth in terms of money. For example, some plants and animals supply materials used to make clothes.

- All species have ecological value. Having ecological value means affecting the other living things in an ecosystem. For example, species depend on each other for food and shelter.

- A **keystone species** is a species that affects whether or not other species in an ecosystem keep living or die off.

Answer the following questions. Use your textbook and the ideas above.

1. Read each word in the box. In each sentence below, fill in the correct word or words.

biodiversity	keystone species	economic value

   a. A _____ is a species that affects whether or not other species in an ecosystem keep living or die off.

   b. The _____ of an area is the number of different species that live in the area.

2. Circle the letter of each sentence that is true about biodiversity.
   a. Biodiversity has no value to humans.
   b. Biodiversity has ecological value.
   c. Biodiversity has economic value.

Factors Affecting Biodiversity
(pages 794–795)

Key Concept: **Factors that affect biodiversity in an ecosystem include area, climate, and diversity of niches.**

- Biodiversity varies from place to place.

- An area's biodiversity can depend on its size. A larger area usually has greater biodiversity than a smaller area.

- An area's biodiversity can depend on its climate. Tropical rain forests, for instance, have great biodiversity.

- An area's biodiversity can depend on its niche diversity. Niche diversity is how many different ways organisms can live in an ecosystem. For example, a coral reef has great biodiversity because organisms can live under, on, and among the coral.

Answer the following questions. Use your textbook and the ideas above.

3. Circle the letter of each sentence that is true about factors affecting biodiversity.
   a. Climate does not affect an area's biodiversity.
   b. Tropical rain forests and coral reefs both have great biodiversity.
   c. A larger area usually has a greater biodiversity than a smaller area.

4. Complete the concept map about factors that affect biodiversity.

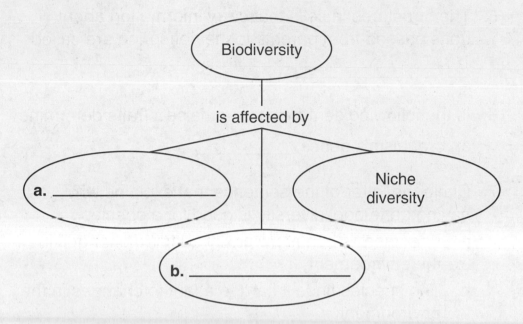

Gene Pool Diversity (page 795)

Key Concept: **The organisms in a healthy population have a diversity of traits.**

- A trait is a characteristic of an organism. For example, traits include the color of an organism and the size of an organism.

- Genes determine an organism's traits. Genes are the structures in cells that carry information about the traits passed from parents to their offspring.

- Each organism has some genes that others in the same species do not have. The total number of genes found in a species is called its gene pool.

- A species with a lot of different genes in its gene pool has a diversity of traits—many different traits. A diversity of traits is also called gene pool diversity. Having gene pool diversity makes it easier for the species to adapt to changes in the environment.

Answer the following questions. Use your textbook and the ideas on page 359.

5. The structures in cells that carry information about traits passed from parents to their offspring are called

_____.

6. Is the following sentence true or false? Traits determine an organism's genes. _____

7. Circle the letter of the sentence that explains why having gene pool diversity is good for a species.

    a. The species can more easily adapt to changes in the environment.

    b. The species finds it hard to adapt to changes in the environment.

    c. The species can never adapt to changes in the environment.

Extinction of Species (pages 796–797)

***Key Concept:* Extinction is a natural process. But in the last few centuries, the number of species becoming extinct has increased dramatically.**

- **Extinction** is when all members of a species disappear from Earth. Species can become extinct naturally. People can also cause species to become extinct.

- An **endangered species** is a species that is in danger of becoming extinct soon.

- A **threatened species** is a species that could become an endangered species soon.

- Making sure that species do not become extinct is one way to protect Earth's biodiversity.

Answer the following question. Use your textbook and the ideas on page 360.

8. Complete the table about terms related to the extinction of species.

Extinction of Species	
Term	**Meaning**
a. _____ _____	The disappearance from Earth of all members of a species
b. _____ _____	A species that is in danger of becoming extinct soon
c. _____ _____	A species that could become an endangered species soon

Causes of Extinction (pages 798–799)

Key Concept: **Human activities can threaten biodiversity. These activities include habitat destruction, poaching, pollution, and the introduction of exotic species.**

- The major cause of extinction is habitat destruction. **Habitat destruction** is when a natural habitat is destroyed. For example, cutting down a forest to build a town is habitat destruction.

- **Habitat fragmentation** is when a habitat is broken up into small areas. Building a road through a forest is an example of habitat fragmentation.

Living Resources

- **Poaching** is the illegal killing or capture of animals in the wild. Hunters kill some animals for their parts, such as their fur or horns.

- When humans carry a new species into an area, that exotic species can cause extinction of species already living there.

Answer the following questions. Use your textbook and the ideas on page 361 and above.

9. Draw a line from each term to its meaning.

Term	Meaning
habitat destruction	**a.** the illegal killing or capture of animals in the wild
habitat fragmentation	
	b. when a natural habitat is destroyed
poaching	
	c. when a habitat is broken up into small areas

10. Look at the picture below. What human activity does the picture show? _____

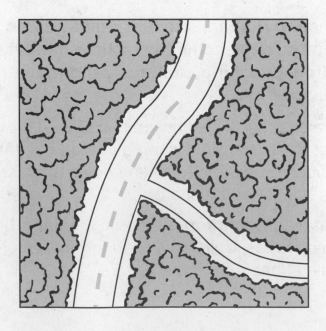

Protecting Biodiversity (pages 800–801)

Key Concept: Three successful approaches to protecting biodiversity are captive breeding, laws and treaties, and habitat preservation.

- **Captive breeding** is having animals in zoos or wildlife preserves mate and reproduce.

- Laws and treaties can protect species. A law in the United States called the Endangered Species Act protects threatened species and endangered species. International treaties can protect species around the world by outlawing the buying and selling of endangered species.

- Protecting a whole ecosystem is the best way to protect biodiversity. Protecting a whole ecosystem protects endangered species living there. It also protects any species that depends on the endangered species.

Answer the following questions. Use your textbook and the ideas above.

11. Having animals in zoos or wildlife preserves mate and reproduce is called _____ breeding.

12. Circle the letter of what the Endangered Species Act protects.
    a. captive breeding in zoos
    b. threatened species and endangered species
    c. animals in other countries

13. Is the following sentence true or false? Protecting a whole ecosystem is the best way to protect biodiversity. _____